1984

THE
REFERENCE
SHELF

THE

REFERENCE

SHELF

THE AMERICAN ENVIRONMENT

edited by JULIE SULLIVAN

THE REFERENCE SHELF

Volume 56 Number 3

THE H. W. WILSON COMPANY

New York   1984

THE REFERENCE SHELF

The books in this series contain reprints of articles, excerpts from books, and addresses on current issues and social trends in the United States and other countries. There are six separately bound numbers in each volume, all of which are generally published in the same calendar year. One number is a collection of recent speeches; each of the others is devoted to a single subject and gives background information and discussion from various points of view, concluding with a comprehensive bibliography. Books in the series may be purchased individually or on subscription.

Library of Congress Cataloging in Publication Data

Main entry under title:

The American environment.

(The Reference shelf ; v. 56, no. 3)
Bibliography: p.
1. Environmental policy—United States—Addresses, essays, lectures. I. Sullivan, Julie. II. Series.
HC110.E5A647   1984   363.7'00973   84–15220
ISBN 0-8242-0698-3

Printed in the United States of America

CONTENTS

PREFACE

Since 1980, when Ronald Reagan was elected president, interest in environmental questions has soared. President Reagan and many members of his administration shared a philosophy of environmental regulation that was radically different from the administrations that preceded them. They believed that although some government regulation might be necessary to protect health, the costs and problems of regulating pollution had gotten out of hand and needed to be sharply curbed. Putting a strong emphasis on economic growth, the administration gave more say to industry and the private sector and less to the environmentalists whose views had influenced the policies of previous administrations.

President Reagan's approach was controversial. After his election, membership in most environmental groups increased dramatically. The Sierra Club, probably the most active lobbyist for the environmental cause, more than doubled its membership. After it became clear that Reagan's appointees in the environmental area were indeed making the changes they had promised, more conservative environmental groups such as the Audubon Society and the National Wildlife Federation began to speak out against administration policies, although in both groups a majority of members had voted for Reagan. In the 1982 congressional campaigns, environmentalist political action groups spent more than $1.5 million on their candidates—75 percent of whom won. The Sierra Club gathered more than a million signatures on a petition asking for the removal of Secretary of the Interior James Watt. Watt, however, remained a popular speaker in the West and in spite of his outspoken ways, which several times caused embarrassment to the White House, the president stood behind him.

In 1983 and 1984, environmental issues were never far from the headlines. In March of 1983, after months of bad publicity, Anne McGill Burford, head of the Environmental Protection Agency, was forced to resign. She had been charged with contempt of Congress for refusing to turn over subpoenaed documents relating to allegations of agency inaction on pollutants, favorable treatment for polluting industries, misuse of funds, and "hit lists" of environmentally oriented employees. Several of her top aides were also forced out, and one, Rita Lavelle, was convicted of perjury. In contrast, Secretary James Watt was considered, even by those who disliked his policies, as a capable administrator. He too came under fire, however, and was forced to resign in October of 1983. Watt and Burford were accused, especially by environmentalists, of being "foxes guarding the chicken coop"—philosophically opposed to the very laws they were charged with administering. The men who replaced them—William Clark as Secretary of the Interior and William Ruckelshaus as head of the EPA—managed to avoid the spotlight and have enjoyed far better relations with all factions in the dispute.

During Mrs. Buford's and later Mr. Ruckelshaus' administration at EPA, the toxic chemicals issue became an increasingly prominent concern. The extent of the problem was well publicized. The federal government bought out the dioxin-contaminated town of Times Beach, Missouri. Vietnam veterans sued the government for compensation for medical problems they said were caused by their exposure to the dioxin in Agent Orange. In Woburn, Massachusetts, a Harvard epidemiological survey carried out with the aid of hundreds of townspeople established a link between chemically contaminated wells and high rates of leukemia and other fatal diseases. In early 1984, a new problem made headlines: EDB, a highly carcinogenic pesticide, was found to have contaminated products ranging from cake mix to baby food. In a 407-page report, Congress's Office of Technology Assessment warned that federal laws did not assure "protection of human health" from "massive annual accumulations of hazardous waste."

Because of space limitations, the editor of this volume has chosen to cover only a few salient issues within the broad field of envionmental topics. Section I includes a broad overview of global environmental problems and attitudes toward them, an account of the socio-political characteristics of the environmental movement, and a speech claiming that environmentalism is a truly popular movement and not, as has sometimes been claimed, a preoccupation of the educated and affluent.

Section II describes the turbulent course of environmental policy in the United States in the past few years. Section III deals with toxic waste and government regulation of polluting industries. Lastly, Section IV takes a look ahead. Will environmental concerns affect our future in unexpected ways?

The editor would like to thank David Winn, Chris Kojm, Alice Demonbrun, and the authors and publishers who have granted permission to reprint the materials used in this compilation.

Julie Sullivan

April 1984

THE STATE OF THE ENVIRONMENT: FACTS AND ATTITUDES

EDITOR'S INTRODUCTION

Depending on who is talking, "environmental problems" can mean anything from acid rain and toxic waste to hunger and unemployment. The first article in this section, by the editors of the Foreign Policy Association, gives an overview of world environmental concerns, including those of the United States, and the effect of these global problems on Americans. At the end of the article, a number of questions point out important issues.

In the second article, William Tucker, in an excerpt from his book *Progress and Privilege,* examines the environmental movement and argues that, though some of their goals are worthy, environmentalists are newly affluent elitists who constitute a "privileged minority" supporting a philosophy of no-growth.

In the last article in this section, Brock Evans, a vice president of the Audubon Society, defends the environmental community from charges of elitism while attacking the Reagan administration's environmental policies. His speech is reprinted from *Vital Speeches of the Day.*

PROTECTING WORLD RESOURCES: IS TIME RUNNING OUT?[1]

If present trends continue, the world in 2000 will be more crowded, more polluted, less stable ecologically, and more vulnerable to disruption than the world we live in now.

Global 2000 Report

[1]Reprint of an article by the editors of the Foreign Policy Association. *Great Decisions '82.* p 49–57. Copyright© 1982 by the Foreign Policy Association, Inc. Reprinted by permission.

What a big 'if' that is.

René Dubos
scientist and conservationist,
of the *Global 2000* premise

Global 2000, a three-year study commissioned by President Jimmy Carter and released in 1980, opened with the words above. Its message was that the world's natural resources are being wasted, abused, and consumed at accelerating and often unsustainable rates. The report warned that "unless the nations of the world act decisively to alter current trends" by the year 2000, fewer than 20 years away . . .

• the world population will climb from about 4.5 billion to 6.35 billion—5 billion in the "third world"; 90% of the growth will take place in the world's poorest countries. Although the rate of growth will have slowed, the number of children born each year will increase from 80 million in 1980 to 100 million in the year 2000.

• although literacy rates, life expectancies and income levels per capita will rise, the larger total number of human beings will include more illiterate people and more people living in absolute poverty than now.

• the real price of food will double; the world requirement for water will also double. The real price of most minerals, including fossil fuels, will rise.

• most accessible forests in many third-world nations will disappear. Firewood shortages will become more severe for the 25% of the world's people who depend on it for fuel.

• desertification (turning fertile land into desert) and soil erosion will increasingly cause floods, famine, and migration, as well as permanently remove huge areas of arable land from productive use each year.

• the extinction of plant and animal species will continue to accelerate, leading by 2000 to the loss of perhaps one out of five of all species now on earth (mostly losses of tropical plants or insects).

• a reduction of the ozone layer of the stratosphere, if it occurs as some scientists suspect, would allow more ultraviolet radiation to reach the earth, causing thousands more cases of skin cancer each year.

• acid rain, air and water pollution, radioactivity, and improper disposal of solid wastes and hazardous materials will endanger increasing numbers of people.

• while food production per capita will increase 15%, little of the increase will go to countries where food is in short supply now. In the Middle East and South Asia, conditions will remain poor; in sub-Saharan Africa, the amount of food per person is expected to decline as Africa's population doubles from the year 1975 to 2000.

The authors of *Global 2000* emphasize that the report is not a prediction but a warning of what *could* happen. They also acknowledge that the figures on which the projections are based were often incomplete or outdated. Critics of the report say it is too pessimistic and does not allow for human ingenuity or the power of science and technology to solve problems as they arise. "'Present trends' involving people typically *don't* continue," remarked Ben Wattenberg of the American Enterprise Institute, a "think tank" in Washington, "particularly if the trends are unfavorable." Julian Simon, an economist at the University of Illinois at Urbana-Champaign, probably the most persistent critic of *Global 2000,* argues that the report was written by well-known "gloom and doom" members of the environmental movement and was carelessly researched and questionably analyzed. "For most or all the relevant matters I have checked," Simon charged, "the trends are positive rather than negative." Simon and other critics have pointed out that *Global 2000* itself projects increases in per capita income, food production, education, and life expectancy, and says that in many places rates of population growth, pollution, and deforestation show signs of declining. In fact, the critics say, historically mankind's lot has been improving, and it will continue to improve.

But both critics and defenders of *Global 2000*—perhaps the largest government survey ever done on world resource trends—agree that the issues it discusses are critical ones.

Links to Foreign Policy

As photographs from outer space vividly remind us, all of humanity shares one planet. In a real sense, the earth is one ecosystem. Significant change or deterioration of one part of any ecological system will affect the rest sooner or later. This "ripple effect" is amplified by modern trade, transportation, and telecommunications, which have made nations more dependent on each other than ever before.

The effects of environmental problems on politics are not obvious, but they are profound. When a country's physical base deteriorates, its economy will soon suffer. The first and most important result of environmental damage on a large scale is that it becomes harder and harder for a country to feed its own people and provide employment. This in turn affects other nations which may supply food to the poorer country or receive immigrants from it. The United States, which exports more grain than any other nation, is said by its own soil scientists to be suffering soil erosion and loss of farmland at an accelerated rate because of these exports. The exports also have the effect of raising food prices for U.S. consumers.

Long-term dependency on another country for food may also have dangerous consequences for a poor nation. Garrett Hardin, one well-known and controversial environmentalist, has suggested that it is inhumane in the long run for the United States and other food exporters to aid countries that cannot feed themselves. While lives may be saved immediately by such aid, Hardin argues, this guaranteed food supply from abroad allows the growth of a population larger than the country's own resources could ever support alone. When food aid stops sooner or later, there will be far more people to suffer starvation. Others have called Hardin's argument inhumane, and make the point that U.S. food supplements can tide a poor nation over till it can build up its own grain reserve— substantially what has happened in India over the past decade.

Almost every major environmental issue in the world has implications for the United States—as the world's largest food exporter; as an international leader in industry, technology, and military security; as a defender of democracy; as a magnet for immigrants; as the world's largest economy; as the home of one of the world's largest populations (only China, India, and the U.S.S.R. have more people).

A Look at the Past

Concern about the environment as a natural system that can be polluted or overburdened in many ways is a relatively recent phenomenon. Two closely related factors explain the rise of this concern in the second half of the 20th century: the global industrial revolution after World War II, and the worldwide population explosion. While in wealthy countries the impact of industry has been the main environmental concern, in poor countries the exponential growth of population has had a more important impact.

Pollution of the air or water is nothing new—complaints of filthy water or smoke in the air have come down to us from ancient times. But most of the pollution of early times was strictly local: wood smoke or coal "fog" over a city, for example. The Industrial Revolution increased the rate of pollution at the same time it helped people live better. But for many years pollution was considered a relatively unimportant side effect of development. After World War II, however, there were more and more incidents that gradually brought international attention to what are now called environmental problems. In 1952, a particularly bad London "fog" killed 3,000 people in a few days. Los Angeles smog was already famous, contributing a new word to the English language. People going back to visit their old "swimming holes" found them filled with scum and bubbles. In 1962, Rachel Carson's book *Silent Spring,* which described the inadvertent killing of birds by the insecticide DDT, focused public concern on the problems of pollution.

During the late 1960s, public support for environmentalists swelled. Along with Britain, West Germany, Japan and other industrialized countries, the United States passed laws and set up agencies to try to clean up the air and water. In the relatively prosperous years of the late 1960s and early 1970s, the costs of environmental protection—estimated in 1970 at $3,500 per person per decade in the United States—were examined less critically than they would be later on. Environmental protection, especially for clean air and water, was overwhelmingly popular with the public, polls showed.

The Stockholm Conference

At the same time, support was growing for international cooperation on environmental issues. In 1968, the Swedish government proposed a United Nations conference on the human environment and offered Stockholm as a site. During the preparations for the conference, held in 1972, a special effort was made to interest less-developed nations, many of which had previously considered the environment to be a concern only of industrialized countries. Before the conference, each country attending was to prepare, if it wished, a report on the state of its environment—forests, water, farmland, and other natural resources. For many nations, this was the first official acknowledgment that environmental problems existed within their borders. It has been said that this awareness alone would have made the Stockholm Conference a success.

When the delegates from 113 countries met in Stockholm, however, they quickly found that the common concern which all their countries shared for the environment did not mean they agreed on what the main issues were. The industrialized countries were primarily worried about pollution, overpopulation, and resource conservation. The less-developed countries, on the other hand, considered environmental problems such as foul air or degraded soils and forests secondary to the more-immediate problems of poverty—hunger, disease, illiteracy and unemployment. Preventing pollution from factories, third-world countries said, was admirable. But for 80% of the people in the world, having sufficient food was far more important. Developing nations saw technology and industry, even with their accompanying pollution, as keys to improving their lives.

By the end of the two-week Stockholm Conference, however, the delegates had managed to agree that the human environment must be protected even as development continues. They adopted an action plan which proposed the establishment of the United Nations Environment Program. UNEP includes Earthwatch, a program to monitor and indicate changes in the physical earth and its biological resources, and other programs.

Ten Years Later

In the decade since the landmark Stockholm Conference, most nations have come to the official recognition that wise management of their natural resources is necessary for long-term prosperity. More important than any single meeting or program that arose from the conference was the awareness it engendered of the earth's ecology as a whole. The environmental dilemmas of both rich and poor nations were for the first time placed in a global perspective. This awareness has meant that even some of the poorest countries that previously concentrated solely on economic development are now taking steps to protect their natural resources, to encourage family planning, and to guard against the worst side effects of industrialization.

During the 1970s, environmental disasters continued to warn the public that vigilance was necessary, even as in many places problems lessened after action was taken. In Seveso (Italy), Minamata (Japan), and Love Canal (near Buffalo in the United States), chemicals poisoned inhabitants and made their towns' names bywords for contamination. At the same time, the river Thames in England came slowly back to life, supporting 95 species of fish, including salmon; air quality in New York and Los Angeles improved; many lakes and streams became safe for fishing and swimming after decades of abuse.

Perhaps the key event of the decade was the Organization of Petroleum Exporting Countries (OPEC) oil embargo of 1973. Although it was an artificial shortage, to many it foreshadowed an "era of limits," in which more and more people would be competing for fewer and fewer resources. During the 1970s, other trends reinforced this perception. The "energy crisis" of the developed world—in oil—was joined by a second energy crisis of the poor nations—in firewood. In many places in the third world, firewood has become prohibitively expensive or is simply unavailable. Population growth rates—perhaps one of the most important factors affecting a country's living standard—began to slow in many countries in the 1970s, but the number of children born each year increased.

While environmentalists and others warn that conservation and resource protection, as well as possible drastic measures to curb population, may be necessary to avert the dire possibilities outlined in *Global 2000,* some analysts believe that the prospects are far from grim. In the early 1800s, it was feared that great cities would be left in darkness as the world ran out of whale oil for lamps. In 1864, Julian Simon points out, the famous English economist William Stanley Jevons predicted that England would soon cease to grow economically because a lack of coal. This stagnation, Jevons wrote, would soon "render our population excessive." In these and other cases, the invention of new technologies made feared resource shortages irrelevant. Optimists believe that the current or predicted "era of limits" will similarly be averted. Simon, for example, believes that "human ingenuity, rather than nature, is limitlessly bountiful." In response to predictions of future scarcity, Simon uses historical trend data to show that prices for most commodities and resources have tended to go down relative to wages, largely as a result of new technologies which have evolved over the past 200 years. Moreover, statistical measures of resource reserves are misleading because typically no one searches for more reserves while supplies are adequate. When more reserves are needed they have historically been found.

Simon also argues in his book *The Ultimate Resource* that high population growth rates are not a problem, contrary to most current public perception. Wealth, according to Simon, is produced or created by people, not just collected by them. Therefore, the more people, the more wealth. As world population has increased in the last hundred years, he points out, indexes of health and prosperity have climbed.

The "no limits" message of Simon, Herman Kahn and other analysts has readily received a hearing. In the late 1970s and early 1980s, public and government opinion has appeared to be swinging back from the "limit to growth" views of a decade earlier. Still, there is a consensus that continued development should include the wise management of resources and a concern for the environment.

Are Resources Renewable?

The environmental questions facing the world today can be separated into two groups. The first concerns so-called renewable resources. If a forest is cut down, another forest can be planted in its place. If a river is polluted, the sources of pollution can be eliminated and natural rainfall will soon allow the river to run clean again. But in the second group, nonrenewable resources such as fossil fuels are consumed but not replaced. (Theoretically, fossil fuels are also renewable, but certainly not on a human time scale.) Animal and plant species are also "nonrenewable"; once they are extinct, they cannot be replaced.

The division between renewable and nonrenewable is not always distinct. For example, topsoil formation is slow, perhaps taking centuries for only a few inches, although it can be speeded with fertilizer. But if topsoil washes away faster than it is replaced, the area may become barren, and it may then take thousands of years before the topsoil returns. In the case of contamination by chemicals, radiation, metals, or other substances, whether or not the resource—air, earth, or water—is "renewable" on a human time scale depends on the duration of the contamination. Minerals are also nonrenewable in the sense that there is a finite amount of each mineral in the earth. However, many minerals can be recycled over and over, and the actual quantity of mineral needed to accomplish a given task may well decrease with improved technology.

Water: Is the Tap Running Dry?

Water is the quintessential renewable resource. It is endlessly recycled through time; new water can also form occasionally in volcanic action. But most of the fresh water on earth is locked in the polar ice caps, and most of what is left is underground. The relatively small amount of surface water in streams, rivers, and lakes has traditionally been the main source of human water supplies.

Although water is the most abundant "resource" on earth, the amount of accessible, usable water is quite small. While the human population may increase greatly in an area, the local water supply does not grow to match it. The result may be that the community stops growing when the limits of water are reached. Or it may build long aqueducts to bring in more water. Los Angeles, for example, draws its water supply from rivers hundreds of miles away. The city's water officials are now looking covetously at rivers as distant as the Columbia in Oregon.

Groundwater is another solution for a thirsty community. Trapped between the surface and an impermeable layer of rock, large amounts of water may underlie even arid regions. But in an arid region, the formation of such a large aquifer may have taken thousands of years, as the water seeped through the soil and rock. In many parts of the world, the demands of a growing population are leading to the "mining" of this water—it is being drawn up so fast that the water table is plummeting. The high plains of Texas, Nebraska, Colorado and Kansas are underlain by such a formation, the Ogallala aquifer. By the year 2000 most of the accessible water in the aquifer will be gone. Farmers in the region—which produces much of the nation's wheat, corn, cotton and beef—will have to depend on another water source to keep up their present yields.

Many analysts have argued that it is unnatural for large cities and irrigated farms to sprout in the desert. But farmers in the Southwest point out that their region, if irrigated, can grow crops all year round, unlike the well-watered but cold East. Still, in recent years there has been more and more discussion of the limits imposed by nature on growth in the Southwest.

Another potential cause of water shortage is pollution. Most municipal water systems in developed countries can deal with biological pollution (i.e. sewage), but they can often do little to remove chemicals. Towns that depend on groundwater, which purifies itself extremely slowly, may find out too late that industrial parks, fertilized potato fields, or cattle feed lots have contaminated their underground supplies for the indefinite future. Pollution in a water supply is harmful to people, of course, but even industry and agriculture, by far the main "consumers," need relatively pure water. Near some major cities, even in developing countries like Korea, rivers may be so polluted that no industrial use is possible.

While in wealthy countries industrial waste and agricultural chemicals are the greatest water polluters, in poor nations the main pollutant is untreated human sewage. Almost none of the rural people in poor countries have latrines or any kind of sewage system. Most of these people also lack the elementary education that would prevent them from using chamberpots to collect drinking water or putting contaminated fingers into their food. Less than half the world's people can get safe drinking water. Many have little chance to wash themselves, their food, their utensils or their clothing—basic sanitation that could prevent disease and death. This lack of safe drinking water is probably the number one preventable cause of death in the world today.

Even if people have the knowledge to prevent contamination, it may be almost impossible to obtain decent sanitation and clean water. Women and children in many parts of the world spend up to eight hours a day walking to and from the well or stream, carrying huge pots of water on their heads. Fuel is often expensive, so boiling water to sterilize it may seem like a luxury, even to someone who knows better. On returning to the States, one American Peace Corps worker wrote,

I used to turn on the water faucet and watch the water flow in disbelief. . . . I remembered how far the village women had to walk for it; how polluted it was when we got it; how expensive the wood was that was needed to purify it; and how we finally had to give that up because we couldn't afford it.

Where the water is contaminated with sewage, as it is in much of the third world, people are inevitably in poor health. Cholera, typhoid, amebiasis, dysentery, hepatitis, schistosomiasis, and many other diseases are spread by people who use nearby water as both latrine and reservoir. While people who live in poor countries do eventually gain some immunity to the microbes in their food and drink, it is paid for in the loss of children's lives. Most deaths in poor countries are of children under five years old, most of whom die from diarrhea and other diseases caused by contaminated water. Perhaps no single step could improve the lives of the world's poor so much as access to safe drinking water for all. In recognition of this need, the UN has declared the 1980s the "International Drinking Water Supply and Sanitation Decade."

The World Bank, the U.S. Agency for International Development (AID), and other organizations have allocated millions of dollars for water and sewage-treatment projects in the third world.

Land Abuse By Rich and Poor

Land abuse includes uncontrolled deforestation, desertification, and their consequences: soil erosion, silting of rivers and reservoirs, flooding, loss of fuel, loss of fertilizer, even famine and drought. It also includes harm that may come from mishandled irrigation, which can waterlog the land or leave so much salt on it that it can no longer be farmed.

The problem of land abuse is global. In the United States, for example, the Department of Agriculture estimates that one-third of the nation's topsoil has eroded since farming began, in most places less than 200 years ago. But land abuse is generally more serious in densely populated developing countries. In these countries with fast-growing populations, the pressure to farm, graze livestock, and cut firewood and timber in new areas is intense. Unfortunately, in most countries that face this kind of pressure, the most suitable land was taken long ago. What is left is marginal land, too steep or wet or dry to be used except in desperate need. But, today, population pressure means that many people are in that desperate need. They have moved high on steep mountainsides in Nepal and onto silt islands miles out in the Indian Ocean off Bangladesh. They make a precarious living from subsistence farming—but they are often helping to destroy their own livelihood.

The uncontrolled deforestation of marginal or hilly land by people struggling to survive is one of the most serious problems the world environment faces today. Trees hold the soil in place, and when they are cut the soil begins to wash away—slowly when the land is flat and the rain is gentle (as in much of Western Europe); very quickly on steep land in the tropics, where many of the forests in developing countries are situated. When the tropical rainy season begins, torrents of soil pour into streams and rivers off deforested hillsides. Often farmers must move on after five or six years because not enough soil is left to grow crops. Terracing, planting hedges, or even contour plowing could help stop the erosion, but the peasant farmers who are now encroaching on forested hills around the world bring with them a tradition of flatland farming. They farm the hills as their fathers farmed the plains, with devastating consequences. In Nepal and Ethiopia, both highland nations, officials joke that their chief export is soil.

But soil erosion is not only destructive to land that loses soil. Almost everywhere in the less-developed countries, flooding caused by upstream deforestation has increased drastically in this century. Silt from soil erosion builds up a river's bed and increases its volume so that it floods more often, bringing disaster to lowland farmers. Waterborne silt can make a new reservoir or hydroelectric dam useless within 25 years. The silting up of rivers can leave a port city stranded in a swamp unless the city can afford the expense of constant dredging; the newly created swamp may become infested with malarial mosquitoes. Thus, soil erosion leaves barren land behind it and brings destruction to new places. In much of the world, soil is disappearing too fast to be replaced for many human lifetimes.

A second effect of deforestation is that continued cutting of trees without replanting eventually means that people cannot find firewood. In the third world, wood is used mainly for fuel to heat houses and to cook food. But the larger and larger populations of most poor countries are relying on fewer and fewer trees each year. In parts of Africa's Sahel desert region, looking for firewood is a full-time, year-round occupation for at least one member of every family. In Katmandu, Nepal, a load of firewood may cost $125—while the gross national product per capita is only $120. In much of the south and southwestern Asia, the Andes and elsewhere, there are virtually no trees, and people can no longer buy firewood. Instead, they burn livestock dung and crop residues for fuel. Soil productivity then declines because the dung and residues are no longer spread on farmland as fertilizer.

The introduction of livestock to arid or steep land can also cause soil erosion and prevent regrowth of plants that would hold down the soil. Sheep and goats especially tend to crop young plants down to the roots. Livestock grazing is the single largest reason for the southward march of the Sahara, and has contributed greatly in the past and today to the barren condition of much of the Mediterranean region and the Middle East.

The governments of developing countries have become more interested in protecting their soil and forests as the gravity of the problem has become obvious in many places. China has doubled its forested land since 1949; South Korea and Israel have carried out major reforestation campaigns. Kenya, the Philippines, Mexico, Cuba, Thailand and other nations officially promote the planting and protection of trees. The UN Food and Agriculture Organization is only one of a number of international organizations that are working to alleviate the problem. About half the world's much-needed forest grows in just three countries of the developed world: the U.S.S.R., Canada, and the United States.

A Change in the Air

Atmospheric pollution is the most universal of environmental problems, because air is constantly moving, respecting no national borders. When China conducts aboveground nuclear tests, the radioactivity may be detected above Seattle.

Smog is one of the oldest—and most visible—environmental problems. During the Middle Ages, coal burning was forbidden in London because of the smoke. The London fog that shrouded Sherlock Holmes was what we would now call heavy smog. In Belgium in the 1930s, after a smog disaster in the Meuse valley, it was found for the first time that smog was capable of making people seriously ill and even of killing them. By the late 1960s, smog was a problem in large cities worldwide, caused as much by automobile exhaust as by industry. But because it was such an obvious health hazard, smog received early attention from lawmakers pressured by an angry public. In many industrial countries today, air pollution is less overwhelming than it was ten or twenty years ago, although it has not ceased to be an important concern. As a result, the countries with the most extreme air pollution problems now tend to be less-developed nations like Mexico—whose capital has perhaps the most smog of any large city in the world. Many of these countries, faced with a choice between development with accompanying pollution and no development, are willing to tolerate some pollution of the air and water.

Acid rain is a second problem, mainly affecting industrial nations. It appears when pollutants from a factory oxidize and fall as rain in areas often far from the smokestacks. The highly acidic rain can eventually eliminate all plant and fish life in lakes and streams. Acid rain has become a touchy issue between the United States and Canada; Canada alleges that most of the acid rain that has killed fish in its wilderness lakes comes from Ohio Valley pollution. The Scandinavian countries likewise complain that acid rain from West Germany, France, Britain and the Low Countries is killing their fish. Since there is no obvious remedy for the condition of these lakes, and since the acid rain has been increasing for several decades, environmentalists have pressed for greater control over factory emissions. But businessmen and economists question the high costs, rigid standards and soundness of scientific data on which the regulations governing clean air are based. They also question whether, particularly in a financial slump, the cost of expensive "scrubbers" for smokestacks is justified—especially since there is no way to prove that any one plant has damaged a particular body of water far away.

Another subject for concern has been the ozone layer, the crucial section of the stratosphere that screens life on earth from the sun's harmful ultraviolet rays. Recent research seems to indicate that chlorofluorocarbons, chemicals used as refrigerants, solvents, and propellants in spray cans, may be destroying ozone molecules as the chlorofluorocarbons float up through the stratosphere, over a period of from 10 to 200 years. The National Academy of Sciences has predicted a 16% increase in human exposure to ultraviolet rays over the next 20 years because of loss of ozone. The main result of increased exposure would be a rise in skin cancer rates. However, the effects of chlorofluorocarbons are still incompletely known. While the United States and Canada, among others, have banned their use except under certain restricted conditions, many nations continue to manufacture and use the chemicals, unconvinced that they may be dangerous.

Conspicuous Wastes:
A Problem That Won't Go Away

As civilization has grown and become more sophisticated, so have the wastes it produces. Disposal of wastes—including biological, chemical, industrial, and nuclear—has become a major problem in modern societies.

The most serious disposal problem is that of nuclear wastes. Every year, the world's nuclear reactors produce millions of cubic feet of radioactive waste, including perhaps 140,000 cubic feet of high-level (i.e. especially toxic) waste containing uranium and plutonium. So far, no permanent storage method for these wastes has been devised. A method that would keep the wastes secure for hundreds of years is not enough; plutonium, one of the most poisonous substances known, has a half-life of 25,000 years, about five times the length of recorded human history. (Half-life is the time it takes for half a radioactive substance to decay. For example, after 25,000 years half the original amount of plutonium would be left; after 50,000 years, one-quarter; and so on.) Any sizable amount of plutonium could therefore remain dangerous to human and other life for up to half a million years. Proposals that have been considered for the storage of these wastes include burial in containers deep in ocean-basin mud; encasing solidified waste in glass or ceramic and burying it in deep granite or salt formations; and sending it in rockets to outer space.

There are serious disposal problems with other kinds of toxic wastes, such as the 30,000 chemicals the United Nations International Register lists as possibly dangerous. Many modern chemicals are synthetic and do not easily decompose; they must be safely contained until they are no longer dangerous. In the United States, disposal of toxic wastes became a highly charged political issue after the publicity given the evacuation of Love Canal, a community built over a chemical dump that had been sold to the city. New laws require safe handling and disposal of toxic wastes in the United States, and most industrial countries now have fairly high standards.

Minerals and Fossil Fuels:
A Burning Issue

Of all the potential "resource shortages," none has generated
so much public discussion as the energy crisis. The world economy
runs on fossil fuels, especially on oil, the leading world energy
source. Fossil fuels, which form from organic matter over millions
of years, are not as abundant as other minerals. While many minerals can be recycled over and over, fossil fuels can be burned for
energy only once. Their relative scarcity and exhaustibility pose
important questions for the future of the world economy. The
present oil "glut" is undoubtedly temporary; it could last into the
1990s—or it could end sooner. When the reserves are exhausted
and production ends, what will replace oil?

While coal and natural gas are more abundant than oil, they
are also potentially exhaustible, in the sense that continued production at high rates would deplete known reserves within several
human generations. While the same is theoretically true of other
mineral reserves, in practice fossil fuels, since they can only be
used once, are in more danger of disappearing. Also, the composi-
tion of the earth's core and mantle is still largely unknown and
many scientists speculate that enormous amounts of minerals may
eventually be mined from deep in the earth. But fossil fuels, because they come from ancient organic matter, are necessarily
found near the earth's crust, and future deep-earth mining offers
little hope of finding replacements for them.

The reaction to possible shortages of fossil fuels has been var-
ied. Many environmentalists believe that conservation, solar energy, and other alternative power sources such as thermal and wind
energy will provide enough energy for the world of the future.
Some analysts believe that nuclear power offers the only hope to
meet future energy needs. And some believe that market forces
and new technology, as in the past, will lead to new, more efficient
and cheaper energy sources. Under the pressure of rising oil prices
since 1973, U.S. oil consumption has declined, supplies have become abundant again, and prices have flattened, they note, and the
pessimistic projections of the past eight years proved wrong.

Most of the world's mineral production, like most of its fossil fuel, is consumed in the developed world. For example, Latin America, Asia and Africa have about three-quarters of the world's people, but they consume less than a quarter of the world's minerals. As energy prices have risen, the cost of producing minerals has also gone up, since mining and processing are energy-intensive activities. This has meant that mineral supplies have not expanded as much as might have been expected from population and development figures. There is not likely to be a major shortage of minerals in the near future; however, some strategic minerals are found only in certain politically unstable nations, or nations unfriendly to the United States. Cobalt, essential in jet aircraft engines, for example, is found mainly in Zaire; chromium, used in stainless steel, is found primarily in South Africa, Zimbabwe, and the Soviet Union. Disruptions in trade with such nations could cause shortages.

Living Species and Wilderness: On the Endangered List?

Animals and plants may not often be thought of as natural resources, but they are so, today more than ever. While past arguments against species extinction—such as the right of nonhuman creatures to life, and their aesthetic and ecological value—are still valid, today there is the added consideration that the promising new technology of genetic engineering, as well as other sciences, depends on existing genes. Every species extinction impoverishes the science of the future by leaving it a smaller "gene pool" to draw on.

Most of the world's plant and animal species live in the tropics, especially in the tropical woodlands that are disappearing at high rates today. Only a small proportion of these tropical forest species (mostly insects and plants) has been classified, and an even smaller proportion has been explored for scientific value. Yet the discoveries made from them have already been immensely valuable. Many useful drugs, including quinine and treatments for various forms of cancer, hypertension, malaria and other medical problems, originated in tropical plants. New strains of crops have also been found in the tropics and bred with "domesticated" varieties to produce hardier, more fertile plants. Sometimes, potentially valuable species are found in only one small place in the world, and that one place may be threatened with human activity that could destroy the species.

But at what cost to humans are species preserved? When the minuscule snail darter held up construction of the multimillion-dollar Tellico Dam in Tennessee for several years, many people were outraged; the dam was eventually completed. On the Serengeti Plain, in Tanzania, millions of animals roam across one of the world's largest game reserves. Tourists enrich the Tanzanian economy on their photographic safaris through the park. But the per capita income in Tanzania is $240 a year. A rhinoceros horn, or the skin of a leopard or cheetah, may bring a poacher enough money to feed his family for a year. Understandably, it has been difficult to halt poaching. How can the interests of people and other living species be reconciled?

Another kind of problem concerns the world fisheries. Fish for eating are in no danger of extinction. But since 1970, when it reached a high, the world fish catch has remained fairly steady. Fish are the only "wild animals" that are eaten in great numbers; it may be necessary to breed them on underwater "farms" to increase the catch, since even ultramodern trawling equipment has failed to bring in more fish over the past ten years. The leveling off of the catch seems to indicate that a natural limit of sorts has been reached. Barring some new development, it seems likely that fish will provide a decreasing proportion of the world's protein in the coming years as the human population grows.

The resource and environmental problems discussed above serve to give some perspective on the scope of such problems. In many cases, the signs are alarming, and environmental damage seems to be increasing. But hopeful signs are also present, and human ingenuity has defeated many resource problems in the past.

Looking For Answers

No one is "against" a healthy environment. When the environment is damaged, it is not because someone set out deliberately to harm it, but because the harm was a side effect of the pursuit of a goal. The goal may be simple survival, or it may be economic growth. The choices that must be made between the pursuit of these goals and environmental protection are seldom easy.

Is environmental protection compatible with economic growth, and if so, to what extent? Must there be a choice between environmental protection and the satisfaction of human needs? How will the growing world population affect these decisions? The answers to these questions may well be different in different parts of the world.

Environment vs. Economic Growth

"Are not poverty and need the greatest polluters?" asked India's Prime Minister Indira Gandhi at the Stockholm Conference. The countries of the third world ask themselves if they can afford to set their environmental standards high, and for the most part their answer is No. Poor nations are usually willing to accept higher rates of industrial pollution both because they have less industry and because they have less money available for regulation than wealthy nations do. For their environmental problems, less-developed nations also have little money. They must often depend on foreign aid for help in reforestation, agricultural extension work, drilling wells, and other projects that the national or local government would normally carry out.

Some believe that a higher standard of living is necessary before concern about the environment is warranted. In this argument, environmental advocacy is a luxury; this explains why environmentalism first arose in wealthy countries. After people's basic needs are supplied, they want a healthy and aesthetically pleasing environment. In a poor country, however, attention must be paid to economic development and social needs before environmental protection becomes relevant. Another argument, however, says that "prevention is better and cheaper than cure" and that without a healthy environment it is impossible to raise standards of living very far. Therefore it is necessary to protect and conserve in order to continue economic development.

In industrial nations, the environmental questions are of a different order. The money is available, and there are usually environmental regulations concerning air and water, but these alone do not necessarily guarantee a better environment. Industries complain that overregulation and rigid standards force them to spend enormous sums on measures that yield only marginal gains in health. The burden of making existing plants conform, they say, prevents them from building new facilities that would be less polluting and at the same time more profitable.

Some environmentalists in return say that regulation is essential and that the costs of regulation—to prevent health-damaging pollution and other problems—are part of doing business. Before regulation, these costs were "externalized"—not paid by industry or agriculture but by "civilians," in the form of higher medical bills, lost time at work, accidents, cleaning bills, and so on. Regulation, according to this argument, merely returns these externalized costs to their originators. For example, a Council on Environmental Quality (a government agency) study in 1978 estimated that while the United States spent $16.6 billion in 1977 to meet clean air standards, the savings in health care and air pollution damage to property came to $21.4 billion. Many supporters of environmental controls, however, also acknowledge that the present system in the United States is costly and in need of reform. The current laws, with permits and requirements, can lead to "analysis paralysis," in which nothing is done for years at a time, while reports are written and analyzed and lawyers argue in court. In the case of the multibillion-dollar Federal sewage-treatment construction program authorized by the Clean Water Act of 1972, critics charge that the program (the second largest public works program in U.S. history) has contributed more to urban sprawl than to cleaning up streams. Communities have used Federal funds to build sewage-treatment plants in anticipation of future growth.

In the Reagan Administration, unlike the Carter Administration, economic considerations are paramount as the White House emphasizes recovery from a decade or more of stagnation and inflation. President Ronald Reagan appointed as Secretary of the Interior the business-oriented—and controversial—James G.

Watt. The Reagan Administration has pushed for relaxation of some environmental standards, including the Clean Air Act of 1970, saying that the standards should be based on "sound" scientific data and "real" health risks. Current antipollution programs are too expensive for the benefits they provide, the Administration believes, adding 0.4% a year to the consumer price index. The coal industry, for example, believes that the Clean Air Act, which mandates "scrubbers" to remove sulfur and solid particles in smoke, has been exorbitantly expensive to implement and has held up the development of coal—abundant in the United States—as an alternative to imported energy.

One proposal that some economists have suggested is for the government to tax polluters according to the monetary value it places on clean air and water. In the past, this argument goes, clean air and water were considered "free goods" that no one need account for, because they were so abundant. But it is now apparent that clean air and water are not unlimited and that they do have an economic value, although it is not clear what that value is. Should business have to pay for its consumptive use of clean air and water?

The conflict between full-scale environmental protection and full-scale economic development is a basic one. Has there been too much emphasis on protection and not enough on the wise utilization of resources? Should there be less or more "environmental protection" than now? The Reagan Administration believes that existing laws are sufficient to protect the natural resources of the United States; when the United States must depend heavily on imported oil, in its view, it is neither right nor economical to keep fossil fuels "locked up" in protected wilderness, national forest, or national park areas. Are regulatory laws due for a reform, as many believe? Is there a risk that reforms would lead to a dismantling of present safeguards? Can environmental protection, as Secretary Watt contends, be compatible with increased development of natural resources? Can the United States afford, in a time of financial trouble, to insist on cleaning up air and water and on preserving the wilderness? Or, as U.S. population continues to increase, are clean air, clean water, and untouched nature more necessary than ever?

The U.S. and the World Environment

Does the United States have an economic or moral interest in the state of the environment in poorer nations? Or should the United States tend to the poor and unemployed of Detroit and New York and Los Angeles before it tries to right wrongs overseas? Many Americans believe foreign aid should be the nation's lowest priority, as many congressmen know from their mail; foreign aid heads the list of favorite budget cuts. Americans often believe that aid leads to dependency without gratitude. The Administration is convinced that the solution to third world development is freer trade, including low tariffs and opportunities for private investment with less regulation of foreign business. Private enterprise and the free market, in this view, brought high standards of living to Western countries and will do the same in the third world. The Administration plans to encourage continued high sales of food, especially grains, to other countries.

Another argument, however, says that foreign aid is necessary because such projects as the building of roads, railroads, and dams in the third world do not draw foreign private investment. Without adequate ports, roads and energy supplies, poor countries cannot attract the foreign corporations that can help their development. Although the proportion of the gross national product per capita that the United States spends on foreign aid has declined drastically over the past 20 years, the OPEC nations and Japan have begun sizable foreign aid programs in the past few years. They have done so, some observers claim, not because they are innately more altruistic but because they believe foreign aid to be in their own "enlightened self-interest," promoting a world in which more people are prosperous and therefore are better trade partners and are more interested in stability.

Is There Enough To Go Around?

The absolute problem of resource sufficiency concerns population more than any other factor. If the world population continues to increase at the rates of the past 20 years, it has been said, all causes are lost ones. While it is unlikely that such high growth rates will continue, and while they are already dropping even in many less-developed countries, the world population will almost certainly continue to grow until well into the next century. Even if the relative problem of unequal distribution of resources were solved, such a continuously increasing population could put a tremendous strain on world institutions and supplies. The economic and political significance of an enormous national population is not yet completely understood. In China, the world's most populous nation, with over a billion people, newlywed couples are now urged to have only one child and are penalized if they go over the limit. While such measures may seem repugnant to people in democratic nations, many Chinese believe that this is the only realistic way to prevent the population from growing to disastrous proportions. What will happen when India, now a democratic nation of 650 million, reaches 1 billion, as projected by the year 2000? Some economists doubt that political freedom can survive in nations where the population reaches such vast numbers.

But population is not the only problem, as others are quick to point out. The distribution of resources is a major consideration. Would a reduction in U.S. consumption of resources, for example, help or hurt the less-developed countries? Some say that it would benefit them in the long run, but others disagree. The United States, as consumer, is a major customer of the developing countries. Its economic growth and prosperity have a "ripple effect" that benefits the global economy. The United States and the other industrialized nations help raise the standard of living in less-developed countries through aid, trade, industrialization, and shared technology.

In 1978, when the English economist Thomas Malthus published his famous *Essay on the Principle of Population,* which argued that population increased faster than food supply, he said, "There should be no more people in a country than could enjoy a glass of wine or a piece of beef with their dinner." Malthus believed that population was the key to world resource sufficiency, and that without control of population growth the world would face catastrophe. In his 1807 book, *Political and Philosophical Essays,* another noted Englishman, William Hazlitt, disagreed:

Mr. Malthus wishes to confound the necessary limits of the earth with the arbitrary distribution of that produce according to the institutions of society or the caprice of individuals, the laws of God and nature with the laws of man.

In essence, this argument is still going on today. Are there by nature "limits to growth"? Or is there no limit to human ingenuity in overcoming limits?

THE CONSERVATISM OF THE LIBERALS[2]

Nineteen-seventy [was] the moment when the liberal coalition of the upper-middle class and the blacks was under its severest strain—and, not uncoincidentally, almost the precise moment when environmentalism burst upon the national political agenda.

The liberal coalition, as I said, was forged mainly by the union of interests between upper-middle-class people and the poor. But by the late 1960s, the whole situation was beginning to fray. Black rage (perhaps egged on a bit by liberal solicitation) had exploded into a series of brutal riots. Quasi-military organizations like the Black Panthers and the Puerto Rican Young Lords were spearheading a new style of political gangsterism. Moreover, the white radicals who had followed their cause into the ghettos were emerging with a strong bent toward violence themselves. Bombings and political terrorism were gaining a foothold in American society.

Into this increasingly dangerous situation, the budding environmental movement introduced a simple but powerful idea. Social conditions were certainly bad, it said. The war in Vietnam was a continuing cancer, and there was much social injustice to be set right. But far more important than that, *the earth itself was endangered.* The spread of pollution, of poisonous pesticides, and of population posed an immediate threat to human society that significantly overshadowed all these social problems. What would

[2]Excerpted from *Progress and Privilege: America in the Age of Environmentalism,* by William Tucker, contributing editor of *Harper's* magazine. Copyright© 1982 by William Tucker. Reprinted by permission of the publisher, Doubleday & Company, Inc.

be the good of solving all these social difficulties, the environmental movement asked, if we destroyed the planet in the process? As Thoreau had put it, "What is the use of a house if you haven't got a tolerable planet to put it on?" And so, in the competition of ideas which plays such a quiet but crucial role in our national life, the environmental movement was born.

I do not mean to downgrade the environmental movement by saying this. I think environmentalism was probably the best thing that happened in American politics in the early 1970s. It is fair to say, I think, that the reason that American student radicalism did not veer into violence and terrorism during the early '70s, the way it did in Europe, is probably that environmentalism absorbed so much of the energies of young people. One of the striking things about the early environmental literature is how many writers are at pains to emphasize that "you don't have to go out and throw bombs" in order to join the ecology crusade. . . .

Put quite simply, the birth of environmentalism represented a withdrawing of upper-middle-class attention from the interests of the poor and a turning in another direction. . . . Tom Wolfe probably captured this moment of realization perfectly in *Radical Chic,* when he described the bad publicity that fell upon Leonard Bernstein and other East Side literati when their efforts to entertain the Black Panthers at a fund-raising party turned sour:

"The panic turned out to be good for Friends of the Earth, somewhat the way the recession has been bad for the Four Seasons but good for Riker's. Many matrons, such as Cheray Duchin, turned their attention toward the sables, cheetahs, and leopards, once the Panthers became Radioactive."

For myself, the most astute description I have ever read of the environmental movement appeared in a small article carried in a Boston counterculture newspaper in 1978 about a recent meeting of antinuclear activists. The organization, called Supporters of Silkwood, was meeting to support the court case of the family of a 26-year-old Oklahoma woman who claimed to have been exposed to plutonium at a nuclear reprocessing plant, and later died in an auto accident. The article, which was entirely sympathetic to the cause, began as follows:

"About 50 members of the Cambridge liberal establishment, including academics, attorneys, journalists, politicians, 'just plain old rich people,' and at least one Nobel laureate, attended a fundraiser at a private home in the plush Observatory Hill neighborhood last week for the benefit of the Karen Silkwood Memorial Coalition."

Without going into the merits of the particular case, the roster of guests expresses perfectly, to my mind, what environmentalism has been all about. Every survey that has ever been taken (including the Sierra Club's extensive polling of its own membership) has shown that support for environmentalism has been concentrated in the upper-middle-class, professional segment of society. Academics, attorneys, doctors, dentists, journalists, and upper-income suburbanites have been, without question, the backbone of the movement. One extensive polling showed that support for environmental causes picks up strongly when income levels reach about $30,000, and then tails off again significantly above $70,000. It is about at this level that the salaries of upper-echelon business executives usually begin. (Academics, who lead comfortably sheltered lives, are usually able to make it into the ranks of the upper-middle class without attaining quite the same salary levels.)

But the key to understanding environmentalism lies in the presence of those "just plain old rich people." Why are they so necessary to the chemistry of the environmental movement? The answer is easy, once we recognize what environmentalism represents. Environmentalism, as I have said, is the ideas of aristocratic conservatism translated onto a popular scale. The "plain old rich people" have brought the ideas and attitudes. (And it is important to recognize just how many "plain old rich people" there are in most of the major environmental organizations.) . . .

Aristocratic values do not come easily but require a great deal of training. The idea of looking on material progress and economic security as an irrelevant and vulgar nuisance cannot be picked up overnight. The old saying was that it took three generations to make a gentleman, and I have the distinct impression that it now takes at least two generations to make an environmentalist. It is usually the sons and daughters of people who have achieved complete material security who make the most strident environmentalists. In families where there is at least some memory of hard times—some generational recollection that economic security is not in the natural order of things—the impulse toward environmentalism usually does not run as strong. (Keep in mind, again, that I am not talking about specific environmental issues, but only the unmistakable loftiness which maintains that "greed," "vulgar materialism," "progress," or simply "people" themselves are the root of the problem.)

Environmentalism has been the mass adoption of aristocratic values by America's burgeoning upper-middle class. It is the "conservatism of the liberals." Once the liberal program of upper-middle-class people creating government programs to sponsor disadvantaged people began to exhaust itself, a very predictable turn of events occurred. Upper-middle-class people decided that *they too* were "disadvantaged" and deserved a liberal program. This accounts for one of the more annoying aspects of the environmental movement—the tendency of its exponents to borrow rhetorical terms from previous liberal programs and try to picture themselves as an "abused minority." The truth is, in fact, the very opposite. One does not become an environmentalist until one achieves some kind of privilege and feels one has something worth protecting. Environmentalists are a *privileged* minority.

In the early days of the crusade, there was a great deal of hope that environmentalism could be characterized as everybody's issue. After all, who could be in favor of pollution, or against saving the earth? This early hope was vastly encouraged by the speed with which the pro-business Nixon Administration picked up the environmental banner and made it a major issue. In his 1970 State of the Union address, President Nixon announced that the deterioration of the environment was a national crisis, and that new environmental legislation would be a major priority of his Administration. Although there has been much criticism that Nixon was only co-opting the issue and was not sincere, there is no question from the record that the Nixon Administration was remarkably sincere in its commitment to environmental legislation.

At the time of Nixon's speech, the National Environmental Policy Act of 1969 (which inaugurated the "environmental impact statement") was the only major piece of legislation that had resulted from the new movement. Over the next two years, the Clean Air Act and the Federal Water Pollution Control Act—both major departures from previous legislation—were pushed through Congress with broad bipartisan support. Memoirs from the inner circles of the Nixon Administration show clearly that the Executive branch pushed ahead on the environmental program with very few misgivings about what some of the limitations might be.

Throughout the period, environmentalism has attracted a broad variety of conservative and liberal support. On Earth Day, 1970, the inaugural moment when the academically based environmental movement "went public," the featured speaker at one very liberal Long Island university was Barry Goldwater, who reminisced about his love of Arizona's natural landscape. James Buckley, the Conservative Party Senator from New York, who was elected to his only term in 1970, was at the time, and has remained, an enthusiastic supporter of environmental causes. As late as 1979, he was still writing articles on protecting endangered species. One of the first books published on the subject, still distributed by environmental groups, was *Arthur Godfrey's Environmental Reader*. *Reader's Digest* also emerged as an enthusiastic and long-term suppporter of environmental concerns.

The question arose, then, if Richard Nixon and Edmund Muskie, Barry Goldwater and Edward Kennedy, Arthur Godfrey and Robert Redford, Republicans and Democrats, liberals and conservatives, could all be in favor of environmentalism, who could conceivably be against it? The answer did not emerge clearly for many years, until the true implications of environmentalism began to make themselves felt.

What environmental enthusiasts unfortunately failed to recognize is that, if environmentalism was indeed everybody's issue, that only held true as long as everybody included people whose status was at least upper-middle class. What environmentalism did was to cut society *laterally*. The enemy-of-the-enemy alignment took on less importance. Environmentalism, because it is oriented toward the status quo, had an inevitable appeal to people toward the top of the social ladder, and a negative appeal to those nearer the bottom. When environmentalists said "we already have enough," and "it's time to stop all this growth-for-growth's-sake," they were very accurately representing their *own* position of economic security. But anyone who was further down the scale and was depending on future growth and progress to improve their lot would be instinctively opposed to the environmental doctrine. The basic flaw of environmentalism—and indeed of all the previous "environmental movements" in history—was beginning to emerge. At heart, environmentalism favors the affluent over the poor, the haves over the have-nots.

But this was not entirely obvious in 1970. What was most surprising at that point was the alacrity with which this supposedly liberal cause was adopted by "conservative" business leaders. Even environmentalists seemed somewhat surprised by this pattern, and were inevitably suspicious that the business establishment was only *pretending* to embrace environmentalism in order to subvert it. In fact, these fears were unfounded.

What emerged instead was a notable split personality among many business people—the executive who worried at the office all day about the costs of curbing pollution but found when he returned to his suburban home at night that environmentalism expressed his interests almost perfectly. Often it was the husband of the family who remained business-oriented while the wife became the strong environmentalist. Perhaps the classic example of this ambivalence is Walter Hickel, President Nixon's Secretary of the Interior and a self-made millionaire who almost wasn't confirmed by the Senate because of his views about the need to proceed with development in Alaska. After less than two years in Washington, Hickel made a complete conversion to environmentalism, and wrote a book worrying about how growth and prosperity were destroying the country. Few college radicals who had begun to swing the banner of ecology could have anticipated the tremendous fervor with which surburban America suddenly embraced environmentalism in the early 1970s. What had been assumed to be a rather radical cause suddenly had all the markings of a middle-of-the-road issue.

Who was against environmentalism then? Initially, blacks were one of the few groups heard expressing some reservations about the sudden turn in liberal thought. On Earth Day, 1970, when a group of California college students buried an automobile

in order to symbolize their renunciation of materialism, the event
was picketed by a group of black students, who said that resources,
rather than being wasted in such a conspicuous fashion, should
be put to work in improving the lot of the poor. (The event did
indeed come perilously close to Veblen's description of conspicuous waste.)

This constant dissent of articulate blacks from the environmental agenda has been a running source of embarrassment to a
movement that has tried desperately for over a decade to preserve
the idea that it is a liberal crusade. As late as 1979, for example,
Vernon Jordan, Director of the Urban League, was asked to at-
tend a joint conference on urban and environmental affairs, intended to heal the breach in the liberal ranks. He responded with
these remarks:

"Walk down Twelfth Street [in Washington, D.C.] and ask
the proverbial man on the street what he thinks about the snail
darter and you are likely to get the blankest look you ever experienced. Ask him what he thinks the basic urban environmental
problem is, and he'll tell you jobs. I don't intend to raise the sim-
pleminded equation of snail darters and jobs, but that does symbolize an implicit divergence of interests between some segments
of the environmental movement and the bulk of black and urban
people. . . .

"[Environmentalists] will find in the black community absolute hostility to anything smacking of no-growth or limits-to-
growth. Some people have been too cavalier in proposing policies
to preserve the physical environment for themselves while other,
poorer people pay the costs."

Bayard Rustin, the veteran civil-rights and labor leader, has
called environmentalists "self-righteous, elitist, neo-Malthusians
who call for slow growth or no growth . . . [and who] would con-
demn the black underclass, the slum proletariat, and rural blacks,
to permanent poverty." Thomas Sowell, the prominent California
economist, has said: "Regulatory rules have impeded people who
are climbing rather than people who are already at the top. There
is a fundamental conflict between the affluent people, who can afford to engage in environmental struggles, and the poor. . . . You
don't see many black faces in the Sierra Club." It is probably some

measure of the way in which black opinion tends to get submerged in the political arena when it does not support the liberal agenda that so little of this black opposition to environmentalism is ever visible in the press.

Labor unions have also been in the forefront of opposition to the environmental movement. By the early '70s, labor columnist Victor Reisel was repeating the joke about God telling Moses that before he parts the Red Sea He is first going to have to get permission from the Environmental Protection Agency. The bumper sticker "If You're Hungry and Out of Work, Eat an Environmentalist!" was originated by labor unions. Considering that many, many environmental campaigns have involved opposition to large-scale construction projects, power plants, highways, and factories that involve blue collar jobs, this is not surprising. Whenever enthusiastic college students go out to picket a nuclear plant, they always find a group of hard-hat construction workers ready to throw bricks at them. As one union official put it: "These environmentalists are a bunch of bloody elitists. . . . If it's 'no growth' they're advocating, then what they're really saying is: 'We've got enough for ourselves, but you stay down there.'"

The working-class, labor-union revolt against both environmentalism and the poor-oriented thrust of the Democratic liberal agenda finally made up the major factor in Ronald Reagan's 1980 Presidential majority, particularly in the Western part of the country. This revolt has often been called Populist, and I think the term is justified. Many of its roots go back to the original conservation movement of the early 1900s and the battles that were then fought about how the country's Western resources should be developed. In general, this neo-Populist revolt against environmentalism has been literally a quarrel between the haves and the have-nots, between the urban and suburban liberal establishment intent on protecting its positions of privilege and the broad reaches of lower-middle-class and poor people, who feel that they do not yet have enough.

Nor does one have to be *absolutely* privileged in order to find environmentalism useful. It need only be a matter of relative privilege. I have often felt that the conversion to environmentalism occurs shortly after an urban, middle-class family finally purchases its first suburban home in, let us say, Maple Grove Acres. The family looks out the window at a beautiful field next door and exclaims, "At last, we're living in the country." Two months later, however, a nearly hysterical neighbor arrives with the bad news: "Do you know our beautiful field next door? Well, it's actually Maple Grove Acres II, and the builder is going before the planning board tomorrow night to get final approval on construction. We've got to go down and stop him." It is at this moment that an environmentalist is born. The problems of endangered species, overpopulation and the deteriorating quality of life suddenly become startlingly real. It is time to stop development and start worrying about fragile ecosystems.

In 1976, Bernard Frieden, an MIT professor of urban studies, visited the San Francisco area with the intention of writing a book on how the suburbs were attempting to exclude blacks. After watching suburban environmentalism in action for two years, he came to a startling conclusion. The suburbs were no longer simply trying to exclude blacks, he said, they were trying to exclude *everybody*. Absurd environmental restrictions (such as requirements that new homes be built on stilts to protect migrating salamanders) were being written into zoning ordinances of hundreds of suburban towns. Their sole intent was to keep other people out. The old suburban game of exclusionary zoning was now being played at a much more sophisticated level. No longer were privacy and economic segregation the issue—now it was all being done under the guise of protecting nature.

The realization that affluent people can serve their own self-interest simply by preventing any more economic growth has been one of the most difficult to make. We ordinarily think of people serving their self-interest by making more money themselves, not by preventing others from doing the same. Veblen, facing the same problem in explaining the anti-industrial attitudes and opposition to progress among the wealthy plutocracy of his day, wrote; "When an explanation of this class conservatism is offered, it is commonly the invidious one that the wealthy class opposes innovation because it has a vested interest, of an unworthy sort, in maintaining the present conditions."

Instead, he argued, it was their insulation from economic stress that kept the elite from adjusting to the idea of further economic change:

"The leisure class is in great measure sheltered from the stress of those economic exigencies which prevail in any modern, highly organized industrial community. The exigencies of the struggle for the means of life are less exacting for this class than for any other; and as a consequence of this privileged position we should expect to find it one of the least responsive of the classes of society to the demands which the situation makes for a further growth of institutions and a readjustment to an altered industrial situation. The leisure class is the conservative class."

All this probably explains why, if environmentalists have been extremely efficient at turning up problems in an industrial society, they have also been ever-so-slightly inclined toward exaggerating them. Seeking to institutionalize the status quo has given upper-middle-class people a peculiar vested interest in the possibilities for impending disaster.

Writing in response to the 1973–74 Arab Oil Embargo, for example, environmentalists Paul and Anne Ehrlich told their audience:

"Unfortunately, there's very little you can do about the international situation, except to keep informed about it. . . .

"The obvious shakiness of the English economy might tend to stiffen your resistance to TV ads encouraging the purchase of English automobiles (where will parts come from if Great Britain's economy collapses?). Knowing that Kenyatta cannot last much longer might persuade you not to put off a long-anticipated visit to the game parks of Kenya."

And even though the Ehrlichs are talking about a complete breakdown of the world order, their tone belies any real concern:

"You should . . . be taking steps to reduce your dependence on the services provided by our complex society and making arrangements to protect yourself and your family against the worst eventuality. . . .

"The best choice is relatively complete independence from the system as a life-style. . . . If you've had extensive camp cooking experience, you're way ahead of the game."

Perhaps the most perceptive criticism of these attitudes was written right at the dawn of the environmental era by Chicago newspaper columnist Jon Margolis. In an article entitled "Our Country 'Tis of Thee, Land of Ecology," published in *Esquire* in 1970, Margolis noted: "Searching for their hundred-fifty-year-old Vermont farmhouses, conservationists wonder how people can actually want to live in a new, $25,000 split-level in the suburbs, apparently never thinking that for most people the alternative is a three-room walk-up in the downtown smog. The suburbs are open to them, as Vermont to the more affluent, because of technology, because draining swamps and dirtying streams and damming rivers and polluting the air gave them high-paying jobs. Shouting about the environmental catastrophe, urging an end to growth, the conservationists are $20,000-a-year men telling all the $7,500-a-year men simply to stay where they are so we can all survive."

Writing in a similar vein about how prep-school boys were adjusting to the "era of limits," Nelson Aldrich, Jr., penned this prescient sentence about modern Doomsday attitudes: "Just discernible in this new Preppie idealism is a wish, barely disguised as a fear, that the era of economic growth may really be finished, and that a New Dark Age may be upon us."

It is this fervent *wish* for an environmental day of reckoning—that hope that some grand historical turning point has been reached where economic growth will be halted—that constitutes the secret of the upper-middle class's fervent embrace of the Doomsday mystique. If further progress will only lead to disaster, then perhaps the status quo will harden and remain forever.

In this kind of framework, the only disappointment occurs when Environmental Doomsday doesn't come.

THE ENVIRONMENTAL COMMUNITY[3]

It is certainly no secret that the environmental movement to-day is united as never before in its long history in its perception that the Reagan Administration has instituted changes in public lands policy of the most radical and extreme nature, breaking almost completely with the 100-year bipartisan tradition that has governed the approach of nearly every other Administration. There has never been anything quite like the approach of this Administration before—at least not for a very long time; and we do indeed have definite and very strong views about this "public lands program" of the Reagan Administration as it unfolds before us. . . .

To understand this, we need to understand a bit about the environmental movement itself: who we are, where we have come from—what is our history?

This is necessary I think, because to believe some of the rhetoric I sometimes listen to at public hearings, or read in trade association journals, one would think that we're just some johnny-come-latelies who just happened on the scene around Earth Day sometime—well meaning but confused folks whose knowledge and understanding of the environment is limited to coffee table books and cocktail parties.

We're either "rich elitists" or "long-haired hippies," depending on who is speaking—and I still can't figure out if those two are supposed to go together or not!

And then finally, there are the comments about the so-called "hired guns," the "paid people" in Washington who work for environmental organizations, and who just sit around all day dreaming up new ways to raise money or whip our members into shape—we don't really care about the environment, and we certainly don't speak for our members—that's at least what's been said.

It's an interesting picture indeed, and as you might imagine, it's not quite how we see ourselves.

[3]Excerpted from a speech by Brock Evans, vice president for national issues of the Audubon Society. *Vital Speeches of the Day.* 48:235–41. F. 1, '82. Reprinted by permission.

First of all, environmentalism is a real, genuine movement; environmentalism, in the sense of commonly accepted goals, beliefs, and values, is widespread and pervasive throughout most of our society, without much distinction between ages, classes, sex, race, or geography. It is a movement of local, regional and national organizations—no one knows exactly how many organizations there are, or how many members there are of these environmental groups. The EPA estimated a few years ago that there are some 12,000 environmental groups around the country, large and small—and that the combined membership of all of these institutions, not counting overlap, was between 6 and 10 million individuals. Although these environmental organizations work on just about every subject under the sun, from solar energy to mass transit, from wilderness to wildlife, we are all bound together by certain broad commonly held beliefs in such things as clean air, energy conservation, wildlife and wilderness and parks.

The second basic fact about the environmental movement goes beyond the membership of the many constituent organizations— right out to the American public itself. By now I think we have all read about the latest Louis Harris Poll regarding the attitudes of the public about the Clean Air Act. In this widespread sampling, Harris found out that about 75–80 percent of the American people, across-the-board: white, black, young, old, liberal, conservative, Republican, Democrat—from all sections of the country— all favored keeping the Clean Air Act as strong as it is or making it stronger.

"—This message on the deep desire on the part of the American people to battle pollution is one of the most overwhelming and clearest we have ever recorded in our 25 years of surveying public opinion—" said Harris.

Over the past 10 or 12 years there have been many, many similar polls, conducted by many different entities and interests. . . . These polls have always shown a very high degree of support for the programs, values, and policies of environmental organizations. Sure, we can always ask the questions in different ways, and we'll get somewhat different answers—we all do that. But we cannot deny that there is a very large degree of public support out there.

To me, the hard test of whether this is so or not comes finally in those votes in the Congress, the actions of our elected representatives, politicians who must by their nature be sensitive to the feelings of their constituents. How do they believe their constituents feel about these public lands issues?

To illustrate, I could take almost any vote on issues of major importance to the environmental movement on public lands questions, whether it be the Alaska Lands bill of 1980 or the Timber Supply Act of 1970, or any of the other hundreds of votes in between.

But let us be more recent; let us turn to some of the most recent expressions of Congressional opinion about the actual or perceived policies of the Reagan Administration concerning our public lands.

The first example might be the vote of the House Interior Committee to withdraw the Bob Marshall Wilderness in Montana from oil and gas exploration last May—a direct reaction to the perceived intent of the Secretary of Interior to exercise his discretion to issue such leases for exploratory oil and gas drilling. This action was taken at the behest of the Congressional representative from the district affected.

The second example would be the action of the House Merchant and Fisheries Committee in adopting language sponsored by Congressman Pritchard of Washington rejecting the Administration's proposal to change the definition of the phrase "directly affecting," when referring to regulations under the CZMA giving coastal states the rights to influence the decision of the federal government regarding OCS leasing and pre-leasing activities. The Administration wanted to prevent states from having such a say, which would mean in our view, a lot less attention to environmental impacts. It would have facilitated more off shore oil drilling without regard to state objections.

The third example might be the recent announcement by Republican Congressman Cheney of Wyoming that he was withdrawing his co-sponsorship of the so-called "Minerals Supremacy bill" due to objections from his constituents or the sponsorship by Republican Representative Lujan of New Mexico of a resolution now in House Interior Committee to withdraw all wilderness lands in the lower 48 states from oil and gas exploration and leasing.

Each of these actions, as noted, was precipitated by a reaction to a perceived or actual policy of the Reagan Administration, policies which had very strong support from industry. Each of these actions taken was initiated by representatives from essentially conservative states, all of which went strongly for the President during the 1980 elections. These actions have to tell us something; and I think that they tell us at the very least that there is a great deal of public support for environmental goals and values, whether the issue is the Clean Air Act or the public lands. They tell us above all that it is not wise policy or politics to see the environmental movement as being a movement without large public support. I can certainly say from my own experience that organizations such as ours which have little financial resources simply cannot hope to prevail in the issues we do without the kind of public support that comes from the whole people, and not just our members.

About a year ago, in Washington, I listened to John Kyl, former Republican Congressman from Iowa, former Undersecretary of Interior under President Nixon, and then an advisor to the Reagan Administration. He addressed a gathering of the timber industry and he told them "many of you have come to us with proposals to change the environmental laws—but only Congress can change the laws, and Congress listens to what the people say. And the environmental movement is a people's movement—that is why we have the environmental laws in the first place. To change the laws you must first change the people—"

So yes, the environmental movement is a people's movement.

No, it does not include all the people—there are many valid interests to be served in this society, we all accept that, but it is very many people, and it is not an elitist movement at all.

I noted before that there has always been a strong bipartisan tradition in the environmental movement for the whole past century; there are many Republicans in it from the greats like President Theodore Roosevelt, creator of the National Forest System and Congressman John Saylor of Pennsylvania, one of the founders and main champions of the wilderness system, or the thousands and thousands of ordinary members who make up our rank and file, for example the two-thirds of the membership of the National Wildlife Federation, who in a recent poll said they voted for President Reagan. If you had been to the hundreds and hundreds of environmental meetings across the country for the past fifteen years that I have been to, you would agree with me that there is a real cross-section of individual people in our movement: young and old, both sexes, all levels of education, conservative and liberal and everything in between—it is a people's movement.

Finally, as to the "hired gun in Washington" statement, just a couple of quick comments will suffice.

First, those of us who are staff of membership organizations know very well that we would not last very long as that staff if our actions and statements did not have the support of the overwhelming majority of our members. Policy in our organization is always made from the bottom up, by the volunteer members, speaking through their elaborate networks of chapter presidencies, regional councils, and Board of Directors.

There is no question that Audubon's policy of strong opposition to the actions of the Reagan Administration against the public lands these days has the overwhelming support of our nearly half million members. We first found this out last May during the time of our annual fund appeal. The appeal this year was rewritten from its normal mild form into a strongly worded call to arms, elaborating the specific policies of the Reagan Administration which we felt were very much antithetical to the cause of protection of the public lands and their wildlife. Eight times more Audubon members gave nine times as much money as ever before in any single fund appeal in response to this letter—laying themselves on the line with their dollars—a sure indication of their strength of feeling! A month later, our 36-person Board of Directors ratified all the actions of the staff vis a vis the Administration unanimously. I have been to many local chapter and regional meetings since, and I can assure you that the feelings of our membership are very strong, deep and intense . . . there is no distinction in our organization, or any of the others of our community at this time, between the feelings of the so-called "hired guns" in Washington, and the overwhelming majority of our rank and file, all of whom share a common love for the land and an alarm for its fate at the hands of this Administration.

All right. That is us, who we are, and what we are like—that is half of what is necessary to understand why we react the way we do. The other half is our long history and tradition as a movement—where have we come from, what have we been working for for so long? This is important to know, in order to understand our reaction to the present also. Environmentalism, concern for the environment, for our public lands is not a new thing—we, and our values, have been around as long as the Republic itself; we go back at least to the writing of William Bartram, who in 1775 traveled through the southern Appalachians marveling at the beauty of the forest wilderness there, lamenting its passing, and pleading for some way to protect some of it. Concern about the American wilderness in those public lands aways off to the west was a central theme of many of the writings of our early authors and poets, James Fenimore Cooper, William Cullen Bryant and many others, in the early part of the 19th century; the uniqueness of America, the things that made us different from other countries—our wild places—were extolled and glorified by painters and musicians in that first half of the 19th century as well.

This rising awareness of the vastness and beauty of the American landscape and wilderness and a concern for its rapid elimination was given a philosophical framework in the writings of Thoreau and Emerson around the mid-19th century, Thoreau specifically calling for saving the wilderness, while there was still time. This cry was taken up by others, newspapermen and writers for popular magazines, especially in New York state where the fate of the Adirondacks was being decided.

But it also reached west, into that vast public domain, and this rising chorus of concern about public lands, a feeling that they had values other than commercial values—that indeed they had spiritual values—was given its first political form and expression in 1872, when a Republican President named Ulysses Grant signed into law legislation creating Yellowstone National Park. This was a significant act indeed because Yellowstone then was a vast wilderness, far more remote to the people of that time than anything in Alaska is to us today—and yet it was consciously set aside by the Congress as a "permanent pleasuring ground for the people—" In other words, for the first time in the history of the world we see the idea that wilderness gives pleasure just because it is—without any embellishment, any ornaments, or even any real access. That is a uniquely American idea, and has been given force and powerful expression many subsequent times in the past century.

Well, that was the beginning, and we all know what came after that in the public lands—the environmental movement grew up in response to the rapidly changing face of these lands, the rapid commercial exploitation of them, and the equally rapid elimination of much of our native American wildlife. The first ornithological societies, which later became the National Audubon Society, were formed in the 1880s; the Sierra Club was founded in 1892—and other great organizations came along in rapid succession. The forest reserves were created in 1891, the Forest Organic Act in 1897, the Forest Service in 1905, the national parks system in 1916—a host of splendid additions to the park system at that time and later—a whole system of bird and animal protection laws, game laws, all designed to begin to restore our wildlife—the beginnings of our national wildlife refuge system in the 1930s—

As we all know, after a brief hiatus during WW II and the Korean War, the wave of enthusiasm surged forward again in the 1960s and the 1970s in the focus of efforts to create an effective pollution control system: the Clean Air Act, Clean Water Act, Resource Conservation and Recovery Act, Toxic Substances Control Act—Superfund; and it surged forward just as emphatically to bring balance, the highest quality of professionalism and orderly planning to our existing public lands systems—hence the Multiple Use Sustained Yield Act of 1960, Forest Management Act and the Federal Land Policy Management Act of 1976, among others.

And finally it created new systems to protect the fast vanishing remnants of our national heritage: Wilderness Act of 1964, Wild and Scenic River Act of 1968, Alaska Lands Act of 1980—Land and Water Conservation Fund Act of 1965—and millions of acres to be added to those systems in many separate laws.

To us, these were great accomplishments and we were very proud. None of these laws were perfect—either from our viewpoint or from that of industry—each one reflected the political balancing and tradeoffs which are such a necessary part of our system.

But from our viewpoint, the way we saw it—and that is what I am sharing with you today—each of these great accomplishments was the realization of a set of dreams, some of them going back decades—each of them representing the achievement of long-standing goals—and each of them, we felt, would benefit our country—would make it not only more a productive, but a more healthy country. Each would make it not only a country with a high material standard of living, but also a nation blessed by an abundance of the things that make life worthwhile.

To us, this whole great network of landmark statutes went to the very purpose of the government itself, as conceived by the founders of our nation: to protect the health and safety of the people, provide for the common welfare, to manage wisely our common resources—

I have said before—and I want to emphasize again—that environmentalism, throughout its long history, has always been a bipartisan concern—leaders of both parties have shaped the American environmental ethic and the laws to back it up; men and women of both parties, of all persuasions, have made up the rank and file of its membership ever since its beginning over a hundred years ago.

And our bipartisan goals have been very consistent for the whole past century; they have never waivered, have not changed much; in reviewing this long tradition and history, it seems that only the place names and names of legislation have changed.

We have always sought the highest quality management of the public lands for the full spectrum of multiple uses, so that the lands will not be abused, but will be passed on to the future intact and not ravaged by short term exploitation.

We have always sought special reservations of our finest scenic vistas, our superlative natural and historic wonders, the remnants of the once-vast wilderness—because they are part of our culture, history and traditions too.

And we have always sought the highest degree of protection for our native wildlife in parks, refuges, and wilderness areas, and through high quality management—so that future generations as well as our own can enjoy this abundance.

These are and always have been the goals of our movement; they have been shared by nearly every Administration, every president, every Congress, since we began this work. These are the goals largely accomplished in the landmark statues and accompanying regulations that I referred to earlier—

But all this has changed now—since the election [of President Reagan] we have seen take place the most radical and extreme changes in perhaps a century, changes of approach and philosophy about the proper use and management of our public lands.

We look around us now at the whole carefully built structure of public land laws, the whole carefully thought out environmental ethic developed over a century, a philosophy of careful management and protection, of husbanding our resources, of reserving from exploitation some places which have higher values—and what do we see?

We see a Secretary of Interior who preaches stewardship and care for resources, but who systematically attempts to undermine, through new or "revised" regulations and budget cuts, key protective statutes such as the Surface Mine Control Act and the Endangered Species Act, the Federal Land Policy and Management Act, the Outer Continental Shelf Act and other laws too.

We see an Assistant Secretary of Agriculture in charge of our public forests who criticizes efforts of the foresters to protect wildlife—one of their statutory duties—as "just creating game farms on the national forests." We see this same official instigating efforts to rewrite regulations so as to cut citizens with no economic interest in the outcome out of the appeals process, to rewrite the regulations to weaken wildlife protection so that logging in key areas can proceed even faster—we see this official calling for a great increase in the cutting of the public forests at the same time that the evidence is strong that such cutting can do grave damage not only to other resources, but the forestry resource itself. We see his emphasis on getting the logs out as the only important mission of the National Forest System.

We see everywhere efforts to accelerate exploitation of the outer continental shelf, of coal lands, and of millions of acres of fragile and sensitive lands within either already protected systems or marked for further study so that they might in the future be protected, and to eliminate the necessary environmental controls on them—We see efforts to open up Wilderness Areas and National Parks to incompatible, damaging uses—and other efforts to transfer lands out of the National Wildlife Refuge System entirely.

We see all this happening, but we see no corresponding effort to maintain already long-standing programs to acquire and protect key park and refuge areas already mandated by the Congress or state and local governments for protection; on the contrary, these programs are marked for extinction. Everywhere, making what we consider to be illegal use of the budget process, we see budget cuts in key areas of law enforcement, research and inventory—all designed to help us protect the resources we have—while at the same time the budget is increased, or at least held the same, in the resource exploitation and development end of things.

Everywhere, throughout the whole public lands sector—we see a pervasive and systematic effort to undo the work of the past 20 years, if not the whole past century.

From the Wilderness Act to the Forest Management Act, from the Land and Water Conservation Fund Act to the Surface Mine Act, from the Endangered Species Act to the Outer Continental Shelf Act—the pattern is overwhelmingly the same: cut or eliminate the budget for the protective, planning and enforcement functions of the laws—and increase the funds for the exploitive parts—get those logs out, and get those minerals and oil and gas out faster—and remove or weaken the laws and regulations designed to protect the environment in the process—

—In a budget cutting year, increase or at least keep nearly the same the funds for big dams, nuclear power, synthetic fuels—but wipe them out for parks, Wildlife Refuges, energy conservation and solar power.

"We will use the budget process to accomplish policy goals," says our Secretary of Interior—and that is what has been attempted.

And this shameful reversal of all past policies of all Administrations is not just confined to the public lands sector, I should add—

It is the same in the pollution control sector—where the crucial regulatory functions of the EPA in administering the Clean

Air Act, Clean Water Act, Toxic Substances Control Act—and other statues are also being systematically eliminated through enormous budget cuts.

No we do not, have never, sought regulation for regulation's sake—we have sought it only to protect the health and welfare of our people. . . .

No, every regulation is not perfect—there is always room for fine tuning and improvement.

But, ladies and gentlemen—what is being done here is not delicate surgery—it is a radical amputation. Under the guise of "regulatory reform"—they are throwing out the baby with the bathwater—

It is a sad pattern that we see, an unhappy chronicle now unfolding before us—and we feel we have no choice but to stand up and fight against it—

"To fail to fight back now would be to fail to protect our history—" said our President of Audubon—Russell Peterson—former Republican Governor of Delaware.—That is what he said, that is how we all felt. We will continue to fight back until at last we can have peace.

Thank you.

POLITICS AND THE ENVIRONMENT

EDITOR'S INTRODUCTION

Increasing American concern for environmental questions is due in part to discoveries of the hazards posed by toxic chemicals, whose threat to public health was not perceived until relatively recently. It is also due, however, to the political battles waged over the policies of President Reagan and his officials, whose stated aims have alarmed Republican and Democrat alike. The second section of this compilation examines the part played in the environmental debate by politics, and shows that the two areas cannot be separated.

In an article from *Blair & Ketchum's Country Journal,* John Mitchell claims that it was Mrs. Burford's unacknowledged purpose to dismantle the EPA and end the government's role as a regulatory of industry. Deborah Baldwin's article from *Common Cause* gives further evidence that William Ruckelshaus inherited a devastated agency from his predecessor. An article from *Nation's Business,* giving another view of the controversy surrounding the Department of the Interior, suggests that the hostility of environmentalists for the Secretary, James Watt, is based on his political views, not on his environmental policies. The result of the political conflict, as a second article from *Nation's Business* shows, is a deadlock in Congress that has prevented the passage of a number of much-needed items of legislation. Reviewing the vast extent of public lands, a *Newsweek* article points out that federal land belongs to the people, and that the people are not likely to agree about how it should be used.

Concluding this section, three speeches by Ronald Reagan trace the President's efforts to rebut the charges of his critics that his staff has betrayed a public trust, and to repair the damage caused by the resignations of Mrs. Burford and Secretary Watt.

ENVIRONMENTAL PROTECTION:
ASSESSING THE RECORD[1]

"Dear Mr. President," the letter began, "I write to you as a citizen with a heavy burden of frustration, concern, and anger. The reasons are not obscure. As I have written previously to your chief of staff, James Baker, 'What the administration is doing in environmental affairs is crazy.'"

Strong stuff. And just who was the audacious crank accusing the White House of administrative insanity? Some wild-eyed eco-freak? An outraged Democrat? No. It was Dan Lufkin, one-time chief of Connecticut's Department of Environmental Protection and chairman of Ronald Reagan's transitional Task Force on the Environment. Lufkin, a lifelong Republican, was telling the President that his "appointments have at best been extreme, at worst bizarre; the stated policies have been retrogressive, catapulting us back to the days of grab and plunder . . . ; the meat-axe approach to gutting programs under the guise of cutting budgets is the wrong weapon, on the wrong victim, at the wrong time. . . . Mr. President, you are now writing the history of the Reagan administration and if you continue as you have begun in the field of the environment, I am very much afraid that history will not be kind to you; for you will be remembered by future generations as the president whose policies led to the destruction of our wilderness land, the corruption of our national parks, the wasting of our irreplaceable resources, the elimination of significant programs of environmental research, the emasculation of regulations vital to clean air and water. . . . "

By most accounts, conservation—or "environmentalism," as we say nowadays—was never a clear-cut partisan issue in American politics. Some presidents, for certain, gave more thought to it than others; some, hardly any thought at all. But neither major political party, reviewing the history of the past hundred years,

[1]Excerpted from an article by John G. Mitchell, field editor for *Audubon* and former editor-in-chief of Sierra Club Books. *Blair & Ketchum's Country Journal.* 10:38–44. Ap. '83. Copyright© 1983 by the author. Reprinted by permission.

could rightly claim itself to be the better guardian of the nation's natural resources; nor, indeed, could one party justly accuse the other of any superiority in the fine arts of burglarizing the public domain. Saviors of the land and wastrels alike have stalked the corridors of the White House. For getting there, neither type has shown much preference as to elephants or asses.

Still, if one had to pick a year, a president, a party, and say that this is where conservation as public policy began, one would do well to pick out 1864 and Abraham Lincoln of The Grand Old Party conveying Yosemite Valley to the state of California to be held "for public use, resort, and recreation for all time." (California later reconveyed the park to the federal government.) Ulysses S. Grant was likewise a Republican. He created the first national park at Yellowstone in 1872. And then there was Theodore Roosevelt of the GOP, who, having given us wildlife refuges and national forests, stood at the brink of the Grand Canyon, saying, "Leave it as it is. . . . "

Resource policy came on some hard times during subsequent administrations. For the GOP, Harding, Collidge, Hoover, and Eisenhower were no great shakes as White House conservationists, but then neither were Democrats Wilson, Truman, and John F. Kennedy, although Kennedy had the good sense to appoint an outstanding interior secretary, Stewart Udall. Lyndon Johnson scored high marks—the highest since the reign of Franklin D. Roosevelt. But Richard Nixon, for all his personal animosity toward environmental "kooks," scored even higher.

In the shadow of other events and issues, we tend nowadays to forget the good environmental things that the Nixon administration accomplished, or allowed to happen: creation of the United States Environmental Protection Agency (EPA) and the first concerted federal effort to force industry to clean up its act, big additions to the national parks and wilderness systems, enforcement of the Endangered Species Act, funding for urban parks, and in general the exercise of stewardship—as in the decision to spare our one-and-only Everglades National Park from the unneighborly intrusion of an ill-sited and redundant international jetport. And the sensible appointments: the energetic and uncompromising attorney William D. Ruckelshaus to head the EPA; the eminent Russell Train to serve as chairman of the first Council on Environmental Quality (CEQ); and, to replace Train (when Train moved over to EPA and Ruckelshaus moved on to other posts in the Justice Department), Russell Peterson, the former Republican governor of Delaware, a state historically in thrall to the petrochemical industry. As governor, Peterson had pushed through a tough coastal zone law barring that industry from despoiling Delaware's 100-mile shoreline. So it went in the Nixon years, and through the Ford and Carter years, too.

In the honeymoon time between Ronald Reagan's election and his appointment of James Gaius Watt as secretary of the interior, Anne McGill Burford (formerly Ann Gorsuch) as administrator of EPA, and others to pivotal resource posts, optimists had every reason to hope that Ronald Reagan might do almost as well by the environment as his predecessors had. Times had changed, of course. There would be a certain tightening of the belt. Jimmy Carter's tree-hugging folks would be replaced by men and women of a more pragmatic persuasion; or—and why not?—perhaps a few seasoned GOP troopers such as Ruckelshaus and Train might be called back to service. One had to judge a man by his record, and Reagan's two terms as governor of California had, on the resources scale, been pretty good. He had actively supported two park bond issues totaling more than $300 million. The state parks system nearly doubled its size. Although Governor Reagan had once said, "When you've seen one redwood, you've seen 'em all," his tenure in Sacramento saw an increase in the number of old groves protected. He vetoed the Dos Rios Dam; the corporate ranchers howled in outrage. In short, he acted like a man who knew—in the words of a one-time supporter—that "conservation is good government."

In Sacramento, Ronald Reagan appointed and then relied on two of the nation's strongest environmentalists: his parks director, William Penn Mott, and Norman "Ike" Livermore, secretary of The Resources Agency. Mott was esteemed for his progressive park policies. "They don't come any better than Bill Mott," says Nathaniel Reed, who served as assistant secretary of the interior for fish, wildlife, and parks during the Nixon and Ford administrations. "He was an innovative genius—one of the most superb park directors in the history of the country." Ike Livermore, Mott's immediate superior and likewise a Reagan appointee, was equally respected throughout the environmental community. "Ike knew how to handle Reagan," Reed says. "He knew he couldn't push the man too far."

Livermore, alas, was not to be a part of the new administration in Washington, D.C. Retired to his California ranch, he was summoned briefly in the transition period to serve on the President-elect's Task Force on the Environment. . . . In its final report, the task force ably translated Ronald Reagan's perceived philosophy into environmental language. . . . The goal of the new administration, the task force said in its preamble, should be "to make the natural and human environment better" when it left office than when it came in. . . . In fact, its report was not even acknowledged.

Now, new men with perspectives out of the rock-'em-sock-'em Old West stood at the President-elect's side. There was James Baker. There was Edwin Meese. There was this sagebrush senator from Nevada, Paul Laxalt. And there was Joseph Coors, the Colorado brewer, contributor to conservative causes (including the John Birch Society), board chairman of the Mountain States Legal Foundation, and influential booster of high public office not only for that foundation's top attorney, James G. Watt, but also for that other Coloradan, Anne McGill Burford.

Watt [was named] secretary of the interior, but he is only one of sixteen top Interior officials nominated by President Reagan and confirmed by the Senate. Together, these men preside over the management of a half-billion acres of public land—land held in trust for all Americans. Common Cause, the public-interest watchdog group, reports that eleven of the original sixteen appointees had prior professional relationships with industries that either lease federal land or have a direct interest in departmental decisions. "Oil and gas, utilities, mining, livestock, and timber," according to the Common Cause guide, *Who's Minding the Store?*, are major industries "strongly represented among the former employers and clients" of these officials. And Common Cause warns, " . . . the potential for conflicts of 'loyalty' among agency decision-makers poses a sensitive problem. . . . "

If the prospects for balance seem bleak at Interior, they appear even worse at Anne McGill Burford's EPA, which operates under a congressional mandate to protect air, land, and water resources in order to safeguard the public's health. Here, twelve of the first sixteen top appointive posts have been handed over to former attorneys, lobbyists, or consultants for industries the EPA regulates.

Meanwhile, over at the Department of Agriculture, Ronald Reagan's choice to serve as the assistant secretary in charge of the United States Forest Service is John B. Crowell, former general counsel of the Louisiana Pacific Corporation. In fiscal 1981, Louisiana Pacific purchased 6.7 million board feet of timber from national forests and other federal lands. Crowell is a firm believer in the principle of multiple use—so long as resource extraction is the dominant use. Although a depressed housing market has resulted in a record backlog—a three-year supply—of sold but unharvested timber, Crowell proposes to increase timber sales in virgin back-country areas of the national forests.

And occupying the head chair at CEQ is Alan Hill, a California businessman whose previous environmental experience was as a subaltern in Ike Livermore's Resources Agency during Reagan's governorship. Hill inherited a council staff long respected, from one administration to the next, for its objective analysis of broad environmental policy issues. But in 1981, the Reagan White House dismissed the entire CEQ professional staff, slashed the agency's budget by nearly 70 percent, and left Alan Hill presiding over an institutional cadaver.

James Watt may have been the first to enunciate the Reagan administration's intent to manipulate resource policy by trimming budgets. "We will use the budget system to be the excuse to make major policy decisions," he told a gathering of national park concessionaires. Critics viewed the ploy with dismay. "What is at stake here is mind-boggling," said Gaylord Nelson, former senator from Wisconsin, organizer of the original Earth Day, and now chairman of the Wilderness Society. "The budget process is being widely used as an instrument for de-facto repeal of laws without congressional debate or public dialogues."

Nowhere has the budget as blunt instrument of policy been so brazenly displayed as in the funding—or, rather, lack of funding—for the EPA. Its budget for fiscal 1983 reflected a 30-percent cut from the previous year. And Anne McGill Burford, testifying before a House environment subcommittee, admitted after repeated questioning by one Republican representative that she had submitted this budget to the Office of Management and Budget without having calculated the minimum personnel and funding resources needed by EPA to meet its statutory responsibilities. The most hurtful swipes of the axe fell on the agency's enforcement and research and development (R&D) programs.

As submitted by Mrs. Burford and approved by President Reagan (though later adjusted somewhat by Congress), EPA's 1983 budget was tailored to reduce the enforcement staff by one third, lopping off some 500 positions and further debilitating the agency's capacity to enforce the laws against dirty air and dangerous water. Already, between June 1981 and May of last year, Mrs. Burford had reorganized her enforcement division *four* times. Partly as a result of this exercise in paper shuffling, and partly because of budget and personnel cuts already in place, enforcement activities fell off sharply. The subcommittee on oversight and investigations of the House Energy and Commerce Committee reported that case referrals from EPA to the Justice Department declined 50 percent, that Clean Air Act inspections fell off more than 60 percent in the first six months of last year, that no penalties were imposed on any one of the 5,000 municipalities with water systems violating the Safe Drinking Water Act, and that referrals to Justice under hazardous-waste laws were down by 37 percent—half of these cases being filed on the last day of the fiscal year. It was a finding that promoted the subcommittee to observe that perhaps "the hurry-up referral process" was merely "a 'bean-counting' attempt to bolster enforcement statistics."

Or perhaps it was something else. David D. Doniger, senior staff attorney for the National Resources Defense Council, may have believed so when he said of the EPA record: "A 'critical mass' of government enforcement is absolutely necessary to maintaining voluntary compliance. When enforcement dips below that level— or when it virtually disappears—the spirit of citizenship, the perception that most people follow the rules, and the fear of detection and punishment all wither away. Voluntary compliance crumbles."

Even *Chemical Week,* the industry magazine, was moved to comment. In an editorial entitled "We Need a Credible EPA," the magazine observed: "Normally, the sight of a regulatory agency in turmoil is not calculated to bring tears to industry's eyes. But an ineffective EPA is not what the chemical industry needs. What it needs and what it expects from the Reagan administration is an agency that will discharge intelligently its responsibility to the American people. That means cleaning up and protecting the environment. . . . Without an effective EPA, industry's contribution to pollution, which has been diminishing, is bound to grow again. In the long run, the American people will not stand for that."

For R&D in 1983, Anne McGill Burford proposed spending $216 million, a sum scaled down considerably from that of the previous fiscal year. Basic research was off by 33 percent; energy-systems research, by 35 percent. In budget hearings before a House subcommittee, Russell Peterson, the former Du Pont chemical company executive, Delaware governor, and CEQ chairman, now speaking in his capacity as president of the National Audubon Society, noted that the R&D budget proposed for national defense was 110 times larger than EPA's request; for space exploration, 28 times larger. "Where are our priorities?" asked Peterson. "[We spend] astronomical sums to prepare to blow up the earth and explore extraterrestrial space while we drastically cut a relatively tiny budget for studying threats to our life-support systems here on Earth." Yet earlier and elsewhere, Mrs. Burford had said: "We need good scientific data on which to base effective regulations." (Congress later attempted to add $51 million to the 1983 EPA budget for R&D, but President Reagan vetoed the authorization bill.)

According to the National Wildlife Federation (the nation's largest and most conservative environmental organization, a majority of whose members voted for candidate Reagan), the 1984 budget would effectively cut the EPA right in half. The 11,400 employees and $1.35 billion authorized for the first year of the Reagan administration (1981) would be slashed to 6,000 employees and $700 million. "Half the agency cannot do twice the job," the Federation predicted in its report, *Shredding the Environmen-*

tal Safety Net. "Accepting [this] proposal means the destruction of the country's institutional capacity to understand and manage the environment."

In addition to the appointments and the budget cuts, the Reagan administration has been busy for two years rewriting the nation's environmental rule books. Consider just a few of the actions taken or proposed in four arenas of resource affairs: air quality, hazardous substances, energy, and the public domain.

Air Quality

The administration has endorsed amendments to the Clean Air Act that would shove some compliance deadlines as much as a decade into the future, weaken automobile emission standards, and rule out protection for regions with pristine air (thereby allowing polluters to locate there). It has turned its back on the problem of acid rain, which Anne McGill Burford prefers to call "nonbuffered precipitation."

By whatever name, sulfur oxides are pouring from the nation's factories and power plants at the rate of nearly 30 million tons a year. In many eastern states, the fallout has been linked to the death of aquatic life in ponds and lakes, and to a loss of forest and farmland productivity. Damage is estimated in the billions of dollars. The Congressional Office of Technology Assessment reports that 50,000 people in the United States and Canada are dying each year as a result of sulfur emissions. The National Academy of Sciences in 1981 urged prompt action to reduce these pollutants; the Reagan administration rewarded the Academy by cutting off some of its acid-rain research funds. Yet the administration has said that not enough is known to do anything about acid rain; and, having said so, has all but eliminated a major program designed to come up with some answers.

Now acid-rain studies are under the supervision of the President's science advisor, Dr. George Keyworth, who believes it is "reasonable" for the president to prefer advice from scientists who share his philosophy. And what might that philosophy be, apropos acid rain? Who knows? We only know that Interior Secretary James Watt once told an interviewer: " . . . every year there's a money-making scare. This year it's acid rain." Reagan's former secretary, James Edwards, said he didn't want to stop acid rain because, in some areas, "it's good for crops." And Reagan's budget director, David Stockman, once told a gathering of manufacturers: "I kept reading these stories that there are a hundred and seventy lakes dead in New York. . . . And it occurred to me to ask the question, 'How much are the fish worth?' . . . "

Hazardous Substances

The Reagan administration has been running from its obligation under law to control the dumping of hazardous wastes, the proliferation of toxic chemicals, and the use of unsafe pesticides. Under the guise of a "New Federalism," it has sought to shift regulatory responsibility to the states even as it would pinch off the grants states need to enforce federal laws.

One might well choose New York as an example, for the Empire State is where the problem of hazardous wastes first emerged in a big way—at the Love Canal. Testifying before the House Appropriations Committee last May, New York's environmental conservation commissioner, Robert Flacke, reported that his agency could not make an inventory of existing dumps and take action to clean them up or close them down because the Reagan administration had cut off the funds to do so. Flacke said the cuts nationwide would result in a "skeleton version" of the waste-control program Congress had authorized.

Under the Toxic Substances Control Act, Congress had also mandated federal monitoring of the production and use of dangerous substances, including known or suspected carcinogens. But, according to Russell Peterson of the National Audubon Society, "Under the Reagan administration, it seems that a toxic chemical is now presumed innocent until we have a body count that proves otherwise."

Item: When the House Public Works Committee proceeded to investigate the problem of hazardous waste disposal, the President directed his Environmental Protection Agency head, Anne McGill Burford, to deny—at risk of contempt of Congress—the committee's request for documents illuminating the EPA's lethargic cleanup effort.

Item: Flying in the face of scientific consensus that what causes cancer in animals may also cause cancer in humans, Dr. John Todhunter of the EPA rejected a staff recommendation that formaldehyde, which has many household uses, be regulated. The recommendation for controls was based on valid animal experiments and a perception of widespread human exposure. Dr. Todhunter chose to ignore the evidence submitted by his own scientists after meeting privately with representatives of the Formaldehyde Institute, a trade association in no rush to embrace regulation.

Item: In 1978, EPA banned the insecticide Mirex after it was found to cause birth defects in rodents and to be accumulating in human tissue in states where the substance had long been used to control the fire ant. Anne McGill Burford tried to lift the ban for three southern states. It took a lawsuit to stop her.

Item: President Reagan personally rescinded a decade-old executive order issued by President Nixon to ban the use on Public lands of 1080, a predator poison used by sheep ranchers to control coyotes. The trouble with 1080 is that it also kills eagles, hawks, bobcats, and bears, not to mention coyotes with no taste whatsoever for mutton. (One pound of 1080 is enough to kill a million pounds of animal life.) Edwin Meese, the president's counsel, explained the decision to a group of environmental leaders. "It's about time," Meese said, "that we listen to the sheep ranchers."

Public Domain

Almost since his inauguration, President Reagan has gambled with recreational, ecological, and even the long-range economic values of the American Commons—the forests, parks, refuges, and rangelands of the public domain—on the shaky proposition that the private sector, after a century of remorseless exploitation of the land, can now somehow husband it and its resources better than government can (or, at least, the *federal* government). To wit:

At his confirmation hearing, Secretary Watt proclaimed that the Land and Water Conservation Fund—financed by motorboat fuel tax and offshore oil lease receipts—was "one of the most effective preservation and conservation programs in America." And indeed it was—until, in one of his first acts as secretary, Watt imposed on the Fund a moratorium on all new national park acquisitions, as well as a freeze on grants from the Fund to the states for regional and municipal parks. In effect, the secretary all but scuttled the authorized uses of the Fund, then attempted to raid it for such unauthorized uses as the maintenance of concession stands, roadways, and sewers.

Having battled the Congress over his plan to open designated wilderness areas to mineral leasing, and having lost, Secretary Watt moved in 1982 to disqualify as many as 5 million acres of de-facto wild lands from further study as potential additions to the wilderness system.

Finally there is the doctrine of "privatization," an economic theory that underlies the Reagan administration's whole approach to resource management. Privatization holds that Americans would be better served if the nation's public resources—land and timber and minerals—were placed in the hands of private owners, who by definition and the profit incentive are best qualified to manage resources in a sensible way. As simple as that: the Trickle Down Theory applied to the public domain. (Or as Gaylord Nelson of the Wilderness Society likes to recall of Franklin D. Roosevelt's famous speech to Iowa farmers during the Great Depression: "Look, you farmers understand the Trickle Down Theory better than any of those economists do. It's the theory that if you feed the horses more oats, the sparrows will eat better.")

Among the leading proponents of the privatization principle is the economist Gordon Tullock of the Center for the Study of Public Choice in Blacksburg, Virginia. Tullock argues that "the national domain should be used to retire the national debt." He advocates the sale both of federal land and subsurface resources. Tullock goes on to note that what "you would obtain from the sale of the national domain would be the use of subsurface resources. Since there doesn't seem to be any obvious reason why these subsurface resources shouldn't be used, even if the property remains part of the national domain, here we would simply have a conversion in which the private motives of the owners would be socially much superior to the private motives of the politicians, pressure groups, and bureaucrats who now control it."

The state of the nation's natural environment is hardly the uppermost issue on the minds of most Americans nowadays. People are out of work—millions of them. Social Security is a question mark. From near and far comes the rattle of nuclear sabers. Hard times. Easy times, too, for a president to lose touch with domestic reality.

Ronald Reagan does not understand the natural environment. But that is no sin, for many presidents before him did not understand it either. Reagan's sin is that he does not *want* to understand. Instead, he wants to be firm, to stay the course. He wants to listen to men who gibe at windmills and dead fish. He wants to believe, as so many of his aides do, that those who deplore his resource policies, who speak in behalf of staying the course for clean air and safe water, for protected wild lands and unscarred mountains, are somehow out of the mainstream, effete and elite, a select few with narrow special interests in locking up the resources America needs now to be strong again. So it is said by the President's men. I sometimes wonder if they read the polls.

The polls indicate that the select few are rather many. Not that polls always provide the last truthful word, but they are the best public opinion measure we have, and they show that a majority (67 percent) of Americans are not willing to sacrifice environmental quality for economic growth (*The New York Times/CBS News Poll*, 1981); that the public (80 percent) wants to keep the Clean Air Act strict, or make it even stricter, regardless of cost (Harris Poll, 1981); and that opinion is evenly divided on the more esoteric question of whether or not oil development should be allowed in designated wilderness areas (*The New York Times/CBS News*, 1981).

Then there is a more recent poll conducted by Research and Forecasts, Inc., for The Continental Group, Inc. This survey finds that more than half of the American public wants to maintain pollution-control standards even if that results in the closing of some factories, that 51 percent of top executives at large corporations believe environmental cleanup should be pursued even if it means higher prices must be charged for goods and services, and that 65 percent of the public wants to preserve certain American places in their natural, undeveloped state. (The Continental Group, Inc., with headquarters in New Jersey, describes itself as a diversified intenational packaging, forest products, and energy company with annual sales of some $6 billion and assets that include 200 manufacturing plants, 1.5 million acres of timberland, and calculated reserves of 8.5 million barrels of oil.)

Sometimes I also wonder if President Reagan and his men (and women, one must add, in particular deference to the EPA) correctly read the results of 1982's congressional and gubernatorial elections. To be sure, the environment was not a big issue in many races, but it was not a small one either. In the Senate races environmentalists working as political action committees threw their support behind three Republicans and eleven Democrats. Of the fourteen, ten won, including the three Republicans. In the House races environmentalists actively supported ninety-seven candidates. Eighty won. In the gubernatorial races environmentalists worked hard for eight candidates. Seven won. "It was our best showing ever," Marion Edey of the League of Conservation Voters said. "It was a clear repudiation of the environmental policies of Ronald Reagan."

A repudiation? Perhaps, although I suspect the real test of public acceptance or repudiation will come in the election of 1984. In the meantime, my best guess is that more and more Americans are beginning to share a puzzlement, a wonder best expressed by a ten-year-old schoolgirl in a letter to Senator Gaylord Nelson shortly after the first Earth Day in 1970. The girl got right to the point. "Do we really have to destroy tomorrow," she asked, "in order to live today?"

PLAYING POLITICS WITH POLLUTION[2]

For the past year the Environmental Protection Agency (EPA) has been saddled with scandal.

[2]Excerpted from an article by Deborah Baldwin, contributing editor. *Common Cause Magazine.* My./Je. '83. Copyright© 1983 by Common Cause Magazine. All rights reserved. Reprinted by permission.

Housed in an isolated complex in southwest Washington, the sprawling Nixon-era regulatory agency has slogged along from administration to administration, grinding out rules, fending off lawsuits from industry and environmentalists alike and hunkering down every time political controversies threatened to throw a wrench into its complex machinery.

And then there was Anne Gorsuch. A telephone company lawyer and Colorado state legislator when Reagan tapped her for the job, Gorsuch—later known by the name Burford—took control of the agency in 1981 with orders from the White House to shake up the mammoth bureaucracy, pare budget and staff, reduce paperwork and relieve industry of burdensome regulations.

She was well on the way when storm clouds erupted over the toxic dump cleanup program called Superfund. For months reporters tracked Burford and her top aides, filing story after story about sweetheart deals Burford and Superfund chief Rita Lavelle allegedly made with top industrial lobbyists.

She was blamed for creating deep morale problems in the agency, misleading congressional committees, selling out her science and engineering staffs and destroying the inner workings of EPA programs. As the place began to unravel, stories surfaced about conflicts of interest among her top officials. Even some business lobbyists privately questioned Burford's competence.

But while press reports focused on the Superfund scandal, little attention was paid to the less spectacular side of the story. In two short years, Burford managed to turn the agency upside down. Some of EPA's most highly respected career officials jumped ship; others were fired. People who stayed felt as if they were on a roller coaster with no end in sight.

But one of the most significant criticisms lodged against Burford, perhaps, was her failure to exploit what some viewed as a rare political opportunity: to make the nation's environmental laws perform better. Working with a delicate alliance of some business interests and environmentalists, Burford could have reoriented EPA's complex legalistic machinery around solutions emphasizing regulatory reform, economic incentives and engineering know-how. Instead she merely gutted many of EPA's rules, angering some companies that found they were at an economic disadvantage because they'd already complied with laws in good faith.

Now all eyes are on William Ruckelshaus, Burford's successor, EPA's first administrator and most recently a Weyerhaeuser timber company executive. Some EPA watchers have high hopes that he will get EPA back on track. But the 13-year-old agency is suffering from more than a temporary derailment of its newest program, Superfund. If the Environmental Protection Agency is going to do the job Congress has set out for it, Ruckelshaus will have to dig deep into more than a dozen equally thorny regulatory briar patches, unearthing countless programs affecting public health that suffer from lack of care and feeding. Many Members of Congress and environmentalists seriously question whether Ruckelshaus has the resources and the White House support to do the job—he has already stated that he will not seek increased funding for an agency devastated by budget cuts even if he has the will.

The agency has yet to come to terms with a six-year-old program aimed at controlling the manufacture and use of staggering numbers of chemicals—many of them believed to cause cancer. Separate programs, created to stem the flow of toxic wastes into the water we drink and the air we breathe, are also hurting. EPA is charged with improving drinking water standards and garbage disposal practices, reducing smokestack emissions and smog, ending ocean dumping and making rivers and lakes "fishable and swimmable."

If Ruckelshaus were to do nothing else over the next two years, he could invest all of his resources in the division that regulates pesticides and herbicides and still not get the job done. According to a recent House agriculture subcommittee study, the pesticides program is a shambles: Dangerous chemicals are being dumped on crops and drained into waterways without adequate safety testing. While the current administration is faulted for stepping up the use of such chemicals, according to the subcommittee report, Burford inherited most of the mess the pesticides program is in today.

Ironically, EPA is not only one of the biggest and best known regulatory agencies in town but one with widespread, bipartisan support from Congress and the public. When news of Burford's questionable decisions first hit the papers, a chorus of Republican voices rose to beg for a reprieve. President Nixon's EPA chief, Russell Train, decried EPA's loss of credibility under Reagan. Russell Peterson, who headed up President Ford's White House Council on Environmental Quality, wrote a scathing attack on the Reagan administration's handling of environmental programs in the Sunday *New York Times Magazine*.

Throughout the controversy, President Reagan managed to keep the spotlight turned on Burford, gracefully stepping aside whenever attention shifted to the White House. Ultimately, however, Ruckelshaus will accomplish only what the White House wants to see accomplished. And exactly what that is remains to be seen.

In reviewing the administration's record to date, critics often point not so much to the things Burford did as to those she did not. The following are examples of recent EPA actions—and inactions.

Superfund

The toxic dump cleanup program, established in 1980, hasn't gotten off the ground yet. Under this administration:
• EPA has yet to compile a required inventory of all abandoned or inactive waste dumps, which may number more than 14,000. Although it has gathered a list of 418 "worst" sites, EPA has forced the cleanup of only four of them, even though 347 of them pose immediate threats to drinking water supplies, according to NRDC.
• Out of $475 million in Superfund monies available to EPA, only $255 million has been spent or earmarked. And the agency is relinquishing its obligation to identify and bring to court major dump users, preferring in some instances to issue warning letters and invitations to negotiate cleanups.

For example, at one site in Santa Fe Springs, Calif., which burst into flames in July 1981, top EPA officials quickly negotiated a private $1.7 million surface cleanup settlement with the biggest dumper and absolved it of future liability. Total cleanup costs, which would cover contamination of drinking water supplies, haven't even been calculated yet and could run into many more millions of dollars, according to one EPA attorney.

Finally, administration officials have failed to set up a special registry designed to track data on the health effects of toxic wastes, as directed under the Superfund law.

Toxic Chemicals

The 1976 Toxic Substances Control Act empowered EPA to crack down on the manufacture and use of toxic chemicals. There are about 55,000 chemicals on the market now, and up to 1,000 new ones are introduced each year. Congress gave EPA similar powers to crack down on toxics in laws affecting air and water quality. And yet, the administration has:
• proposed exempting half of the new chemicals from agency screening requirements, allowing industry to carry out its own safety tests and not requiring manufacturers of those chemicals to give EPA advance notice of potential hazards;
• reduced funding for a program created to help schools identify and remove asbestos from school buildings, despite health risks to an estimated three million students and 250,000 teachers;
• proposed weakening rules governing lead in gasoline, despite long recognized lead pollution problems in heavily trafficked areas. (Lead has been added to gasoline to reduce knocking, and it is scheduled for increasingly tighter restrictions.) After enormous public outcry, EPA backed down.

The current EPA also:
• failed to propose air pollution standards for the chemical formaldehyde (which is used in many consumer products and which has been shown to cause cancer in test animals), despite authority to do so and requests for immediate action from a number of environmental health experts;
• issue rules telling industries how to dispose of hazardous wastes that were criticized by the congressional Office of Technology Assessment because they "do not effectively detect, prevent or control the release of toxic substances onto the environment, particularly over the longer term." The study pointed out that "cleaning up a

site and compensating victims might cost 10 to 100 times today's costs of preventing releases of hazardous wastes." According to an analysis by 10 environmental groups last spring, weakened standards fail to protect aquifers, underground sources of fresh water.

• EPA also proposed allowing the dumping of liquid wastes in landfills, which had been barred earlier because liquids can easily contaminate ground water. After enormous outcry and charges that the decision favored a firm represented by a consultant to Burford, the proposal was withdrawn—but not before the firm dumped thousands of gallons of liquid wastes in a Colorado landfill, according to congressional investigators.

• Rules developed under this administration allow industries to burn toxic wastes as fuel in industrial boilers, even though burning such wastes could pose health hazards.

• It exempted companies from toxic waste controls if they fall into a category called "small generators." Environmentalists say all sources of toxic chemicals should be controlled.

Water Pollution

• EPA reversed earlier policy by dropping a proposed appeal of a court decision allowing New York City to dump sewage sludge in the ocean. The sticky residue left over after dirty water goes through sophisticated water pollution filters, sludge contains chemicals suspected of being carcinogenic and heavy metals like lead that harm marine ecosystems and wend their way through the food chain.

• EPA, while moving ahead with rules designed to reduce the flow of industrial toxics into municipal wastewater plants, proposed so-called pretreatment standards that are so weak they don't do the job, according to the Natural Resources Defense Council (NRDC).

• The administration also adopted changes in clean water policies that will give states—instead of EPA—the right to determine how clean is clean. There is concern that such policies encourage states to get into a bidding war to attract polluting industries—and jobs—and undermine federal laws aimed at creating nationwide

clean water goals.
• Related proposals would allow states to downgrade water quality without public hearings or debate.

Air Pollution

• During the 1981–82 debate on proposed revisions to the Clean Air Act, the administration supported changes in the law which would have weakened environmental standards. (The legislation didn't pass, but Congress is expected to consider it again.)
• Under the previous administration, EPA identified seven particularly hazardous air pollutants and managed to set rules to control four of them. The remaining toxic pollutants—benzene, arsenic and radionucleides—haven't been acted on by the current administration.
• The previous administration was carrying out research on an additional 37 hazardous air pollutants singled out several years ago for priority action (many are believed to cause cancer), but the Reagan EPA cut back efforts in this important area.
    In other developments affecting air quality:
• EPA reduced funding for research on acid rain, which many scientists believe is caused by a chemical reaction to the sulfur dioxide in smokestack emissions. Acid rain is linked to ecological damage and reduced fish and timber productivity. While cutting research efforts in this area, the agency maintained that "more research needs to be done" before action can be taken.
• Sulfur dioxide emissions standards for industrial plants, meanwhile, have been weakened, increasing the risk of acid rain and respiratory illnesses, according to environmentalists.
• The agency also eased the rules governing so-called "emissions trading," also known as the "bubble concept," a regulatory reform effort devised under the Carter administration that would reward industry for cutting down air pollution in one area by allowing it to increase pollution in another. Rather than maintain air quality, the changes will allow pollution to increase, say environmentalists.
• EPA proposed to weaken or delay emission standards for gasoline-powered trucks and diesel-powered cars, and took no action

to establish overdue standards for diesel trucks.

Pesticides and Related Chemicals

• All told there are at least 35,000 pesticides on the market, containing about 1,400 active ingredients. In 1972 Congress directed EPA to begin reviewing them, opening up safety data to public review and comment. Burford ended the process, opting instead for private "decision conferences" with industry.

• Public health advocates were already concerned that the pesticides safety program wasn't working under Carter, whose EPA officials allowed 240 "emergency" exemptions to rules governing which pesticides are used and how. Burford opened the door to many more such exemptions, granting 650 of them during 1982 alone.

For example, EPA approved DBCP for "emergency use" on 20,000 acres of South Carolina peach orchards last year when peach growers raised fears of an invasion by root nibbling insects. Most uses of DBCP were outlawed in 1979 when some male orchard workers exposed to the pesticide became sterile. DBCP is also believed to cause cancer.

• EDB, a potent carcinogen that is used to fumigate citrus fruits before shipment, was singled out two years ago for immediate action. The Reagan EPA decided not to tighten regulations governing the fumigant.

• Many uses of the herbicide 2,4,5-T were banned under Carter. Herbicide manufacturers brought suit, but rather than settle their differences in court, EPA initiated discussions with industry regarding potential changes in those restrictions.

BEHIND THE CAMPAIGN AGAINST WATT[3]

Environmentalist groups are throwing their expanding political power behind liberal causes that could undermine the nation's economic foundations, two new analyses conclude.

The studies, conducted independently, also agree that an all-out attack by environmentalist groups against Interior Secretary James G. Watt is actually aimed at Reagan administration policies designed to stimulate economic growth.

One of the analyses is in a book, *At the Eye of the Storm—James Watt and the Environmentalists,* by Ron Arnold, a former environmental activist. He writes:

"The implicit goals of environmentalism—to drastically reduce or dismantle industrial civilization and to impose a fundamentally coercive form of government on America—are real."

The second study is *The Politics of Broken Faith—Whom Do We Believe?* by Hank Cox, editor of *Washington Watch,* the monthly newsletter of the Regulatory Action Center of the U.S. Chamber of Commerce. In documenting the no-growth stance of major environmentalist groups, Cox notes a paradox:

"While the militant preservationist groups continue to carry out their political campaign against the Reagan administration and its probusiness policies, they also continue to receive millions in annual contributions from corporations and corporate-funded foundations. . . . As the environmental movement has been corrupted by an extremist element more interested in liberal politics than in protection of the environment, there has been no corresponding reduction in corporate aid."

The two published perspectives come at a time of growing controversy and uncertainty over trends in the environmental movement, which has enjoyed tremendous legislative success and public support for more than a decade.

Among the measures of that success:

[3]Reprint of a staff-written article. *Nation's Business.* 71:56–8. Mr. '83. Copyright© 1983 by the Chamber of Commerce of the United States. All rights reserved. Reprinted by permission.

• There are 28 major environmental laws on the federal statute books and thousands of such laws at the state and local level.

• More than 20 federal agencies have major responsibilities in the environmental area.

• Committees and subcommittees of Congress have been restructured or created to deal with environmental issues.

• Environmental requirements or constraints affect virtually every area of business and commercial life in the nation.

As a result of those successes, some critics say, the environmental lobby is now trying to move beyond its original goals and exercise political power in areas not directly related to those goals. The opposition of some environmental leaders to the MX missile program is cited as an example of this trend. Environmental groups say their concern over MX is related solely to its potential impact on the environment, but critics argue that those leaders are using their political clout in areas far afield from ecological issues.

Explaining his shift from environmental activist to critic, Arnold writes in his book:

"As my involvement grew deeper, it became apparent to me that the movement was concerned with more than simply protecting environmental quality. I began to see deliberate alarmism, calculated political moves and a difficult attitude toward basic American values, such as individual liberties and private property."

Both authors view the core of the environmental movement as the province of an elitist group reluctant to share with others the fruits of its own economic progress.

Says Cox: "The preservationists are adamantly opposed to anything that smacks of construction and development, and they use trumped-up environmental issues to block action. They have virtually destroyed the nuclear power industry, fought successfully to prevent exploratory drilling for oil and gas on public lands and continue to wage war on strip mining. The only form of energy production they do not object to is probably the most dangerous—deep coal mining.

"Their indifference to the plight of unemployed blue collar workers, like their contempt for coal miners, is rooted in their own elite status. They have benefited greatly from our economic system but now, instead of wishing to extend the same opportunity to others, prefer to maintain the status quo."

Arnold agrees. The major environmentalist organizations, he says, "have remarkably few members among the poor, ethnic minorities or the goods-producing sector; the vast majority of environmentalists are middle- or upper-class, highly educated and have abundant leisure time."

He traces the growth of the modern environmental movement (from 1960) to such factors as the outdoor recreation boom, media-shaped perception of pollution problems, consumerism, the counterculture that evolved in the Vietnam War protest era, an antitechnology trend and an anticivilization concept holding that "man's basic nature is thwarted by the constraints of civilized living," so the collapse of civilization might not be such a bad thing after all. Arnold sees an antihumanity outlook at work, describing this as the view that "humans should somehow apologize for being the dominant species."

In addition to describing the evolution of today's environmental movement, Arnold recounts the career that brought Watt to his present position, where he is one of the most controversial individuals in public life.

A native of Wyoming, Watt graduated from the University of Wyoming and its law school. He first came to Washington in 1962 as an aide to Sen. Milward Simpson (R-Wyo.) after serving as a volunteer in Simpson's campaign. He had met the senator-to-be through Simpson's son, Alan, a college friend of Watt's. (Alan Simpson is now a U.S. senator from Wyoming himself and was a key ally of Watt's in the hard-fought battle that preceded Watt's confirmation as Interior Secretary in 1981.)

Watt later served as a natural resources specialist for the U.S. Chamber of Commerce, where he helped develop Chamber policies and programs on mining, public lands, energy, water and environmental pollution. That experience, combined with his congressional staff work, qualified him for his next career steps— key posts in the Interior Department and service as a member of the Federal Power Commission.

He later became head of the Mountain States Legal Foundation, established to represent the free enterprise perspective in public interest litigation, which had become increasingly dominated by antigrowth forces.

Arnold recalls an ironic twist in Watt's next move, which was into his current position. Watt volunteered to serve on President-elect Reagan's transition team on Interior Department policy, but he was rejected as too conservative. Watt was tapped for the top job at Interior only after the first choice, former Sen. Clifford P. Hansen (R-Wyo.), turned it down.

But what brought him into the massive controversy that has surrounded him from the day his appointment was announced?

Arnold's book explains:

"The most obvious answer is Watt's predevelopment policy, his opening of federal lands to mineral leasing, his support for a strong economy in general and other views that do not sit well with the environmental leadership.

"Another dimension of this feud is also obvious: Jim Watt's conservative politics clash mightily with the liberal philosophy of most environmentalists. Watt's belief in reduced and decentralized federal power and in the private enterprise system automatically sets him at odds with the large environmentalist organizations that have spent the last 20 years lobbying successfully for stronger federal power to deal with matters of ecology. Democrats have taken up the cudgels against Watt as a campaign issue."

Watt's own formulation of the dispute has served as the focal point for much of the conflict between himself and many of his critics:

"The battleground is not what our critics would like you to believe it is, protecting the environment. It is over ideology, over forms of government that lead to a centralized, socialized society."

At the same time he has warned industry: "Do not mistake our programs, policies or pronouncements as signals that the coal or another industry is free to despoil the land and pollute the environment. This administration is in the mainstream of the environmental movement, and we will be good stewards of our natural resources. Your responsibility is not only to follow rules on environmental protection but to be constantly in search of ways to do a better job of protecting the environment. . . . You must treat with care the land which serves your industry and upon which this generation and untold generations to come must depend.

"You also have an obligation to the free enterprise system. People who care about free enterprise care about the environment. People who run rough-shod over the environment in the name of free enterprise are despoiling the free enterprise system."

In his analysis, Cox of the U.S. Chamber reviews the increasing politicization of the environmental movement, as dramatized by a September, 1980, gathering at the White House.

Representatives of the Audubon Society, Wildlife Federation, Sierra Club and similar groups joined President Carter in the Rose Garden and announced their strong endorsement of him in his election fight against Ronald Reagan.

"When the environmental groups claim they oppose the Reagan administration because of its environmental policies, they conveniently forget they entered partisan politics before there was a Reagan administration and before it had any environmental policies," Cox writes.

Why the opposition to Reagan and his policies? Cox writes:

"In a sense, the hysterical rhetoric being hurled against the Reagan administration is a smoke screen diverting attention away from the tumult within the movement itself—the long-standing quarrel between the conservationists and preservationists."

Conservationists traditionally have advocated balanced use of land resources, whereas preservationists have fought against any incursions on unspoiled lands.

"In the early days of the environmental movement," Cox writes, "the conservationists called the shots. Today, however, the preservationists have gained the upper hand, and their concept of environmental protection is much more extreme and far-reaching.

"During the Carter administration, preservationists moved from the environmental groups into powerful government positions, imposing their single-minded will on the nation's land-use policies. Hundreds of millions of acres were placed off limits to exploration and development in a veritable frenzy of wilderness activity designed to benefit practically every type of plant and animal life except one—humans."

While noting the millions of dollars that corporations and corporate-funded foundations pour into the environmental movement, Cox cites current efforts that three recipients of business largess are making to block business supported revisions of the Clear Air Act.

The Wilderness Society asserts "Powerful economic interests, polluting industries and the Reagan administration are working together to dismantle the act." The Sierra Club says, "The Reagan administration and a host of big business allies are working to destroy the Clean Air Act." And the Wildlife Federation claims that the law "is in danger of being destroyed."

Against that rhetoric, Cox cites views of both business and labor that some aspects of the act hamper economic expansion and could be modified without harm to the legislation's basic goals.

He quotes Robert A. Georgine, president of the Building and Construction Trades Council of the AFL-CIO: "The problem with the Clean Air Act is not its goals and objectives. It is the law's many requirements which add little or nothing to the protection of air quality. These requirements put unnecessary obstacles in the path of new construction of industrial and energy plants."

The environmentalists' increased militancy, Cox says, may result from past victories that leave relatively few new battles to fight. They must continue to find new targets, but sometimes the effort backfires.

For example, the National Wildlife Federation contended after a survey that "our rank-and-file members overwhelmingly rejected Secretary Watt's announced positions on 10 of 11 issues." It quickly became apparent, Cox says, "that, of the 11 policy questions in the survey, eight either did not represent Watt's position, had no relation to existing laws or dealt with subjects the Secretary had not addressed. In only two questions could Watt's real position be discerned, and on both the federation's members supported him by percentage votes of 80 to 11 and 62 to 12."

In his report of corporate funding of antibusiness activities, Cox recalls the parting words of Henry Ford II, when he resigned from the board of the Ford Foundation because of his concern over its support of liberal causes.

"I'm just suggesting to the trustees and the staff," Ford said, "that the system that makes the foundation possible is very probably worth preserving."

ENVIRONMENTAL GRIDLOCK[4]

The Clean Air Act, one of the nation's landmark environmental laws, expired more than two years ago. The Clean Water Act, another basic statute, expired more than a year ago.

They are among seven major environmental laws that Congress failed to renew by their respective deadlines and that are still awaiting reauthorization on Capitol Hill.

Enforcement of the statutes continues, however, because Congress has provided funding through the appropriations process, a legislative channel separate from the reauthorization machinery.

Washington frequently operates on the cynic's version of the golden rule: He who has the gold makes the rules. Regulators are powerless to enforce duly enacted laws for which no funding has been provided, but they can enforce even expired laws as long as they have the money to do so.

Says a spokesperson for the Environmental Protection Agency: "Just because a law's authorization expires, our mandate to enforce it does not change."

In addition to the air and water acts, environmental measures that have expired but are up for renewal include those dealing with hazardous wastes, drinking water, pesticides, ocean dumping of wastes and toxic substances.

Congress is also considering reauthorization of legislation to revise a 1980 law that created an industry-financed fund to clean up dumps for hazardous waste.

Why the logjam on environmental legislation? "Congress has been unable and unwilling to address these laws from a policy perspective," says Mark Gallant, environmental issues specialist for the U.S. Chamber of Commerce.

Competing interest groups are making so many contradictory demands on environmental requirements, he adds, that Congress has become neutralized on many of the pending issues.

[4]Excerpted from an article by Mary-Margaret Wantuck, staff writer. *Nation's Business.* p 70–72. N. '83. Copyright© 1983 by the Chamber of Commerce of the United States. All rights reserved. Reprinted by permission.

Other factors have contributed to the delay, Gallant says. They include highly sophisticated analytical techniques—developed since the first environmental laws were passed—that permit identification of more and more substances that one group or another insists should be regulated.

"Just because you can identify something doesn't mean it's a threat," Gallant says, "but a lot of people want Congress to use that assumption when it is framing environmental laws."

Capitol Hill sources also cite the year's upheavals at EPA as a factor in delaying action on regulatory laws enforced by that agency.

This is the status of the major environmental bills pending on Capitol Hill.

Clean Air Act. Action on renewing this law, which expired Sept. 30, 1981, was delayed by a sharp conflict within the House Public Works Committee's Democratic majority. Since then acid rain has become a major issue in discussions about reauthorizing the act. Proposals for dealing with the problem would, if adopted, cost billions—money that would be added to consumer bills. Extensive debate on the subject is expected to continue for some time.

Clean Water Act. This law expired September 30, 1982, but proposals under consideration in the House and Senate are so far apart that final congressional action is unlikely until next year. The Senate has moved faster than the House on this reauthorization; the House has a long way to go even to complete committee consideration.

Hazardous wastes. A key issue in renewal of the Resource Conservation and Recovery Act, which expired Sept. 30, 1982, is whether to reduce the threshold at which a generator of hazardous waste comes under regulation by the act. One pending proposal would put controls—and the attendant paper work—on many small businesses now exempt from the act because of the small amount of waste they generate.

Drinking water. Proposed House amendments to the Safe Drinking Water Act, which expired Sept. 30, 1982, would require EPA to set allowable levels of 14 chemicals found in water supplies and establish monitoring programs for more than 125 others. The reauthorization bill also contains prohibitions against ground-water contamination. Controlling disposal of brine from oil and gas drilling operations is one of the proposed steps.

FIFRA. The House has passed a one-year reauthorization of the Federal Insecticide, Fungicide and Rodenticide Act (it expired Sept. 30, 1982) in response to an environmentalist strategy designed to achieve major revisions. A longer authorization would have eased pressure on Congress to meet the environmentalists' goals. A bill for a two-year extension is pending in the Senate Agriculture Committee, but that panel has no plans to consider major revisions this year.

Ocean dumping. The ocean dumping section of the Marine Protection, Research and Sanctuaries Act expired in September, 1982, and the marine sanctuaries section expired a year later. The House Merchant Marine Committee has passed a reauthorization bill requiring designation of permanent dump sites and setting permit fees. Amendments pending in the Senate Commerce Committee would recognize rights of holders of offshore oil and gas leases in sanctuary waters and would give fishing interests a role in the regulation of their industry within protected areas.

Toxic substances. There has been relatively little controversy over implementation of the Toxic Substances Control Act, which expired September 30, but Congress has been in no hurry to enact the reauthorization bill. Any legislative activity could lead to environmentalist pressure for amendments to require testing of new chemicals—and to counterarguments that any such program should be voluntary.

Superfund. The Comprehensive Environmental Response Compensation and Liability Act—the Superfund law—does not expire until September, 1985, but bills to change it are pending. At present the fund, which covers costs of cleaning up hazardous waste dumps, is financed by a tax on petrochemical feedstocks. Proposed changes would replace that arrangement with a system of fees for disposal of wastes on land. Other Senate measures would extend the Superfund for five years and increase its ceiling to amounts ranging from $3.2 billion to $6 billion.

The general expectation is that Congress will not complete action before next spring on the major environmental laws still awaiting reauthorization. There may be further delays even then.

The 1984 political season will be well along by next spring, and the lawmakers may be wary of making controversial environmental decisions.

BATTLE OVER THE WILDERNESS[5]

Roland Falcioni scans the scores of campers and trailers lining the beach at the Cape Cod National Seashore and wonders how long it will be before the environmentalists evict them. The National Park Service has already taken steps to protect the fragile dunes from the ravages of human feet and tire treads. But three environmental groups have sued, demanding a ban on off-road vehicles. Falcioni's group, the Massachusetts Beach Buggy Association, has joined the fray and negotiations between the two sides have broken down. "It seems like every year they come up with more ways to deprive people of recreational activities," says Mary-Jo Avelar, chairman of the Provincetown Board of Selectmen. "You can't take your dog out there, you can't pick the flowers. What are the dunes for? You can't admire them if you can't get on them."

Woody Guthrie got it right when he wrote "This land is your land, this land is my land." That's just the problem: the federal government owns one-third of America, and citizens are battling over virtually every acre from California to the New York island. The disputes are older than the range wars and as basic as preservation versus development. The extremes among partisans range from Earth First!, the radical environmental group that tolerates sabotage in the cause of preservation, to conservative think tanks that view public ownership of land as nothing short of socialism.

But even Americans who simply want to get away from it all this summer are fighting among themselves over who gets to use Uncle Sam's land—and how. There is now a 10-year waiting list to float a private raft down the Colorado River. Ticketron is han-

[5]Excerpted from an article by Melinda Beck, staff writer. *Newsweek*. 102:22-4+. Jl. 25, '83. Copyright© 1983 by Newsweek, Inc. All Rights Reserved. Reprinted by permission.

dling scarce camping reservations, and "backcountry permits" have been sewn up for months at some of the most isolated spots. The bitterest battles are raging over the right to love nature in different ways. One hiker in the Pecos Wilderness near Santa Fe became so incensed when he encountered another walking his dog on a trail that he slit the puppy's throat. At the nearby Rio Grande Wild and Scenic River, fist fights have broken out over the right to eat lunch on a limited number of sandbars.

At the center of the storm is Interior Secretary James Watt, who, as one of his first acts in office, symbolically turned the bison on the department's seal to face right instead of left. Since then, environmentalists say Watt has freed more federal acreage for oil, gas, coal and geothermal exploration than any interior secretary in history. He has also relaxed strip-mining controls, streamlined rules requiring environmental-impact statements and virtually halted national-park acquisitions in favor of restoring man-made facilities. [In 1982] Congress thwarted his plan to open wilderness areas to oil and gas development, but a federal court upheld his proposal to release the entire U.S. outer continental shelf to offshore oil drilling. . . .

The controversies over public lands go far deeper, however, than one interior secretary or one administration, raising questions that go to the very heart of democracy and the national character. How much access should the people have to their land? What if one man's recreation is another's noisy interruption? Should a government dedicated to the principle of private property own more than half of Utah, Idaho, Oregon and Nevada and nearly 75 percent of Alaska? In addition to splendid forests and awesome canyons, federal lands contain 40 percent of the nation's salable timber, 50 percent of its coal, 80 percent of its shale oil and most of its copper, silver, asbestos, lead, berylium, molybdenum, phosphate and potash. How much land should be put into commercial production? How much should be saved for future generations or preserved just as it is?

The debate is complicated by the bureaucratic wilderness of federal agencies that have jurisdiction over the lands—including the Bureau of Land Management, the National Park Service, the U.S. Fish and Wildlife Service and the Forest Service, an agency

of the Department of Agriculture. The departments of Defense,
Energy and Transportation also have small tracts, as do NASA
and the Army Corps of Engineers. There is a Talmudic tangle of
separate land classifications such as Wilderness Areas, National
Trails, Grasslands, Seashores, Lakeshores, Monuments, Battle-
fields, Historical Sites, Wild and Scenic Rivers and Recreation
Areas—some of whose boundaries overlap. And the laws governing the lands are sometimes contradictory. The National Park
Service, for example, is charged with protecting the natural resources *and* serving the public on its 79 million acres. Much of
the remaining land is held by law for "multiple use"—a somewhat
implausible doctrine that requires federal land managers to juggle
hunting, fishing, timbering, grazing, oil, gas and mineral development, watershed protection, wildlife preservation and recreation
on the same lands.

The needs of still other government agencies affect public
holdings. The Department of Energy, for example, is considering
building a high-level radioactive waste dump within viewing dis-
tance of the Canyonlands National Park in southeastern Utah.
Many communities and special-interest groups in the West hate
the Bureau of Reclamation, the nation's dam operator—and some
blame it for mismanaging the flood of the Colorado River in recent
weeks. (When not in flood stage, the mighty Colorado, which
carved the Grand Canyon over 200 million years, is controlled
these days by a computer in Montrose, Calif., which regulates its
flow according to the electricity needs of bustling Western cities.)
Last year the House of Representatives passed a bill that would
require Interior to consider the impact of other federal-agency actions on adjacent parklands. But Interior officials oppose the measure, claiming it would foster still more paperwork—and more
lawsuits—over public-land policies.

Given the vast range of competing interests they must serve,
many beleaguered federal land managers figure that if everyone
is mad at them, they must be doing something right. Aside from
the major philosophical disputes, they also have to contend with
such minor annoyances as pot hunters who illegally forage for ancient artifacts; pot *growers,* who use national forests to raise marijuana crops; cactus rustlers feeding a chic new market in

Southwestern landscaping; "survivalists," who occasionally hold paramilitary maneuvers on federal lands—and even Satanists seeking a bit of isolation like everybody else. "It's real life in the parks," marvels Walter Herriman, superintendent of New Mexico's Chaco Culture National Historical Park, where one ranger was shot at while confronting a pot hunter.

Twenty years ago, residents near Moab, Utah, decided that the spectacular array of needles, arches, mesas and basins carved by the confluence of the Green and Colorado rivers was so dramatic that it ought to be a national park. Town fathers went to Washington to press the idea. Congress accepted and in 1962, Park Service drew up a proposal envisioning a road, an observation area and tasteful motel accommodations. Today there is no observation area and no motel, and the road dead-ends four miles from the river confluence. Park officials are managing most of Canyonlands National Park as a de facto "wilderness area," accessible only to those with Jeeps or the stamina to hike hours into the desert.

"We created a monster," laments Ray Tibbetts, former chairman of the Grand County Commissioners. "Now we know how the Indians feel about broken promises from the federal government," agrees another leader, Cal Black. Locals are so furious that several years ago, when the BLM was considering other nearby parcels for wilderness designation, county commissioners ordered roads cut in the land in hopes of disqualifying it and organized a picnic to watch.

Of all the concepts in federal land-management policy, none arouses more passion than "wilderness." Technically, the term applies only to 80 million federal acres designated by Congress since 1964 to remain in their most pristine, natural state, "where man is a visitor who does not remain." In theory, that means no roads, no cabins, no water systems, no toilet facilities, no mining, no drilling, no timber harvesting and no mechanized anything. There are inevitable exceptions, but the law is quite serious. The Forest Service cannot use chain saws to cut trees that fall on trails in wilderness areas. When a service helicopter crashed in a wilderness area several years ago, rescue workers had to take it apart and carry it out on foot.

Environmentalists see wilderness as the last refuge against man's ravages—a place that has "answers to questions we haven't learned how to ask yet," says Richard Beamish of the National Audubon Society—and in the environmental heyday of the 1960s and '70s, there was a rush to designate new areas. But the pace has slowed in recent years, in part because of local opposition. "A lot of people who hike up here are not very experienced," says Reuben Rajala, a trail supervisor for the Appalachian Mountain Club, which is leery of more wilderness designations in New Hampshire's White Mountains. "They may not want a Howard Johnson's, but they want toilet facilities and water." In northern California, where the timber industry says a proposed 2.4 million-acre wilderness would cost the local economy 1,300 logging and sawmilling jobs, one popular bumper sticker reads: "Sierra Club—Kiss My Axe."

As contentious as designating wilderness areas is, the question of managing the nation's wildlands is worse, and the problem applies not only to official wilderness areas, but to "backcountry" sections of national parks as well. Ever since a 1963 report by biologist A. Starker Leopold recommended that national parks be run as "vignettes of primitive America," many park officials have stopped interfering in natural cycles, even letting some forest fires burn. But man's efforts to erase his own imprint have sometimes proved futile—and often controversial. As rangers in Yellowstone closed down the garbage dumps that fed grizzly bears for decades, the hungry grizzlies started foraging in campsites and off park boundaries where they sometimes maul humans and end up being shot. Last year, to the horror of locals, Yellowstone officials allowed some of the park's magnificent bighorn sheep to walk off cliffs to their death rather than treat an infection of pinkeye that was blinding the herd.

Managing people in wilderness is even more troublesome—in no small part because of the growing enthusiasm for isolated areas. "We're in danger of loving wilderness to death," warns preservationist author Roderick Nash, who admits that environmentalists have been their own worst enemies. "Sierra Club calendars have done for wilderness what Playboy did for women," Nash says. As New Mexico BLM official Forrest

(Frosty) Littrell puts it, designating an area wilderness sometimes has a "neon-sign effect": suddenly, everyone wants to see it. To maintain some semblance of solitude in such areas, many national parks have had to limit access to backcountry areas—a seeming contradiction that troubles some wilderness enthusiasts. "'Wilderness' is unrestrained freedom—and that doesn't jive with regulations," says Michael Scott of the Wilderness Society in Denver. "But unrestrained freedom will destroy the area. What do you do?"

Many backcountry managers learned the need for such limits from experience. At Grand Canyon National Park, the epiphany came on a fateful Easter weekend in 1971 when nearly 1,000 people showed up at Bright Angel Campground, a narrow strip of campsites at the base of the canyon designed to accommodate fewer than 100 campers. "These people hadn't escaped from anything," recalls canyon District Ranger Larry Van Slyke. "The very thing they had hiked down to avoid was confronting them." Since then, canyon officials have required permits for overnight camping in the canyon, and beginning in October, they went further, assigning campers to one of 78 separate "zones" in the backcountry based on their equipment and experience. Far from resenting the hassle, most hikers appreciate the system. "It's sort of like buying tickets for a rock concert," shrugged Robert Bachmann of California, one of dozens of people standing in a predawn line outside the Grand Canyon's "Backcountry Reservations Office" for a chance at a permit cancellation. "If you want to go bad enough, you'll do just about anything."

Nash would go still further. He has advocated dividing public wildlands into five categories—from well-developed areas with clearly marked trails, to the most remote Alaskan mountainscapes—and requiring visitors to qualify for licenses by demonstrating their wilderness skills. (No humans at all would be allowed in "Class Five" lands, which would be left undisturbed as a genetic pool for the future of the earth.) "You wouldn't allow an untrained person to examine a rare piece of art," Nash argues. "When you have increasingly rare environments, you don't want to turn people indiscriminately loose in them."

To more populist nature lovers, Nash's scheme conjures up the specter of "vacation police," and many argue that even now, wilderness is an elitist notion that discriminates in favor of the healthy, wealthy and fit. Even there, however, there is widespread disagreement. "Those who say wilderness is only for the young, wealthy elite are wrong," says "W" Mitchell, former mayor of Crested Butte, Colo., who has run five different wild rivers despite being confined to a wheelchair. "I don't need my $20,000 mobile home, my $10,000 four-wheel drive or my $5,000 dirt bike to enjoy wilderness. It's the great equalizer."

While some long-running disputes over recreational rights have been settled, others are just beginning. Last year Grand Canyon officials ended their 10-year motorboat-versus-oars battle with a compromise (Sept. 16 to Dec. 15 it's "oars only" on the Colorado River). But they have yet to take on the 40-odd companies that operate scenic flights over the canyon, disturbing the "natural quiet" for hikers. Whose interests take precedence is often a matter of political clout or just plain tradition. "The hikers were there first, and that's all they have going for them," says Andy Lundstrom, who has been apprehended three times for running the Yellowstone River in his kayak against park regulations. "We could claim we don't like to see them hiking along with their aluminum and nylon packpacks and digging up the trails with their shoes."

By 1984, visitors to the Grand Canyon will not even need to venture into the park to "experience" its splendors. At a $5 million complex going up less than a mile from the park boundary, they can view a 30-minute film of the canyon's four seasons in a 100-foot-high theater. Next door, 32 tourists at a time can brave a five-minute simulated raft ride through four feet of artifically swooshed waters, riding rafts just like the ones real river runners use. "We'll show [visitors] what they can't see by standing on the rim and looking in," says Toby Rowe, a spokesman for FORMA Properties, which is planning similar thrill centers outside Yosemite and Yellowstone.

Indeed, the debate over backcountry usage is lost on the vast majority of national park and forest visitors, to many of whom a "wilderness experience" means bad TV reception in a park lodge or campground Winnebago. "Wilderness is largely a state of

mind," says National Park Service Director Russell Dickenson.
"A lot of people enjoy a 'windshield vacation,' driving through the
park and stopping at the overlooks. Who's to say that's better or
worse than a canoe trip in 50 miles of isolation?"

But catering to the "windshield visitors" (also known as the
"Winnebago tribe" or the "subspecies *touristica*") presents its own
set of dilemmas. Tourist facilities in most national parks reflect
the recreational tastes of past generations, and some park planners
are trying to introduce a more natural, 1980s element. In Yellowstone the Hamilton Store at Old Faithful long ago stopped serving
"geyser-water coffee"—made from water pumped in, naturally
hot, from the geyser basin—and the bathhouses that once stood
over the hot springs have been removed. At Yosemite, after receiving comments from 63,000 individuals and groups, park planners
decided to reduce the number of parking spaces, banking and post-
al services and overnight accommodations. Auto repairs and car
rentals are no longer available in Yosemite Valley. "The feeling
was that if you wanted a resort atmosphere, you could go somewhere else," says Park Service official John Adams. (The swimming pool will remain by popular demand, however, as will the
beauty shop at the Ahwahnee Hotel.) In parts of many national
parks, private automobiles have been banned in favor of free shut-
tle buses. "Instead of people problems, we have auto problems,"
says Dickenson.

*Reeking of pot, swarming with humanity and rocking to the
beat of countless oversize radios, Gateway National Recreation
Area is the electric Kool-Aid acid test of federal land policy.
Sprawling over 26,000 patchwork areas of Brooklyn, Queens,
Staten Island and New Jersey, the park boasts such unnatural
wonders as an abandoned airport, a nudist colony, a video-game
arcade and a bay polluted with toxic wastes. On weekends, 50 U.S.
Park Police come up from Washington to help keep order, and an
average of 30 arrests are made. Many park-service veterans think
Gateway shouldn't be a national park in the company of Yellowstone and Yosemite. But Gateway rangers say this park is important for different reasons. For city kids, Gateway provides a first
campout under scraggly pines, a first glimpse of open sea and a
chance to learn, as ranger Patricia Resignio puts it, that "all vege-
tables don't come from cans."*

While some conservatives think the federal government owns too much of America, conservationists point to the growing crowds and say more land is needed—particularly for the newest "urban parks." But the pendulum has swung away from park acquisitions since the mid-1970s, when the late Rep. Phil Burton of California pushed a "park-a-month" plan through Congress, a measure fondly dubbed "park-barrelling." Watt has argued that the parks should fix up the facilities they have before acquiring new lands, and some groups applaud his five-year, $1 billion rehabilitation program. But others charge that he has tied up acquisition funds approved by Congress and warn that some choice land parcels— such as those around the Santa Monica Mountains National Recreation Area in Los Angeles—may be lost to development or rising prices if not purchased quickly.

Another argument for acquiring more federal lands is the need to protect fragile ecosystems on existing public holdings. Booming oil, gas, timber, housing and geothermal developments in the region around Jackson, Wyo., for example, threaten five national forests, two national parks, a wildlife refuge, elk migrations and even Yellowstone's geysers. Jackson residents worry about the menaces to the region's natural beauty but county officials cannot legally deny subdivision applications on environmental grounds. Federal officials, meanwhile, throw up their hands at the notion of "buffer" acquisitions. "Where does the buffer end?" asks Assistant Interior Secretary Ray Arnett. "Does it stretch from the Atlantic to the Pacific?"

Additional land purchases would not solve many of the environmental problems public lands are facing. Resource specialists at the Grand Canyon, for example, can do little about the smog from Los Angeles that is reducing visibility, one of the park's most critical features. Other park officials have made progress through simple cooperation. When rangers at Montana's Glacier National Park noticed high levels of fluoride in park flora and fauna, they notified a nearby Arco plant, which voluntarily installed smokestack scrubbers and launched a monitoring program. But a nascent cooperative effort may come too late to save the Everglades National Park. Used for decades as a "pumping station" for South Florida's urban and agricultural needs, the fragile water system that is home to many threatened wildlife species "is sick and dying with a limited prognosis," says former Assistant Interior Secretary Nathaniel Reed.

When Bernard Vandewater of Quinault Lake, Wash., says "this land is my land," he can show you the actual deed. One of perhaps 1 million "inholders" who live or own property inside national-park boundaries. Vandewater personifies perhaps the thorniest public-land problem of all. According to Charles Cushman, director of the National Inholders Association, more than 70, 000 Americans have lost their homes to National Park Service "land grabs" since 1966. (Park Service officials say that most inholders have been offered generous settlements or "easements," and that actual condemnations are rare.) For his part, Vandewater says he's not budging. He and other inholders at Olympic National Park have signed a pact not to sell and are working instead to have Quinault Lake deleted from the park.

While inholders struggle to keep their land from Uncle Sam, proposals to sell public lands also spark uproars. In 1983, when the Reagan administration proposed to sell several million acres of federal land to help reduce the national debt, there were coast-to-coast protests as citizens realized that private ownership might shut them out. Some feared that religious cults or foreign speculators would buy the properties; ranchers worried about higher grazing fees. "I know of no other issue in the last year and a half that has drawn more controversy, concern or misunderstanding," says Rep. Larry Craig, Republican of Idaho. [The proposal was abandoned.]

If the federal government is so intent on raising revenues from its land, why doesn't it charge more for the oil, gas, timber, coal and other resources it sells and leases? Grazing fees on federal rangelands are only about one-fourth of those charged by private range owners. The Forest Service *spends* more money building roads and administering logging operations that it takes in from timber sales, according to some calculations. (It may be illegal, but Steven Hanke, an economist with the conservative Heritage Foundation, says that marijuana is the biggest revenue generator on Western forestland.) "Any resemblance between federal resources management and market value is pure coincidence," says Pat

Parentau of the National Wildlife Federation. If the government exploits the nation's resources at the expense of wildlife and wilderness, it should at least insure that taxpayers get their money's worth, environmentalists insist.

Critics are particularly incensed that the Reagan administration is increasing oil, gas, coal and timber sales at a time when there are surpluses of those commodities. The prices they fetch amount to little more than fire sales: the GAO estimates that Watt's controversial coal lease in the Powder River Basin cost the federal government $100 million in lost revenues. "These are supposed to be people who know about supply and demand!" marvels National Audubon Society president Russell Peterson. "The lasting legacy of this administration will be a large-scale transfer of publicly owned lands to private hands at below-market rates in a short period of time," agrees Geoffrey Webb of Friends of the Earth. . . .

Could private business manage the lands any better? Some critics think so. "A private owner has incentive to take care of the land," argues Hanke, who says that public lands aren't really controlled by the public, but by politicians, bureaucrats and special interests. That "tragedy of commons" notion is echoed at the Center for Political Economy and Natural Resources in Montana, where a small group of scholars thinks that government's need to balance competing interests virtually guarantees mismanagement. Even wilderness would fare better in the free market, the group maintains: without government subsidies, only profitable forests would be harvested and the rest would be left alone. "The history of private ownership of forests has been 'cut out and get out'," counters Rupert Cutler, John Crowell's predecessor under Jimmy Carter and now a National Audubon Society vice president. "That's why the Forest Service was established."

Curiously, much of the land now owned by the federal government is land nobody wanted. Through America's first two centuries, Uncle Sam gave land away, through homesteading, deeds to states and grants to railroads as an incentive to move westward. To the first settlers, wilderness was an evil that had to be tamed. It was only after the 1890 census, when historian Frederick Jackson Turner declared the frontier closed, that many Americans began to view wilderness as a treasure to be protected.

Even today it is hard for most Americans flying, driving or hiking across the country to believe there is a shortage of wilderness, so much of the land looks empty. Indeed, according to Frank Popper of Resources for the Future, 383 million acres of Western land—17 percent of the country—have never been surveyed. There is enough frontier left, he notes, that great wonders like Leviathan Cave in eastern Nevada and Indian rock carvings in Lassen County, Calif., were discovered just in the last two decades.

Will there still be wondrous surprises from the land in the decades to come? Will Yellowstone someday be seen as America's Acropolis—or will future generations wonder why we saved it? If there is any consensus in the current wilderness wars, it is that this land is *their* land and that the decisions made now will affect it profoundly.

ON THE NOMINATION OF WILLIAM D. RUCKELHAUS AS ADMINISTRATOR OF THE E.P.A.[6]

Remarks and a question-and-answer session on the nomination of William D. Ruckelshaus to be administrator. March 21, 1983

The President. Good morning.

Over the past week, it has become crystal clear that there is one man in this country better qualified than anyone else to take charge of the Environmental Protection Agency. And today, I'm pleased to announce my intention to nominate that man, William D. Ruckelshaus, to become the next Administrator of the EPA.

No one could bring more impressive credentials to this important job than Bill Ruckelshaus. He has proven his ability and integrity as Deputy Attorney General and as Acting Director of the FBI. As the first Administrator of the EPA, he played a critical role in shaping and launching the Agency. He is staunchly committed to protecting the Nation's air and water and land.

[6]Excerpted from the U.S. Government publication *Weekly Compilation of Presidential Documents.* 19:428–32. Mr. 28, '83.

I have given him the broad, flexible mandate that he deserves. Bill Ruckelshaus will have direct access to me on all important matters affecting the environment. I've also authorized him to conduct an agencywide review of the personnel and resources to ensure that the EPA has the means it needs to perform its vital function. And I've urged Bill to run an open, responsive operation, a goal that I know he shares with me.

Let me add a personal note. Back in the early 1970's, as Governor of California, I had the opportunity to deal personally with Bill Ruckelshaus as Administrator of the EPA. We were rightly proud of our State's environmental record, and in many ways, California led the Nation environmentally. But there are always going to be some things that could stand improving, and there are always bound to be some differences in policy and perspective between State and Federal authorities. In reconciling those differences, in enforcing the law, and in creating a constructive working relationship between his Agency and its State counterparts, Bill Ruckelshaus deeply impressed me. He was tough, fair, and highly competent.

Now, I'm proud of my environmental record as Governor of California, and I deeply believe that this administration has done a good job over the past 2 years. But I also believe that we can do better, and that after the dust settles and the country sees Bill Ruckelshaus at work in the EPA, our people will recognize that this administration's commitment to a clean environment is solid and unshakeable.

Mr. Ruckelshaus. Thank you very much, Mr. President, for your kind remarks. I witnessed—from the Pacific Northwest— some of the problems that my old Agency has had. And needless to say, I witnessed that from afar, and it did not occur to me until very recently that I would have anything to do about it. Last week, Mr. President, you asked me to consider helping out. And it's my belief, as a citizen of this country, if the President of the United States asks you to assist on a matter that's important to the country, you have an obligation to take that request seriously.

As far as my own views on the environment are concerned, the question of whether we are going to clean up the environment of this country is long over. That debate occurred back in the 1960's and resulted in all kinds of address to environmental problems by States and the Federal Government in a massive outflow of laws and regulations.

The question of today is not "whether," the question is "how"—how do we proceed to deal with this enormously complex mix of problems involving air pollution, water pollution, solid waste, and all of the problems that EPA has to deal with that affect public health and the environment?

I guess my immediate task, as I see it, is to stabilize EPA, is to re-instill in the people there the dedication to their task, to their job, that they have had from the outset of that agency and to get on with this enormously complicated job of cleaning up our air and water and protecting our citizens against toxic substances.

I believe that the President has given me the tools that I need to do the job, most important of which are his personal support. He has given me the flexibility to define the problems and to suggest solutions and, on that basis, I'm going to do the best job I can for him and for the country to divine and to serve the public interests.

I would be glad to try to respond to any questions, or either one of us would.

Q. We have one for the President first. Mr. President, let me—let us just ask you if you think that it was the philosophy that your appointees brought to the EPA or what they thought was your philosophy on the environment that caused some of the problems over there in the first place? That's been suggested. **The President.** No, my philosophy has been one and the same. It's been the same since I was Governor of California: to enforce the laws and to use common sense in doing this. And very frankly, I think that the attack that was leveled was unwarranted. **Q.** But some of the folks that were there seemed to be tilting toward business because they thought that's what your administration wanted. **The President.** I think that was a misreading and, as I say, I think a misunderstanding. All that I've ever proposed is that we be fair. **Q.** Somehow you're getting tougher, though, now, Mr. President. Will your policies become more, say, pro-environment now with the mandate that you've given Mr. Ruckelshaus? **The President.** They've always been pro-environment. **Q.** Are they changing at all starting now? **The President.** I'm too old to change. **Q.** Mr. President, will Mr. Ruckelshaus be able to be truly independent of both interference from the White House on political grounds and interference from industry? Does he have a mandate to be independent of that kind of interference? **Mr. Ruckelshaus.** Let me try to respond to that. When I was there before there were always—a constant flood of speculation, charges about various industrial intervention into EPA. There was never any substance to it when I was there, and there won't be any substance to it now.

It is our job, my job, the job of that agency to serve the public interest. That includes all of the public. And when we have charge—we are charged with regulating a segment of our society, we're going to do so fairly. It's very important to underscore "fairly." We are going to do our best to interpret the mandate that Congress has given us and interpret that in a way that achieves environmental improvement in this country. I don't think that necessitates confrontation. I don't think it necessitates us shaking our fist at anybody. It entails a lot of hard work and a lot of dedication to seeing that those laws are properly administered. **Q.** To follow up, what do you think of the testimony that has been heard on Capitol Hill about political interference, about Dow Chemical rewriting reports in the past? What about the stewardship of the agency so far? **Mr. Ruckelshaus.** Well, my concern is the future, not the past. My concern is the future of that agency and to ensure that it does its job.

To the extent that any charges are leveled, I have no idea whether they're right or wrong. We will do the best we can to investigate the substance of those charges, and if they prove to be correct, why, appropriate action will be taken. But I don't want to prejudge that, because I have no idea. **Q.** Mr. President, a lot was made last week of your statement about environmental extremism and trying to turn the White House into a bird's nest. I mean, is that the way you feel about environmentalism? **The President.** No. But as in any movement, there are going to be zealots on both sides who are going to want something more than what is happening. And I think Bill has been answering this question, in a way, with what he was saying about the purpose. There are some people, and they've always been there, who are so zealous that they literally would stop all progress. But by the same token, why don't you give some circulation to a remark that I made when I was Governor? I said, "There are also people in the country that believe that they won't be satisfied unless they can pave over the entire countryside."

Now, that was an extreme statement, too. But it was about those people that believed that in the name of progress it warranted destroying the purity of our waters and the quality of our air and so forth. **Q.** Do you feel, sir, though, that the environmentalists have legitimate concerns about what's been going on at EPA? Are there any legitimate concerns there? You say the charges are unwarranted. **The President.** I think the—and then we have to leave with this one. I'm sorry. . . .

Now, if you understand and go back, you've got to remember that there was a time when the so-called toxic waste, and not too long ago, was being simply disposed of the way we've disposed of any kind of garbage—put it in a hole some place, do this with it and that. But it was not being villainous or venal; we didn't understand those drugs or those things. It was like in California, not too many years ago, discovering, for the whole Nation, what caused smog. No one had known before. And so things were done without evil intent.

Now, there are thousands and thousands of those dumps throughout the country. And the EPA has the task of not only finding and identifying all of them but then determining which constitute the most immediate danger and, therefore—because you can't deal with all of them at once—going to work on a priority basis on those.

And evidently, there were some disputes—and particularly on the part of some on the Hill—as to whether right decisions had been made on some of these. I think that they had made sizable progress and were well underway toward establishing—they had already some several hundred that they believed were the prime and the priority dumps to be cleaned up.

And this is what I think all of the fuss was about. And I would like to point out that in all the allegations and everything—accusations, just like so many other things, no one has presented any facts at all. . . .

Q. Mr. Ruckelshaus, one question? **Mr. Ruckelshaus.** Sure, I'd be glad to. **Q.** Mr. Ruckelshaus. After years on the industrial side of the fence, have your views toward regulation changed any since you were at EPA? **Mr. Ruckelshaus.** When my views on regulation and on the environment and the protection of the public health changed, to the extent they've changed, was when I was at EPA. I went into EPA with a lot of assumptions about scientific certitude, about pollutants, about our ability to measure them, about our ability to abate them with the technology that was available at a reasonable cost, and the only thing necessary to gain compliance with the environment was to start enforcing the laws.

After I got there and after I was, frankly, there about 3 months, I discovered this problem was a lot more complex than I realized when I first arrived, and that we have a whole mix of extraordinarily complicated, difficult problems to solve under the calmest of circumstances. And when you add to that complicated mix the emotion that can be generated around some of these problems, it just becomes four or five times as complicated. . . .

IN DEFENSE OF JAMES WATT[7]

Radio address to the nation. June 11, 1983

My fellow Americans:

I think it's time to clear the air and straighten out the record on where my administration stands on environmental and natural resources management matters. I know you've heard and read a million words about where others think we stand. Now, how about 5 minutes of the truth?

The Secretary of Interior, Jim Watt, is the prime target for those who claim that this administration is out to level the forests and cover the country with blacktops. Someone in the press the other day said if Jim discovered a cure for cancer, there are those who would attack him for being pro-life.

[7]Excerpted from the U.S. Government publication *Weekly Compilation of Presidential Documents.* 19:863-4. Je. 20, '83.

Let's go back a little first and set the stage. Jim rides herd on all the national parks and most of the 80 million acres of national wilderness. There are other things, like wildlife refuges, which up the total considerably. In fact, the Federal Government owns one-third of all the land of the United States.

When he came to Washington 2-1/2 years ago, Jim found that visitor facilities in our national parks had been allowed to deteriorate to the point that many failed to met standards for health and safety. It's being corrected. The National Park Service has made a major effort to improve maintenance at the parks that so many Americans love and love to visit. And today, they provide a wider, more beautiful variety of outdoor splendor than you can find anywhere else in the world.

Not too long ago, however, a new firestorm was raised about our wilderness lands. The perception was created that Secretary Watt was turning some of these lands loose from wilderness classification and government ownership. I should point out that wilderness lands are areas of such wild beauty that they're totally preserved in their natural state. No roads violate them, and no structures of any kind are allowed, and there are now almost 80 million acres of such land.

So, what was the fire-storm all about? Well, hang on, and follow me closely. As a result of legislation passed several years ago, a study was made of some 174 million acres of land to see if any or all of it should be declared wilderness and added to the present 80 million acres. Conditions were imposed in the review procedures to ensure that wilderness standards would be met.

If, for example, there were roads on the land, it was ineligible. It was ineligible if there was any dual ownership by other levels of government or if title to mineral rights was held by individuals or governments. Also, with limited exceptions, any package had to contain no less than 5,000 acres to be eligible. The study had been going on under the previous administration, and some 150 million of the designated 174 million acres had already been turned down by previous administrations as being ineligible for wilderness classification.

Now, think hard now. Do you recall hearing one word about this or any attack being made on anyone at the time? I don't.

When we arrived, there were still about 25 million acres to be studied. A few months ago, another 800,000 acres—that's a fraction of what the previous administration rejected—were disqualified as not meeting wilderness qualifications. Yet, the reaction this time was instantaneous, volcanic in size, and nationwide in effect: "Jim Watt was giving away wilderness land. Our children and grandchildren would be deprived of ever seeing America as it once was."

Well, nobody bothered to mention that our administration has proposed to the Congress addition of another 57 wilderness areas encompassing 2.7 million acres. That's more than three times as much land as was disqualified. Nor did anyone mention that I've already signed legislation designating sites in Indiana, Missouri, Alabama, and West Virginia as new wilderness areas.

The truth is that our National Park System alone has grown to 74 million acres, and almost 7,000 miles of river are included in our National Wild and Scenic River System. We have 413 wildlife refuges totaling some 86.7 million acres. This record is unmatched by any other country in the world.

Our environmental programs also are the strongest in the world. Last year, expenditures by business and government to comply with environmental laws and regulations were estimated at over $55 billion, or $245 per man, woman, and child in the United States.

We have made a commitment to protect the health of our citizens and to conserve our nation's natural beauty and resources. We have even provided financial and technical support to other nations and international organizations to protect global resources. Thanks to these efforts, our country remains "America the Beautiful." Indeed, it's growing more healthy and more beautiful each year. I hope this helps set the record straight, because it's one we can all be proud of.

Till next week, thanks for listening and God bless you.

CLARK IS APPOINTED[8]

Radio address to the nation. November 26, 1983

My fellow Americans:

There's a change of management over at the Department of Interior. James Watt has resigned, and Judge William Clark has taken his place.

When Jim became Secretary of Interior he told me of the things that needed doing, the things that had to be set straight. He also told me that if and when he did them, he'd probably have to resign in 18 months. Sometimes the one who straightens out a situation uses up so many brownie points he or she is no longer the best one to carry out the duties of day-to-day management. Jim understood this. But he also realized what had to be done, and he did it for more than 30 months, not 18.

Our national parks are the envy of the world, but in 1981 they were a little frayed at the edges. Since 1978 funds for upkeep and restoration had been cut in half. Jim Watt directed a billion-dollar improvement and restoration program. This 5-year effort is the largest commitment to restoration and improvement of the park system that has ever been made.

You, of course, are aware of the economic crunch we've been facing. Yet, even so, Secretary Watt set out to increase protection for fragile and important conservation lands. In 1982 he proposed that 188 areas along our gulf and Atlantic coasts be designated as undeveloped coastal areas. And that proposal became the basis for the historic Coastal Barrier Resources Act. This act covers dunes, marshes, and other coastal formations from Maine to Texas— lands that provide irreplaceable feeding and nesting grounds for hundreds of species of waterfowl and fish. And, under Secretary Watt, we've added substantial acreage to our parks and wildlife refuges and some 15,000 acres to our wilderness areas.

[8]Excerpted from the U.S. Government publication *Weekly Compilation of Presidential Documents.* 19:1617–18. D. 5, '83.

Interior is also in charge of preserving historic sites and structures. In the economic recovery program we launched in 1981 we gave a 25-percent tax credit for private sector restoration of historic structures. The result has been private investment in historic preservation five times as great as in the preceding 4 years. Secretary Watt has explored other ways to involve the private sector in historic preservation. And one of the efforts we're all proudest of is the campaign to restore Ellis Island and the grand lady in New York Harbor, the Statue of Liberty. This campaign is being led by Lee Iacocca, the chairman of Chrysler, and is being financed almost entirely by private contributions.

Preservation of endangered species is also a responsibility of the Department, and the approval and review of plans to bring about recovery of endangered plant and animal species has nearly tripled in the 30 months of Secretary Jim Watt. From the very first, Jim pledged to the Governors of our 50 States that the Department would be a good neighbor, that they would be included in land planning, and that small tracts of isolated Federal lands would be made available to communities needing land for hospitals, schools, parks, or housing. He also stated that isolated small tracts would be sold to farmers and ranchers.

An example of what I'm talking about is a strip of land 1 mile long and only 2 to 20 feet wide that was recently sold. I think you can imagine how these efforts must have erased some problems private landowners had with clouded title to their property.

Of course, all this was distorted and led to protests that he was selling national parks and wilderness. What he actually did was sell, in 1982, 55 tracts that totaled only 1,300 acres, and this year, 228 tracts totaling a little over 10,000 acres. The largest parcel was 640 acres; that's 1 square mile. None of it was park, wildlife refuge, wilderness, or Indian trust lands. They are not for sale. And not one acre of national parkland was leased for oil drilling or mining, contrary to what you may have read or heard.

When territories were becoming States, they were promised title to Federal lands within their borders, some lands to be used for public education. But as more and more Western States joined the Union, there began to be a delay; in fact, a permanent delay in turning over these lands. Jim Watt promised the Governors that if they'd identify lands they had a right to claim under their statehood acts, we'd make the Federal Government honest. The Governors responded, and as a result, by the end of this year more land will have been delivered to the States to support their school systems than at any time since 1969.

Changes have been made in the management of forest lands which are eligible for multiple use. Those lands will provide lumber on a sustained-yield basis. This will benefit Americans who cherish the dream of owning their own home.

We've made giant strides in implementing a national water policy which recognizes State primacy in managing water resources. People must be a part of our planning, and people need a reliable, safe drinking water supply, water for generating power, and water for irrigation.

Since I've mentioned energy, let me touch on that for a minute. It's estimated that 85 percent of the fuel we need to keep the wheels of industry turning is on Federal-owned property, including the Outer Continental Shelf. Efforts to increase the supply of energy have been carried out in full compliance with environmental stipulations. We can and will have an increased energy supply with an enhanced environment.

James G. Watt has served this nation well. And I'm sure William Clark will do the same.

Till next week, thanks for listening, and God bless you.

TOXIC WASTES AND REGULATION

EDITOR'S INTRODUCTION

No environmental concern is more urgent than the issue of toxic pollution. This section points out the seriousness of the problem, and its effects on public health, offering some suggestions as to how the toxic by-products of industry can be handled more safely.

"The Toxics Boomerang," adapted from Lewis Regenstein's book *America the Poisoned,* describes the extent of the dangers caused by toxic waste. In the second article Jeremy Main, writing in *Fortune* magazine, looks at another side of the problem: the huge economic and social costs of compensating the victims of pollution.

Next, an article from *Public Relations Journal* reports that, contrary to the assertions of environmentalists, many industries attempt to control pollution, and that their efforts far exceed legal requirements. The fourth article, reprinted from *Technology Review,* suggests that in future it will be both practical and desirable for federal regulations to be replaced by the constraints imposed voluntarily by manufacturers upon themselves. Lawsuits brought by victims of pollution against the manufacturers of the toxic waste, the article argues, will have an important effect on the future actions of industrialists.

Concluding this section, two articles, reprinted from *Technology Review* and the *New York Times,* discuss the possibilities of disposing of toxic wastes in the oceans, and of recycling them for industrial purposes.

THE TOXICS BOOMERANG[1]

In the tens of thousands of years that we humans have ruled the Earth, we have wrought increasingly severe, and in some cases irreversible, damage on the planet's life-support system, a structure that we call "the environment." We have done more ecological damage to the world in the last few decades than in the entire preceding period of recorded history. If we continue at the current rate, or even at a greatly reduced level, our planet may soon be unfit for habitation by most higher life forms, including humans.

In the United States, no environmental problem (with the possible exception of habitat destruction) is of greater magnitude and importance than the pervasive contamination of our society and food chain with a variety of deadly chemicals. A multitude of toxic compounds known to cause cancer; birth defects; miscarriages; heart, lung, liver and neurological damage; and other severe disorders are found regularly in our food, our air, our water, and our own bodies.

There is increasingly alarming evidence that the widespread contamination of our environment may be linked to the high incidence of adverse health effects that are occurring across the nation—in epidemic proportions in some areas. For example, a recent study by the University of Medicine and Dentistry of New Jersey found that areas of the state where toxic waste dumps were located had extraordinarily high cancer death rates, up to 50 percent above average in some cases. (The amount of hazardous waste generated each year in America is now estimated at between 150 and 275 million metric tons, somewhere around a ton for every man, woman, and child in the country. The overwhelming majority of this waste—90 percent or more—is disposed of in a way that represents an actual or potential threat to the public health.)

[1]Reprint of an article by Lewis Regenstein, vice president of The Fund for Animals. *Environment*. D. '83. Adapted from his book *America the Poisoned*. Copyright© 1982 by Acropolis Books. Reprinted by permission.

In 1980, officials of the U.S. Environmental Protection Agency (EPA) called this toxic chemical crisis "the most grievous error in judgment we as a nation have ever made," describing it as "one of the most serious problems the nation has ever faced." Yet, the response of our government over the last few years has been to weaken or cripple the very laws and agencies that were set up to cope with this situation.

The Pervasive Toxins

Today, every Ameican is regularly and unavoidably exposed to dangerous, health-destroying chemicals. Several hundred pesticide ingredients used on our food are known or thought to cause cancer and birth defects in animals—in some cases at the lowest doses tested. By the time restrictions were placed on most uses of some of the deadliest carcinogenic chemicals, such as DDT, dieldrin, benzene hexachloride (BHC), and PCBs, they had contaminated virtually the entire populace: these poisons were found in the flesh tissues of literally 99 percent of all Americans tested, as well as in our food, air, water, and almost all mother's milk samples. In fact, breast milk has become so contaminated with banned, cancer-causing chemicals that it would be illegal to sell it in supermarkets. (This does *not* mean that mothers should avoid nursing their children. Women can significantly reduce their levels of contaminants by following a sensible diet, and by avoiding or minimizing their consumption of foods that concentrate toxins, for example, food high in animal fats—especially high-fat meat and dairy products—and freshwater fish.)

Moreover, "banned" and restricted chemicals, whether used in this country or not, still represent a serious threat to the U.S. public. In recent years, EPA has adopted a policy of routinely issuing "emergency" exemptions for the use of such products. In 1981, 298 of 462 of these requests were approved; in the first half of 1982, 350 out of 548 were granted.

Export Trade in Death

Our food supply is also contaminated with numerous carcinogenic chemicals that have been banned in this country but that can be and are exported abroad for use on food grown for export to the United States. American firms routinely export to foreign, underdeveloped nations hundreds of millions of pounds of extremely hazardous pesticides and other chemicals that return to us on bananas, tomatoes, coffee, tea, sugar, cocoa, chocolate, beef, and other imported food that is consumed by those in the United States. Such banned chemicals thus remain part of the U.S. diet.

For example, DDT was generally banned in the United States in 1972 because of its potent carcinogenicity and its devastating impact on birds, fish, and other wildlife. Yet, over 40 million pounds a year of DDT have continued to be manufactured in the United States and shipped abroad, much of it distributed at taxpayer expense by the U.S. Agency for International Development (U.S. AID).

Less than 1 percent of imported food shipments are checked by the Food and Drug Administration (FDA) for illegally high pesticide residues. The General Accounting Office has reported that "half of the imported food that FDA found to be adulterated was marketed without penalty of importers and consumed by an unsuspecting American public."

Almost half of the green (unroasted) coffee beans that are imported into this country and tested have been found to contain illegally high residues of pesticides that have been banned or greatly restricted in the United States because they cause cancer. Among the chemicals that the FDA has found on imported coffee from South America, Asia, and Africa are such generally banned carcinogens as DDT, BHC, dieldrin, heptachlor, and others. Such contamination may help account for the otherwise unexplained link shown in some studies between coffee consumption and cancer of the pancreas.

In addition, the World Health Organization (WHO) estimates that some 500,000 people around the world are poisoned each year by pesticides, many by chemicals from America. However, these official, reported figures are thought to represent only a small fraction of the actual total.

Shortly after entering office in 1981, President Reagan revoked the modest export restrictions on such hazardous substances that had been implemented by executive order a month earlier. Moreover, the administration has drafted plans to expedite the ability of U.S. firms to export banned products on the grounds that such restrictions "placed U.S. exports at a competitive disadvantage."

As a result, U.S. citizens as well as foreign nationals will continue to be exposed to chemicals that cause death and disability and to other products that are so hazardous they cannot legally be sold in this country. As long as our government continues to permit this "export trade in death" the American people will remain among the victims of such a policy.

The Cancer Epidemic

Our massive use of toxic chemicals has been accompanied by an alarming rise in the incidence of cancer, which kills over a thousand Americans every day. Each year, more Americans die of cancer (430,000 in 1982) than were killed in combat during World War II, Korea, and Vietnam *combined.* The disease kills about eight times more Americans than do automobile accidents.

In June 1982, the National Cancer Institute reported that Americans have an almost one-in-three chance of developing cancer during their lifetimes, pointing out that "the probability of developing cancer from birth to age 74 is approximately 31 percent." This means that, in America, some 60 to 80 million of us now alive can expect to get cancer.

Around 1900, cancer caused only about 3 percent of all deaths, and ranked between 8th and 10th as a cause of mortality. Today, the disease causes about 20 percent of all deaths, and is the number two killer of Americans (after heart disease). Cancer ranks first as the cause of death for women between 30 and 40, and for children aged 1 to 10. It is clear that, despite the claims of the chemical industry, the increased cancer rate of recent decades is not caused by people living longer; it has now become a disease of the young as well as the old, and is second only to accidents as the chief cause of death for Americans under 35.

Less than one-third of these annual cancer deaths (perhaps 130,000—mainly lung cancers) are thought to be caused by cigarette smoking. The remaining almost 300,000 deaths are caused by other factors, with the pervasive presence in our society of deadly chemicals thought to play a major role.

Moreover, chemicals that cause sterility are regularly found in human semen samples, and studies show that the sperm count of American males appears to have dropped 30 to 40 percent in the last 30 years, with toxic chemicals being largely to blame. This may help account for the dramatic increase in sterility among males that has occurred over the last few decades. In 1938, the rate of sterility among American males was reported to be just 0.5 percent. Studies done in the 1980s show a rate of 10 to 23 percent in areas sampled.

In 1980, after three years of study, the federal inter-agency Toxic Substances Strategy Committee (TSSC) issued its report that clearly demonstrated that synthetic chemicals are a threat to the lives and health of millions of Americans, and that confirmed the alarming rise in the cancer rate in the 1970s. In announcing the findings, Gus Speth, then chairman of the President's Council on Environmental Quality (CEQ), emphasized that "man-made toxic chemicals are a significant source of death and disease in the United States today." And CEQ member Dr. Robert Harris pointed out that it is no coincidence that the production of such chemicals greatly increased between 1950 and 1960, with a dramatic increase in the cancer rate showing up 20 to 25 years later—"the lag time one might expect."

In August 1980, the Surgeon General of the United States, Julius Richmond, released an assessment of the threat to public health caused by toxic chemicals, calling it "a major and growing public health problem." An accompanying report prepared by the Library of Congress makes it clear that this problem is not confined to the United States but is of worldwide dimensions:

"In the case of chemicals such as some of the pesticides . . . these are so long-lasting and so pervasive in the environment that virtually the entire human population of the Nation, and indeed the world, carries some body burden of one or several of them. . . . A significant proportion of the world's population, perhaps all of

it, is exposed to the cumulative if unknown effects of a plethora of man-made pollutants from a number of diverse and often distant sources."

Dioxin

One of the most alarming and possibly dangerous aspects of this problem is the fact that virtually the entire American population is potentially at risk of being exposed to dioxin (TCDD), the most deadly synthetic chemical known. In early 1983, the community of Times Beach, Missouri, contaminated with just a few ounces or pounds of dioxin, had to be largely abandoned by its residents, as had happened a few years earlier at Love Canal in upstate New York.

Yet, even while Times Beach was being evacuated and bought up by EPA because of dioxin pollution, the agency was, and still is, allowing over a million pounds of herbicides containing dioxin to be sprayed throughout the country—including urban areas and agricultural lands where food and cattle are raised.

In 1979, EPA formally recognized the dangers of these dioxin-contaminated herbicides by announcing that it would ban 2,4,5-T (one of the two ingredients of Agent Orange) and silvex on the grounds that they presented an unacceptable threat to human health and the environment. The agency cited data showing that 2,4,5-T was killing unborn children in areas where it was being sprayed on forests to kill off unwanted vegetation. As EPA Assistant Administrator for Toxic Substances Steve Jellinek put it, "Now we have human evidence. We have dead fetuses."

Declaring 2,4,5-T to be an imminent threat to human health, EPA proceeded to apply emergency restrictions on several applications of it, suspending its use on forests, rights-of-way, and "pastureland." Yet, inexplicably, it permitted other uses to continue (such as on rice, "rangeland," fences, industrial sites, buildings, parking areas), thereby perpetuating wide public exposure to dioxin.

Silvex, which was similarly restricted with its sister chemical 2,4,5-T because of dioxin contamination, can still be used for these allowed applications as well as on sugarcane and even on fruit orchards (apples, prunes, and pears).

In the rice-growing areas of Arkansas, for example, these herbicides have been used for over three decades to kill weeds. In 1981, Arkansas county's cancer mortality rate was almost 50 percent higher than the national average. A lengthy front-page story in the *New York Times* of April 9, 1983, describes some of the effects of spraying 2,4,5-T and silvex:

"'Sickness touches every family here,' said Aileen Brasko . . . whose brick ranch house . . . is surrounded by rice fields. 'People say they don't feel good all the time.' . . . Mrs. Brasko said her husband, George . . . has suffered from severe headaches and allergies. Their 17-year-old daughter has leukemia and once had a brain hemorrhage, apparently from a birth defect. Another daughter, 20, has diabetes. 'These things are rampant,' she said, 'but nobody pays any attention.'

In an informal telephone survey of 20 rice farming families in the country, most families complained of a year-round sinus condition that Mrs. Brasko described as chronic nasal congestion.

. . . a physician at the hospital closely familiar with cancer admissions . . . said that cancers of the colon and pancreas were so frequent in the region as to constitute 'a remarkable observation.'"

Another extremely toxic herbicide that has been associated with the deaths of numerous human fetuses is 2,4,-D, the other ingredient of Agent Orange. This weedkiller—perhaps the most widely used in the country—is known to cause cancer, miscarriages, and birth defects in animals, and appears to have similar effects upon humans.

In the Swan Valley area of Montana, 9 out of 10 pregnant women lost their children during a year-long period when 2,4-D was being heavily sprayed. And around Ashford, Washington, where the surrounding forests and highways were being treated with the herbicide, a total of 12 pregnancies resulted in 10 miscarriages during a period of a little over a year; one of the two live-born children died shortly after birth. Numerous similar accounts abound from communities across the nation.

EPA is still allowing massive amounts of these two ingredients of Agent Orange to be sprayed throughout the nation in a sort of chemical warfare that we are waging against ourselves. (Ironically, these phenoxy herbicides, as they are known, were developed during World War II as chemical warfare agents.) Moreover, the continued use of 2,4,5-T and silvex is causing dioxin to build up in the environment and in the food chain; it has turned up in such food products as fish, beef, and even mother's milk.

The presence of dioxin wastes across the nation also represents a serious potential problem. For example, there are thought to be *several thousand* pounds of dioxin located at the Hooker Chemical Company's Hyde Park, New York, dump site, which is located near Love Canal. (This compares to just 55 pounds of dioxin that caused the contamination of Times Beach and 100 other suspected sites in Missouri.) Dioxin is so deadly that a drop of it is believed to be sufficient to kill a thousand people; an ounce could kill a million. Thus, the dioxin at Hyde Park is theoretically sufficient to kill every human on Earth if consumed in equal amounts. No one can predict the results of this dioxin seeping into the local groundwater or otherwise escaping into the environment, nor has anyone come up with a viable solution for dealing with dioxin-contaminated soil and other wastes when places such as Times Beach are "cleaned up."

Health Effects of Dioxin

Dioxin has proved incredibly toxic at the lowest levels at which it has been tested, and has caused devastating effects (including death) at the lowest doses imaginable. At levels of just a few parts per billion (ppb) or even per trillion (ppt), dioxin has caused miscarriages, birth defects, cancer, and death in laboratory animals. (One ppt is the equivalent of 1 second in 320 centuries.) EPA considers dioxin in soil to be unsafe at levels above one ppb—the equivalent of 1 second in 31.7 years. Yet, 2,4,5-T commonly contains concentrations of dioxin several times higher than that level. Dioxin has been found in Missouri at levels of several hundred ppb, and, in the case of some riding stables, at 30,000 ppb.

No one known the damage dioxin now causes to the public health, but it has been associated with numerous human deaths and disabilities over the last few decades, sometimes showing up in the form of cancer decades after exposure. Among the studies

and evidence showing such a connection are the following:
• At least two Swedish studies done on agricultural and forest workers regularly exposed to 2,4,5-T and 2,4-D showed extraordinarily high rates of extremely rare and fatal forms of cancer known as soft tissue sarcomas. These rare cancers have appeared at high rates in other population groups exposed to dioxin (such as workers at Dow and Monsanto chemical plants) and are now being found at alarming levels in Midland, Michigan, where Dow Chemical has for years produced (and dumped) products containing dioxin.
• EPA's studies on pregnant women exposed to 2,4,5-T (such as in Alsea, Oregon) found an association between the spraying of 2,4,5-T and a high rate of miscarriages.
• A 1982 trial verdict resulted in 47 railroad workers who were exposed to dioxin being awarded some $58 million. They complained of such illnesses as cancer, liver damage, loss of sex drive, neurological problems, dizziness, and breathing difficulty. Vietnam veterans who were exposed to Agent Orange (a 50/50 mixtureof the herbicides 2,4,5-T and 2,4-D) have manifested these same symptoms.

In late July 1983, preliminary reports by EPA were released that conclude there is a probable link between dioxin and human cancer, and that rank the compound as the most powerful carcinogen—100 million times more potent than vinyl chloride. Instead of acting to rectify the dioxin situation, EPA has in recent years done just the opposite. In 1981, the agency halted the process begun in 1979 to ban 2,4,5-T and silvex, and began conducting private negotiations with Dow Chemical on lifting the partial ban on 2,4,5-T. (In October 1983, in a surprise move, Dow announced that it would no longer market 2,4,5-T or silvex in the United States and that it would abandon its efforts to have EPA certify the chemicals as safe. Shortly thereafter, EPA said that it intended to ban further uses of the herbicides. However, there are still some 60 other companies involved in the fight over 2,4,5-T, so it remains to be seen what final action will be taken.)

Additionally, Dow's Midland, Michigan, plant is still dumping 25 million gallons of wastes a day into the Tittabawassee River, which feeds into Saginaw Bay, the source of commercial fish that are sold throughout the United States and that have recently been found to contain significant levels of dioxin. After an EPA study concluded that "Dow's discharge represented the major source, if not the only source of TCDD contamination" there, and advocated a ban on the consumption of such poisoned fish, agency officials submitted the report to Dow and allowed the firm to delete this information.

Dow denies that it is the source of this pollution (even though fish caged downstream from the plant absorb far more dioxin than those caged upstream), but refused to allow EPA to gather on-site data or to furnish the agency with information about its discharges or chemical processes. Thus, at the same time it is spending $33 million to buy up Times Beach because of dioxin pollution, EPA has refused to take action to halt the further spread of this deadly contaminant.

Sealing Our Doom

Dioxin is but one of the dozens of toxic, cancer-causing chemicals that are frequently found in the environment and the food chain, exposing virtually the entire populace to a variety of deadly compounds. While many of these chemicals have been tested individually, the real question is, What will be the effects of regular exposure to a combination of dozens or hundreds of such chemicals, reacting with each other in ways that are little understood and that cannot be predicted?

It is ironic that in so casually trying to wipe out other forms of life that were not perceived as immediately useful or convenient to us, we may well have sown the seeds of our own destruction. Our greatest mistake was to assume that our chemical poisons could be selective, that we could kill off numerous other forms of life and not be affected ourselves.

We should have known better than to think we could poison our environment and our wildlife but not be affected ourselves. A book written long, long ago warned us that we could not kill off the birds and beasts of the Earth without jeopardizing our own survival. As the Bible tells us in Ecclesiastes 3:19, the fates of humans and of animals are intertwined:

"For that which befalleth the sons of men befalleth beasts. Even one thing befalleth them: as the one dieth, so dieth the other: yea, they have all one breath, so that a man hath no pre-eminence above a beast."

In light of what we have learned in recent years, we can no longer plead ignorance. Yet we are continuing down a road that we should know full well could be leading us to a disaster of unprecedented proportions. And every day that passes the problem becomes greater, as does the price we will inevitably have to pay when the day of reckoning arrives.

THE HAZARDS OF HELPING TOXIC WASTE VICTIMS[2]

Congress is on the way to enacting a law that answers some large emerging questions about what our society owes people who may have been injured by hazardous chemicals. Among the questions: Under what circumstances can they collect from a company that manufactured or dumped the wastes? What if several companies are involved and it is unclear which wastes caused the cancer, or birth defects, or other medical tragedies? What if there is doubt that these misfortunes are even related to the toxic wastes? What if there is little or no doubt about this but the company was breaking no laws when it acted, years ago, or had no reason to believe that its actions might turn out, years later, to be harmful to innocent bystanders? Is our society prepared to tell these bystanders that nobody can be held liable for their misfortunes—that life in an industrial society carries with it some inescapable risks?

The toxic waste compensation bills now making their way through Congress attempt, in various ways, to make it easier for those who have been injured to seek damages. However, the bills would have some other major effects. The consequences could in-

[2]Reprint of an article by Jeremy Main, staff writer. *Fortune.* 108:158–60+. O. 31, '83. Copyright© 1983 Time Inc. All rights reserved. Reprinted by permission.

clude yet another costly federal benefit, complete with the bureaucracy needed to administer it. The bills would create basic and sweeping changes in our concepts of evidence and liability. And they represent a threat to the competitiveness if not the solvency of many corporations.

The potential cost of compensating victims of toxic wastes can be seen in the special case of asbestos. Asbestos workers have brought thousands of suits against their employers of decades ago. These suits involve occupational rather than hazardous waste claims and in other ways are quite different from the problems that Congress is considering. But in terms of costs and numbers, the portents are clear.

Asbestos manufacturers have already spent $1 billion on claims, and at that only about $4,000 out of 25,000 claims filed have been closed. Hundreds of new suits are filed every month. Dr. William J. Nicholson of the Mount Sinai School of Medicine in New York City believes that 165,000 people will die from past exposure to asbestos between now and the end of the century. Manville Corp. and two other companies among the 300-plus defendants have sought protection from the blizzard of claims under Chapter 11 of the bankruptcy law. Several manufacturers are suing their insurers over disputes about their coverage.

The toxic waste claims typically concern companies in the chemical and oil industries, some of which are beginning to find themselves in the same fix as the asbestos companies. The cases are piling up. One big case involves Agent Orange: after trying to get disability benefits from the Veterans Administration and being rebuffed, Vietnam veterans have now turned on the manufacturers and sought payment for the illnesses allegedly brought upon them and their children by the defoliant. A class action by 17,000 veterans against five chemical companies is expected to come to trial in federal district court on New York's Long Island next year. Another center of toxic waste litigation is the area around the notorious Love Canal dump in Niagara Falls, New York, where past and present residents have filed over 1,400 individual suits, for a total of at least $1 billion against Occidental Petroleum, which inherited the problem when it acquired Hooker Chemical, and other defendants. In idyllic Silicon Valley, 270 residents are suing Fairchild Camera & Instrument Corp. for leaking a solvent that they say got into their water supply and caused miscarriages and heart defects among their children. In Fort Edward, New York, 35 residents are suing General Electric for over $100 million, claiming that the company allowed a solvent called TCE to get into their drinking water. These cases are likely only a beginning.

Hardly anyone is happy with the way the cases are handled. The plaintiffs find it hard to win in a legal system designed to deal with the obvious damage caused by something like a bullet or a car, but not with the hidden processes of chemistry. Developing the scientific evidence to back the plaintiffs' claim is extremely expensive and usually inconclusive, particularly when current illnesses may have been caused by exposure decades ago. The defending companies are unhappy because they often face incalculable penalties for damage in connection with actions they may have taken years ago that were then legal and not known to be harmful.

These dissatisfactions have created an irresistible political pressure to do something, and quickly. Congress has before it a score of bills, some designed to help the victims of hazardous waste in general, others targeted on such specific problems as Agent Orange. Recognizing what it belatedly sees as one of the most sensitive issues of the 1980s, the Administration set up a Cabinet-level work group three months ago to pull together the fragments of policy developed by various federal agencies—and to figure out how to hold down the government's liabilities. California, Minnesota, New Jersey, and Washington have enacted compensation laws, and other states have them in the works.

The evidence thus far suggests that politicians are going to find it hard to vote against compensating victims. It also suggests that politicians will have difficulty making some critical distinctions. When should victims be compensated? Certainly not, we would all agree, when they fall victim to risks that are a normal part of living. By driving cars, smoking cigarettes, and drinking alcohol, most Americans tacitly accept some risks (far greater than those posed by toxic chemicals) in return for certain pleasures and conveniences. Presumably the public will accept some heightened level of general exposure to toxic risks in return for the benefits of the chemicals that produce them. On the other hand, we could presumably agree that the victims should be able to collect when an illness is demonstrably related to a company's negligent handling of dangerous chemicals.

But between these two clear-cut scenarios is a huge gray area in which there is quite a lot to argue about. The legislators and lawyers writing the new laws seem inclined to push the definition of compansable damage to a point at which it pretty much fills up the gray area.

In doing so, they seem to be operating on the unproved assumption that toxic wastes have claimed some enormous number of victims. But it is clear that some who believe themselves victims are wildly wrong. Consider, for example, the phantom toxic leak that affected Memphis in the late 1970s. There were all the usual details—reports of unexplained diseases, picketing, emotional meetings, even a congressional hearing. The only thing lacking was a dump or other source of poisonous chemicals. It was never found and a study by the federal Centers for Disease Control determined eventually that there was no unusual incidence of illness. Since it deals with the unknown and the mysterious, chemical terror spreads fast—and the press does its part to pass on each unexamined piece of evidence.

How many have been affected is unclear. The effects of some poisonous substances, such as dioxin and PCBs, seem to have been exaggerated. On the other hand, still unrecognized dangers might lurk. The reality lies somewhere between the claim of Senator Robert T. Stafford, the Vermont Republican who has offered one of the compensation bills, that there are "millions upon millions" of potential victims and the Chemical Manufacturers Association's soothing words that there is no "evidence of a significant health problem from hazardous wastes."

Science and medicine are far from knowing how to link toxic waste and disease. In the case of asbestos the connection is clear— the plaintiffs were heavily exposed to asbestos, mostly as construction and shipyard workers, and asbestos is the only cause of asbestosis and a fatal cancer of the lung lining called mesothelioma. If the workers are suffering from either disease, there's very little doubt how they got it.

But most cases hold no such clear connection. The chronic effects of many chemicals are still being studied. The effects vary with dosage, length of exposure, the individual, and even the combined effects of several chemicals. Often the dosage was low, making the link harder to establish. When a longtime three-pack-a-day smoker gets lung cancer, it seems reasonable to link it to smoking. But what if a three-cigarette-a-day smoker gets lung cancer? Were the cigarettes the cause, or did they combine with other factors, or did they have nothing to do with the cancer? Medicine just doesn't know. Most exposures to toxic chemicals are at the three-cigarette rather than three-pack level.

The case of Agent Orange shows how difficult it is to know or prove what happened. This chemical, used as a defoliant in Vietnam, contained traces of dioxin, which is highly toxic. It causes cancer and other chronic diseases in animals, but so far as humans are concerned, an acute skin disease called chloracne is the only illness that all the experts acknowledge to be caused by dioxin. Many Vietnam veterans claim that their cancers, liver ailments, nervous disorders, deformed children, and other woes were caused by Agent Orange. They may be right, but the proof is not yet there. In fact, it is not even clear that they suffer from these afflictions more than other Americans.

The limited studies conducted by the government so far tend to support its contention that Agent Orange is not responsible. The Air Force announced in July part of the results of a study of 1,269 airmen who were massively exposed to Agent Orange when they handled it during the war. The rate and causes of death among these veterans are normal. Results of the more important part of the study, dealing with illness rather than death, will be announced this fall. The government is planning to spend $140 million on Agent Orange research, half of it on a massive study by the Centers for Disease Control, which had no trouble getting the Office of Management and Budget to approve the full amount of its request. But the study won't be completed until 1987 and even then may not contain the kind of clear answers lawyers need in court. Many of the veterans' ailments are vague—things like fatigue, headaches, and loss of memory, which could have many causes.

Whatever the study may show, by the time it is out, Congress and the courts will long since have acted. Science can be patient, but the victims and the politicians clearly won't wait. When a lame-duck session of Congress hurried through the Superfund law in 1980 to provide for the cleanup of hazardous dumps, a section providing for compensation to victims was dropped at the last minute. The final act provided, however, for a study of victims' compensation. The 12 lawyers appointed to the so-called 301(e) study group—named after the section of the Superfund act that created it—finished their work last year and issued a two-volume report. In rough outline, all the bills before Congress are similar to this report.

The report recommends a two-tier system for helping victims. To get the bulk of claims cleaned up efficiently without swamping the courts, it suggests a federal Tier I to cover medical costs and lost income, but not pain and suffering, through a no-fault administrative system similar to workers' compensation. If plaintiffs wanted to make claims for pain and suffering, they would have to go through the full legal process in state court under Tier II; however, the rules would be altered to strengthen the plaintiffs' side.

A major unanswered question about the Tier I federal fund is how it would be financed. Should the present $1.6-billion Superfund simply be expanded without changing the way it collects money? That would impose the whole burden of the system on a few companies, since 88% of the Superfund's money comes from oil and chemical companies, which pay on the basis of the feedstocks they use. And even these contributions to the fund do not exhaust the companies' liability for cleanups—a fact dramatically evidenced by the U.S. Army's recent $1.8-billion claim against Shell Oil Co. (The claim was related to the costs of cleaning up some leased Army property on which Shell had been manufacturing pesticides.)

Simply expanding the present Superfund tax base would surely be unfair. Just five companies, Arco, Dow, Exxon, Shell, and Union Carbide, contribute more than half the total. One way or another, the oil and chemical industries will almost inevitably pay for most of the fund. Still, the burden could be spread more fairly than it would be under an expanded Superfund.

The amounts a victim could recover from the Tier I fund would generally be limited to medical expenses and two-thirds of lost income, up to $2,000 a month. However, in a presentation made to President Reagan and his Cabinet council in May and then leaked to the press, OMB cited as a warning the case of black-lung compensation, established in 1970 to help coal miners. It was at first billed as a limited plan that might cost $20 million to $40 million a year. But over the years, miners and their dependents came to be treated more and more liberally; today the program costs $2 billion a year.

Not only might the Tier I fund swell into a monster, but the victims receiving payments from it might also be free to pursue unlimited compensation in the courts under Tier II. The OMB paper said these recommendations add up to "the worst of both worlds; an administrative compensation system with liberal evidentiary standards and generous benefits, as well as continued availability of traditional tort law."

The liberalized court standards being proposed are at least as significant as the potential costs. Since the states have a hodge-podge of common law, mostly making it difficult for victims to claim recompense, all the major bills before Congress would create a "federal cause of action." In other words, plaintiffs could sue under federal, not state, law. And under the federal law the rules of the game would be made easier for the plaintiffs.

To pursue a toxic case in state courts is difficult under present rules. "Proof of the causal connection between exposure and injury is an almost overwhelming barrier to recovery," said the 301 report. Negligence is hard to document if a spill took place 20 years ago and witnesses have died and documents been discarded.

Getting proof is expensive. Anthony Z. Roisman, a Washington attorney who has fought many environmental battles, says it costs $100,000 to $200,000 just to gather the necessary scientific and medical evidence. Expert witnesses may charge $1,000 or more a day for their testimony. Most plaintiffs and lawyers just can't spend that kind of money in advance. Roisman gets foundation support for his work, and so he is able to carry the expense of developing cases, but most lawyers can't. In a major toxic case that he is handling in Woburn, Massachusetts, Roisman has been able to make use of some extensive research collected by the Environmental Protection Agency, which is studying pollution in the local area.

Another difficulty about proving causal connection is that it may not exist. Science often can't give clear answers. Consider Woburn, where eight families have each had a case of leukemia in the last decade. The families are suing two companies: W.R. Grace, which has operated a small manufacturing plant producing food-wrapping equipment in Woburn since 1960, and Beatrice Foods, which at one time owned John J. Riley, a local tannery. The suit says, for example, that the solvent TCE was dumped by Grace in its backyard, found its way into the water supply, and contributed to causing the leukemia. Anne Anderson, whose son Jimmy died of leukemia in 1981 after a long illness, is convinced she knows what killed her son. "I've always had a feeling it was the water," she says. "We were told it was OK, but it was always very, very bad." Grace admits to having used small amounts of TCE and to burying several drums of unidentified waste in its backyard, 2,500 feet from the contaminated wells. Their contents are being examined now. But the whole area is a mess of pollution and has been since the 19th century. Woburn used to call itself the tannery capital of the world. The wells lie near the Aberjona River, which drains a whole industrial area. An industrial sewer that has overflowed at times runs nearby. Many other plants are in the area, as well as cemeteries for old cars and for discarded drums and tanks. Woburn offers "an incredibly complex scientific case," according to an EPA official on the scene. To win his case, Roisman will have to prove that TCE got into the wells, that TCE contributes to causing leukemia (not an accepted scientific fact), and that there was enough TCE to do the damage.*

The proposals before Congress would make this kind of case easier to prove. Since scientists are never likely to agre that TCE caused the leukemia, the supporters of victims' compensation are pushing for a form of evidence known as "rebuttable presumptions." These have been used in the black-lung law. For

*In February 1984, a Harvard study concluded that there was definitely a connection between the Woburn wells and the health problems of people who drank from them. [Ed.]

instance, if a man had worked in the mines for ten years and later died of a respiratory disease, he was presumed without any need for further proof to have died of black-lung disease, and it was up to the mining company to prove that he died of something else. Congress eliminated this particular presumption in 1981, but other presumptions remain.

If presumptions are included in the toxic victims legislation, the lawyers plan to develop statistical evidence. For example, if a given city normally had 100 deaths a year from liver cancer and that rate went up to 110 some time after dioxin was dumped locally, lawyers could try to use the increase to create a presumption of liability. But this approach would raise a lot of intriguing questions. Would the dioxin be blamed for all 110 cases, or only ten cases, and if so which ten? Leslie Cheek III, a vice president of the Crum & Foster Insurance Companies, said in testimony before a congressional committee that any such use of presumptions "would so weaken the evidentiary and burden-of-proof requirements of the common law as to cast upon defendants and their insurers the impossible tasks of identifying which of the millions of Americans with long-latency diseases and other health problems did *not* contract them through exposure to hazardous substances."

Along with easier rules of evidence, the lawyers and legislators are pushing for tougher and broader rules of liability. Normally a plaintiff has to prove negligence to collect damages. But common law has applied "strict" liability—that is, liability without regard to negligence—to extremely hazardous activities such as blasting. In the 1970s the courts began to apply strict liability to suits over defective products. If strict liability were now extended to toxic wastes, then it would do a company no good to plead that it had obeyed the laws and followed approved procedures when it disposed of its wastes. It would still be liable, even if the hazards are seen only in retrospect.

On top of strict liability, the new legislation might create what is known in legal language as "joint and several responsibility." It means that a single defendant can be made to pay all the damages even in situations where many defendants may be guilty. Like strict liability, joint and several responsibility opens up some fearsome risks to business. Will the company that contributed 10%

or 20% of the waste in a dump be held responsible for all the damage caused by its toxic releases?

Lawyers can be expected to refine these statutory changes by looking for ways of creating new common law to reinforce their cases. For example, in the Woburn case, Roisman plans to ask for damages not just for those afflicted, but for the other family members, too, the argument being that drinking the polluted water has made them more susceptible to disease in the future.

Clearly these proposed changes add up to a huge potential burden on society. "The plain goal of these proposals is to provide *all* hazardous-substance victims with the best of both nonfault and fault-based remedies: eased evidentiary burdens coupled with generous awards," says Crum & Foster's Cheek. "As laudable as this objective may be in theory, it cannot realistically be achieved if the system's costs are to be controllable, predictable, and, ultimately, insurable." Joint and several responsibility could double or triple insurance rates; it might even create risks that insurance companies would refuse to cover. Says Michael J. Horowitz, general counsel of the OMB and co-chairman of the Cabinet work group: "I know of no greater fiscal threat for the Nineties than the whole question of toxic torts and victims' compensation."

Furthermore, the reforms might discourage what should be their ultimate objective: motivating companies to undertake a real cleanup so that there wouldn't be any victims. Fear of a hefty judgment might make a company take better care of its wastes, but if strict liability removes the need to prove negligence, then the negligent company will suffer no more in court than the company that did its best to clean up. With joint and several responsibility, plaintiffs will tend to go after the company that has the deepest pockets, rather than the dirtiest company.

Taken together, the proposals suggest the possibility of one company being held retroactively responsible for an offense committed by another company at a time when the offense was neither illegal nor known to be harmful. George C. Freeman Jr., a Virginia lawyer who served on the 301 study group, believes that a new law including joint and several responsibility and strict liability might conflict with constitutional due process requirements, especially if applied retroactively.

The choice facing Congress is between an existing system that satisfies no one and a set of proposals that could prove enormously costly. Of course, doing nothing could also be costly. The present system for compensating victims is appallingly inefficient and wasteful. A recent Rand Corp. study showed that of the $1 billion spent on asbestos cases by the end of 1982, only $236 million had reached the hands of the plaintiffs. The rest was absorbed by legal fees and costs. In economists' terms, the "transaction costs" paid by society were steep.

All four of the major bills before Congress follow the basic two-tier formulation of the 301 commission report, but differ substantially in detail. They have been proposed by Senator Stafford, Representative John J. LaFalce (whose district includes Love Canal), Senator George J. Mitchell of Maine, and jointly by Representatives Edward J. Markey (who represents Woburn) and James J. Florio of New Jersey. All four would create strict liability, and three would establish joint and several responsibility. The LaFalce bill provides for a modified form of joint and several responsibility. The Mitchell and Stafford bills would pay for victims' compensation simply by extending the Superfund, with its present tax system; however, the Markey-Florio bill would spread the burden a little more fairly. It would add a tax of 79 cents a barrel to domestic and imported oil, paid by the refiner or importer, and another tax of $2.13 per dry-weight ton of hazardous waste received at the dump, this tax to be paid by the dump operator. None of these bills is likely to come to the floor before next year, although this fall Markey may try to get part of what he wants for the plaintiffs by tacking onto another bill an amendment creating the federal cause of action.

Whatever legislation is finally adopted, the outcome will inevitably be uncomfortable. However, the costs could be contained by a number of limitations, which some of the bills already have. Perhaps the most important is in the Markey-Florio bill, which, surprisingly, would prevent the plaintiffs among Markey's own constituents now in state court in Woburn from collecting damages in federal court: it does not allow retroactive claims. The bill specifies that to be actionable in federal court, the exposure to a chemical must take place after the date of enactment. The Stafford and Mitchell bills would allow the use of rebuttable presumptions in Tier I and Tier II cases, while the other bills would limit their use to Tier I cases. The Markey-Florio bill would soften joint and several responsibility by making generators and transporters of toxic waste responsible for the waste only during the period when it is in their hands. Other limitations of liability desired by industry include a requirement that plaintiffs choose between Tier I and Tier II, and not pursue both types of actions, and the use of Social Security, workers' compensation, and health insurance payments as an offset to awards.

Congressman Thomas A. Daschle, a South Dakota Democrat, has some other approaches that would contain costs related to Agent Orange. His bill, the most likely to succeed among a dozen that have been offered to help Vietnam veterans, would pay compensation for only three ailments: a rare type of cancer, a rare liver disease, and chloracne. Together, they make up less than 1% of the claims based on the use of Agent Orange, but they are the diseases most closely connected to dioxin. The Daschle bill would expire automatically when the Centers for Disease Control finish a major study of the effects of Agent Orange. The idea is that when we know more, we can take a fresh look at what we are doing. These are only some of the means of containing the costs and the claims and at the same time helping people with the most serious problems.

Given the large lingering uncertainties about the damage done by toxic chemicals in the past, Congress shouldn't rush to comprehensive legislation. A minimal and temporary no-fault compensation system seems reasonable, however, provided that the standards for accepting claims are fairly tough and the compensation covers only medical costs, lost pay, and property damage. People who feel entitled to collect more should be free to take their chances in court, but it would be a mistake for Congress to fundamentally transform U.S. tort law in an effort to make things easier for plaintiffs and tougher for defendants in toxic waste cases.

Congress is talking about holding business to a stricter standard of responsibility, but the bills now in the pipeline seem unfair in critical respects. Some might even be unconstitutional. They will almost certainly represent bad news for the oil and chemical industries. And in some form or other, at least one of these bills will almost certainly pass within the next year or so.

INDUSTRY AND THE ENVIRONMENT: A COMMUNICATION GAP[3]

Throughout the decade of environmentalism, symbolically commencing with Earth Day in April 1970, industry was viewed as a reluctant partner in the nationwide commitment to curtailing pollution. However, the Bureau of the Census conservatively estimates that, in the period from 1973 to 1980, industry spent more than $100 billion for pollution control equipment and operation costs. This does not take into account an estimated $6 billion the Census Bureau calculates was spent on research and development related to pollution abatement. Yet, in spite of this substantial investment in maintaining and improving environmental quality, industry continues to be viewed as doing only the minimum required by law.

As the current Administration has pursued sometimes controversial approaches to environmental regulation, business is seen as tacitly approving actions relaxing existing standards, delaying deadlines for compliance, and weakening or eliminating those organizations charged with enforcing a complex array of environmental statutes. It remains to be seen whether new leadership in the nation's major environmental agencies may help change this impression.

In fact, the general image of business insensitivity to environmental concerns is largely inconsistent with its record. It reasonably can be argued that industry did not anticipate the emergence of environmentalism as a major domestic policy issue. Yet, it is also true that over the last 10 years, industry has taken an increasingly active role in pollution control, both by investing in pollution

[3]Excerpted from an article by Gerald Prout, director of public affairs for FMC Corporation's Industrial Chemical Group. *Public Relations Journal.* Winter 1983. Copyright© 1983 by the Foundation for Public Relations Research and Education. Reprinted by permission.

abatement technology and by becoming more directly involved in the policy-making process. Industry generally has increased its say over the future direction of environmental management, and in most cases, has done so responsibly.

Nonetheless, industry's continuing failure to publicly communicate this involvement in maintaining and improving environmental quality has left public opinion malleable to the rhetoric of others. Environmental activists are consistently able to stir the public conscience and define the policy agenda in this important area. Though industry may not be a reluctant partner, it is largely silent about its role.

From the pronouncement in the late '60s that Lake Erie was dead to Love Canal—the cause célébre of the '80s—for over a decade, environmental activists have effectively communicated in a now familiar pattern. Sources of pollution—usually industrial—are identified and public attention drawn to their effects; the effects become the subject of intense sloganeering and hyperbole; a local (but often national) constituency is aroused to take action; the episode becomes pretext for new or more stringent legislation; and the legislation is translated into an often intricate set of regulations with which industry must comply.

Leadership of public opinion on environmental matters has thus tended to gravitate to environmental activists; spokesmen such as Russell Peterson or Barry Commoner, or politicians such as Cecil Andrus or Gaylord Nelson, have been able to arouse public concern over the "imminent" dangers of neglecting our natural endowment. While industry spokesmen have consistently acknowledged that an appropriate regard for the environment is part of a broader concept of corporate social responsibility, the communications initiative has belonged to others. Environmentalism continues to be a public relations problem for industry. . . .

The prevailing view of a Great Society at the turn of the last decade did not include polluting industries. Environmentalism became an integral component of a broader philosophical attack on the legitimacy of corporate power and the very economic system in which the invisible hand had purportedly failed. As William Schambra wrote recently, these critics of the system "promised prosperity, while harboring suppressed hostilities toward the traditional sources of progress." But environmentalism was and is a movement with broad appeal across the entire spectrum of political thought. It is a phenomenon which attracts those who hold to an ever-expanding definition of American abundance and those who shrink from such a vision and openly worry about the exhaustibility of our resource base. . . .

Rhetoric vs. Performance

Even in the first generation of environmentalism, there were those who understood the scope and nature of environmental cleanup. As Peter Drucker warned in a *Harper's* article almost 10 years ago:

The sewage treatment plants that are urgently needed all over the world will be designed, built and kept running not by purity of heart ballads or Earth Days, but by crew-cut engineers working in very large organizations, whether businesses, research labs or governmental agencies.

Indeed, over the last decade, more than $30 billion in federal monies was committed to the construction and upgrading of sewage treatment plants nationwide, one of the largest public works projects in U.S. history. Yet the resultant improvements in water quality are so gradual they typically escape national attention. In some cases the quiet success stories of this program are remarkable, given that it has only been in effect in a significant way for 10 years. The resuscitation of Lake Erie, for example, is now largely attributed to the federal municipal sewage construction grants program.

From the beginning, the control of pollution in its various forms has entailed this type of technological solution. The details of addressing the environmental agenda have been left to those truly able to grasp the complexity of the task. In fact, an entire industry has evolved over the last decade to address the needs of industry and government in meeting the requirements of various environmental statutes. While the pollution control equipment industry's health is peculiarly tied to politics, it remains an industry with substantial growth opportunities as it confronts the task of safely disposing of vast quantities of solid waste.

In its approach to environmental management in the "real world," industry is increasingly finding that many forms of pollution represent the uneconomic use of valuable resources. The application of pollution reduction and recovery techniques in some cases can turn what would otherwise be expenses into profits. Many industrial wastes are thus now being reprocessed for use as energy or recycled as raw materials for use again in the industrial process itself. As early as 1975, 3M Company began a program it called "Pollution Prevention Pays," stressing four essential concepts: product reformulation, process modification, equipment redesign and the recovery of waste materials for reuse. In three years, total savings to 3M's domestic facilities were $17.4 million. 3M eliminated the equivalent of 75,000 tons of air pollutants, 500 million gallons of polluted wastewater and 2900 tons of sludge per year. Other companies have also found similar economic incentive to control pollution. . . .

Most businesses seems reluctant to draw attention to their efforts to improve the nation's environment. While other capital expenditures or facility expansions are usually announced with some fanfare, expenditures for a new pretreatment system, scrubber or baghouse are seldom announced unless through the most routine of statements. More importantly, the cumulative accomplishments of individual manufacturing facilities in reducing pollutants are seldom placed in perspective for employees, shareholders or the community. Nor typically have industry's major trade associations effectively assembled the record for their industry group and put it before the public.

Industry's Reluctance to Communicate

Business's failure to draw attention to its record of accomplishment can be explained by several conditions:
• The very installation of pollution control equipment or modifications in an industrial process to reduce pollution implies that a problem may have previously existed and thus gone unaddressed;
• The installation of equipment is often piecemeal and the results sometimes uncertain and undramatic;
• The installation of the equipment is often the final step in a pro-

cess of negotiation with government authorities in which the very
scope and/or design of the project has itself been at issue;
• Planned or actual reductions in various pollutants cannot be
easily correlated to actual environmental improvements.

As Robert Crandall of the Brookings Institution noted recently, "It seems ludicrous to me that we regulate air and water pollution extensively without being able to tell whether the regulation
is working." Nonetheless, after years of concerted effort, it is difficult to measure actual results.

In addition, while the process and expense of compliance pro-
ceeds at a technical level for industry and government technocrats,
leading environmental activists seek to move the environmental
agenda relentlessly forward at a *political* level. Thus, while American industry proceeded to meet the requirements of much of the
environmental regulation of the '70s, a new environmental issue—
the disposal of hazardous wastes—has percolated, becoming the
environmental priority of the '80s. It is difficult for industry to
proclaim substantial accomplishment in one area when its defi-
ciencies in another area are the subject of emotional community
and national debate. Nonetheless, it must. If industry fails to effectively communicate what it has done and is doing for environmental quality, it may begin to relinquish its hard-won role in shaping
future environmental policy at a time when the environmental
movement is itself seeking to reshape its own identity. . . .

The extent of industry's dollars and cents commitment to the
environment was indicated previously. This record of performance—of actually having to find what works best in practical,
real-world applications to curtail pollution—provides industry
with growing credibility to assert itself more broadly in the area
of environmental policy-making.

As examples of such involvement, two broad concepts, largely
conceived and supported by industry, are now having some initial
impact on the environmental policy process. While these ideas,
largely being put forward by industry representatives, are complex and have many specific applications, a brief summary of each
provides insight into how business has assumed a new role in environmental policy making.

The Application of Good Science to Environmental Policy

As Victor Hugo observed, "Science says the first word on everything and the last word on nothing." By definition, uncertainty surrounds virtually every political decision in the environmental area, decisions which must be made on often conflicting and indefinite scientific information.

In the current debate over acid rain, for example, general agreement exists in the scientific community that much of the Northeastern United States and Southeastern Canada are receiving much more acid rain than would be expected to come from a "pure" atmosphere. But experts cannot agree as to whether the acidity of the precipitation is increasing, or the extent to which local versus longer-range sources of pollution are responsible for such precipitation. Decisions must, by definition, always be made with some significant degree of uncertainty; the issue, however, is how to reduce the uncertainty level and the emotion surrounding the debate, by application of the best science available. The recent popularity of cost-benefit analysis has only served to heighten the problems generally associated with scientific uncertainty and increase the costs of bad science.

Science has also become increasingly political. In her recent study of the Love Canal situation, Adeline Gordon Levine suggests that the announcements of various "scientific" findings by government and private sector experts were timed to coincide with political factors, and the procedures used in the studies themselves adjusted to meet various political exigencies. The Carter EPA's own 1980 study of chromosomal damage to Love Canal residents, looked to by many as the final word in an already emotional debate, was so obviously flawed that any remaining shred of credibility to which local residents might have gravitated in their hour of desperation was lost.

Long before the Love Canal incident and increasingly since, conscious effort has been made by industry to upgrade the quality of science which serves as a basis for political decision-making, and to create greater consensus within the scientific community on key issues in order to expedite the decision-making process. Since consensus on basic scientific questions, particularly those elevated to a level of public policy concern is difficult and time consuming to achieve, a consortium of six companies (Dow, duPont, Exxon, Mobil, Monsanto, and Rohm and Haas), are currently funding a study on the practicality of "state-of-science conferences"—a mechanism designed to air conflicting views on basic scientific questions in hope of achieving a consensus which will have broader public (and therefore political) acceptability. . . .

Applying Marketplace Incentives to Environmental Regulation

. . . Several notable spokesmen have urged the charging of pollution taxes as a means of controlling excessive degradation of our common resources. Such effluent or emission charges may indeed represent a more efficient means of controlling pollution and would certainly have reduced the costs. . . . However, initial skepticism over the extent to which industry might prefer to pay the fines rather than curtail pollution led to the alternative command-control regulatory structure under which we presently operate. Under the current regulatory scheme, some opportunity does exist for the economics of regulation to at least be considered. Under the Clean Air Act, for instance, a company may locate in areas that are considered "non-attainment" if the company installs the best available technology and pollution from new sources is offset by reduced pollution from other sources in the area. Similarly, under the Clean Water Act, variances for industry can be permitted if a lower level of control represents "the maximum use of technology, within the economic capability of the owner or operator."

Yet such examples of economic considerations being factored into the existing regulatory scheme are rare. By and large the system remains largely inflexible to economic considerations. Moreover, the costs of complying with regulation continues to grow. The Council on Environmental Quality estimates that between 1979 and 1988, $735 billion will be spent for all pollution control capital and operating costs. In recognition of the growing expense of this and other forms of regulation (which constitute a major component of the "Great Inflation" of the last decade), the Reagan

Administration sought to give higher priority to analysis of the costs of any proposed regulation, and to weigh the benefits against the effects of regulation on productivity, a healthy economy and adequate energy supplies. Industry, for the most part, supports such cost-benefit analysis. . . .

Yet, as survey data suggests, there exists a threshold of public tolerance for deregulation, even in the name of economic growth.

. . . As noted previously, the public, while sensitive to the exorbitant costs of regulation, is not insensitive to the goals set forth. Discarding regulation on the basis that it is too expensive is but the first step in a process of reregulation: designing a regulatory structure which acknowledges the need for providing greater flexibility and economic incentive for compliance with practical, achievable environmental goals, which the public still seems to support. As Robert Crandall suggests:

Study after study documents the inefficiency of the current regulatory approach and its lack of enforceability. By simplifying the traditional air and water pollution programs through use of market incentives, while improving monitoring and enforcement techniques, the agency could contribute substantially to both regulatory reform and regulatory relief. . . .

Both the application of good science as well as the introduction of new economic incentives to the process of environmental policy-making, suggest that industry is, by and large, seeking to play a constructive role beyond merely complying with existing targets. The results of such efforts are as yet unclear, but industry participation in the process should only help to strengthen its credibility and the soundness of environmental regulation. But industry's role in developing and promoting such innovative new approaches to environmental management stands to go largely unnoticed by the public unless industry can undertake to communicate its own role more effectively. . . .

CONTROLLING HEALTH HAZARDS WITHOUT
UNCLE SAM[4]

Over the last decade, four administrations have sought to make the regulatory process less dependent on federal intervention. The current administration is making an especially concerted attempt to deregulate health, safety, and environmental hazards. By executive order, President Reagan has not only required federal agencies to conduct cost-benefit analyses of major new regulations before issuing them; he has also drastically reduced agency budgets, cut back on enforcement, and appointed officials committed to these goals. While many of these appointees have been replaced in recent months, the Reagan administration still appears unlikely to pursue aggressive new regulatory initiatives.

This does not mean that we, as a nation, have forfeited our right to control the panoply of environmental, health, and safety risks we face every day. Since federal regulation cannot do the whole job and will certainly not be used to its fullest extent in the near future, private alternatives must be found.

In cases of well-understood risks and technologies, the most obvious substitute for federal regulation is for industry to regulate itself. Toward that end, private firms invest considerable resources in developing health and safety standards for their own activities, often relying on industrywide or professional standards.

Industry currently follows as many as 60,000 such nongovernmental standards. These "consensus" standards cover products and services in the construction, electrical, metal, chemical, textile, and nuclear industries. To the extent that these standards define acceptable product quality and design in a particular industry, they keep nonconforming products and practices off the market. For example, compliance with standards developed by Underwriters Laboratories, Inc., is a minimum condition of marketability for many electrical products.

[4]Reprint of an article by J. Raymond Miyares, lawyer specializing in environmental, health and safety matters. *Technology Review.* 86:14–16. Jl. '83. Reprinted by permission.

But many health and environmental risks are not as easy to define. Acid rain, pesticide misuse, the toxic by-products of industrial manufacturing, and defective products—all are sources of risk that arouse debate over how they should be controlled. In such cases, the development of voluntary consensus standards is difficult. And even if standards were developed, a lack of consensus would probably undermine their widespread use.

The Legal Remedies

Lawsuits are another alternative to federal regulation. In the past, the threat of legal liability stimulated many firms to adopt voluntary standards of conduct. Before various regulatory programs were created in the 1960s and 1970s, injuries from a perceived health hazard were almost exclusively remedied through law suits. Damage suits against product manufacturers proliferated. Today, hardly a week goes by without news of a large out-of-court settlement, or judgment, won by an injured plaintiff. For example, a California court recently awarded $6 million to the victims of a fire caused by the explosion of a gas tank in a Ford Pinto during a rear-end collision.

Such awards have certainly improved product safety—not only the products of the company held liable but also those of other manufacturers in the same industry. Heat sensitive shutoff switches in hair dryers and collapsible steering columns in automobiles are examples of design improvements implemented because of judgments against manufacturers. These settlements put those engaged in similar enterprises on notice as to what level of safety will be demanded of them in the future. Furthermore, some unsafe products such as flammable children's pajamas have been driven from the market—or "voluntarily" withdrawn—because of the fear of liability.

More and more victims of exposure to toxic industrial chemicals are also seeking redress through the courts. In a federal district court in New Jersey recently, B.F. Goodrich was held liable for the death of a nearby resident whose cancer was determined to have been caused by exposure to the company's vinyl-chloride emissions. In Oregon, a federal district court ordered Martin

Marietta Co. to pay damages to nearby residents because the emissions from the company's aluminum smelting plant were damaging fruit crops.

But proving that injuries are environmentally caused can be quite difficult. Evidence of the levels and duration of exposure may be hard to produce, and other causes may have contributed to the alleged health effects. Epidemiological data—statistical assessments of the incidence of disease in certain populations—are often too imprecise to shed much light on the specific case being tried. Furthermore, the long latency period of many diseases has sometimes proven to be a barrier to judicial relief. That's because some states have statues of limitations, requiring that damage suits be filed within a set number of years after initial exposure to a toxic substance.

Clearly, some reform is needed if litigation is to effectively redress injuries incurred from exposure to hazardous substances. Environmental groups and others are stepping up their efforts to promote legislation that would make it easier for victims of exposure to hazardous waste to be compensated.

Insurance, a third alternative to federal regulation, is perhaps the oldest way of addressing risk. Insurance against marine perils existed as early as the twelfth century. Fire insurance first appeared in the seventeenth century, and product-liability insurance was introduced in the late nineteenth century.

In setting rates, insurance underwriters take into account the product or activity being insured, the ways in which it poses risks, the magnitude of potential injuries, and the laws governing such risks. Thus, insurers can identify at least the most unsafe clients and charge higher rates for risk-producing behavior. For example, auto insurance premiums usually reflect individual driver safety records. So drivers must maintain a safe driving record to prevent their rates from going up. Worker compensation insurance, in contrast, is more often based on general loss expectancies for a particular industry. Flood insurance rates, meanwhile, are based on federal flood estimates.

Of course, the value of insurance in encouraging safer management of risks depends on the insurers' ability to assess those risks. For some insurance lines such as environmental-impairment insurance, past experience is limited, and making detailed assessments of loss may be difficult and costly. Thus, insurance companies set uniformly high rates to protect themselves, and variations in safety practices have little effect on rates. In the 1960s and 70s, for instance, product-liability coverage was prohibitively expensive because insurers didn't know what the extent of the risk would be and priced their insurance coverage on the high side to protect themselves. Many companies could not afford such insurance and were ill-equipped to compensate the victims of defective products. However, this problem was remedied as insurers collected the information necessary to permit them to better evaluate risks. Today, product liability coverage is underwritten on a more precise and affordable basis.

A fourth alternative to regulation, providing information to consumers, can be quite effective. The National Highway Traffic and Safety Administration's *Car Book,* which rated new models on safety and performance features, was so powerful in swaying public opinion that it was withdrawn from publication after intense lobbying by automobile manufacturers. The book was later published with private funds. When consumers became aware of the possible effects of fluorocarbons from aerosol sprays on the earth's ozone layer and boycotted certain products, the industry decided to use other propellants or replace spray nozzles with pumps. And a product safety rating of "unacceptable" from *Consumer Reports* magazine may induce a manufacturer to alter that product quickly.

However, the Reagan administration seems very reluctant to distribute information on environmental, health, and safety risks to consumers. The administration recently rejected a proposal from consumer groups to require ingredients to be labeled on wines and beers, many of which contain chemical additives. Mandatory labeling showing the energy consumption of major appliances is being discontinued, even though there is evidence that such labels substantially alter consumer choices. For example, while consumers prefer heavily insulated water heaters that cost more but save on energy, buyers may well choose models that are cheaper in the short run if such information is no longer readily available.

An administration committed to letting free-market mechanisms operate might do well to rethink its position and make such information available. If product information were widely available, consumers would probably make choices that would encourage industry to make safer and more environmentally benign products.

Contract negotiation is a fifth alternative to regulation. Labor unions have often bargained for better and safer working conditions, sometimes trading higher wages and more fringe benefits for such improvements. The United Steel Workers and ASARCO, a multinational company that processes ore, recently negotiated an agreement to protect workers against exposure to arsenic. The International Labor Organization has also relied on collective bargaining to improve protection of chemical industry workers.

Bargaining for Better Health

Negotiations are also being used to settle public environmental controversies. For example, the Massachusetts law governing siting of hazardous-waste treatment facilities provides funding to communities to negotiate with developers and hire consultants. The law requires developers to obtain community approval for the waste facility's design, construction, operation, and maintenance and to compensate local residents for any adverse effects. The idea is to facilitate a trade-off between the environmental risks of such a facility and the economic and social benefits its developers can provide to the community.

Such negotiations can, of course, be unwieldy and slow. In Massachusetts, developers have been unable to win community approval for any waste facilities. But if all parties could agree on the safety measures to be adopted, the need for federal regulation would be lessened.

Each of these alternatives is most effective in certain contexts, and none is a complete means of regulating hazards. Indeed, all remain subject to the same criticism that led to heavier reliance on federal regulation in the first place. Industry is sometimes indifferent to safety or health concerns that conflict with its financial interests. The threat of liability for injuries created by industrial activity can be too remote to have a geniune impact. Insurers may not take into account the huge variations in safety practices when setting rates. Corporations may manipulate consumer preferences for clean air, pure food, and safe products. And multiparty contract agreements regarding health risks may be difficult to achieve.

Nevertheless, federal regulation is not the only game in town—perhaps not even the most important one. Even the most efficient regulations cannot eliminate all health, safety, and environmental hazards. Therefore, we must rely more heavily on private alternatives even while regulators are taking their ball and going home.

THE CASE FOR OCEAN WASTE DISPOSAL[5]

Love Canal, Times Beach, Valley of the Drums—these names are giving nightmares to every community confronted with the problem of waste disposal. Residents living near toxic waste sites are becoming increasingly alarmed about the potential health hazards, and the demand for "Superfund cleanups" is growing. In many states, local opposition to newly proposed disposal sites has sprouted overnight, and older sites continue to fill up and close down.

With America facing a crisis in the disposal of its wastes on land, more and more eyes are turning to the sea. Many businesses and municipalities see the ocean as a cheaper alternative to building landfills, advanced treatment plants, and incinerators. They also recognize that the sea has virtually no political constituency fighting to protect its health and environmental rights. As a result, a growing number of waste generators are seeking ways to dispose of their wastes at sea. Millions of tons of waste are already being dumped into the ocean each year, and federal guidelines have failed to effectively regulate such practices.

[5]Reprint of an article by William Lahey and Michael Connor. *Technology Review.* 86:60-8. Ag./S. '83. Reprinted by permission.

At the same time, recent studies of marine life around specific dumping sites show that the ocean is not as fragile as we once believed. There are many unanswered questions about the impact of waste disposal on our oceans—how much is safe and at what sites. But there's little doubt that the ocean, particularly its deep-water areas, has some capacity to assimilate both sewage and industrial wastes. Today, scientific forces as well as powerful economic and political ones are pushing us into a policy that permits the use of the sea as a major dumping site.

That doesn't mean we should subject our oceans to the 10 million tons of dry sewage sludge, 30 million tons of sludge from air purification processes, 300 million cubic yards of dredge spoil, 65 million tons of fly ash, and 100,000 cubic meters of low-level radioactive waste that America's disposers, according to recent EPA estimates, would like to dump there. If ocean waste disposal is not to become a disaster of similar (or worse) proportions to the problem of disposal on land, we must first evaluate the ocean's capacity to assimilate waste and then regulate its disposal accordingly. Major changes are needed in the way we now approach ocean waste disposal. Specifically, we must devise a policy that relies on economic incentives to limit environmental and health risks. One approach would be to charge a fee for ocean waste disposal according to the amount of wastes to be dumped and their level of toxicity.

Protecting the Clear Blue Sea

But before we can discuss the future, it is important to put the past into perspective. In the late sixties and early seventies, the American public seemed determined to protect the ocean. The generally heightened awareness of environmental issues during this period was only one of the catalysts for concern over ocean dumping. Public ire had also been aroused by the dumping of a large amount of nerve gas into the ocean by the U.S. Army in 1970. In the same year, the President's Council on Environmental Quality (CEQ) released a report concluding that stringent legal measures, both nationally and internationally, were required to protect the ocean. The CEQ reasoned that uncertainty regarding the environmental effects of ocean dumping should inspire caution, and its report concluded that until proven harmless, the dumping of materials that appeared environmentally sensitive should be discontinued.

Congress took its cue from the public. On a single day in 1972, it passed into law three major marine-protection bills: the Marine Protection Research and Sanctuaries Act, the Marine Mammal Protection Act, and the Coastal Zone Management Act.

In 1972, Congress also sought to control piped discharge of wastes into local rivers and estuaries. It amended the Federal Water Pollution Control Act, making it unlawful to discharge a pollutant into water without a permit from the Environmental Protection Agency (EPA). The amendments set an ultimate goal of eliminating all discharge of pollutants into navigable waters by 1985. They also required many communities to build secondary sewage treatment plants by 1977. In contrast with primary treatment, which uses only mechanical means such as screens to remove suspended solids from wastewater, secondary treatment uses microorganisms to break down organic compounds in waste. The objective is to decompose these compounds sufficiently so that when the liquid effluent is released into the nation's waters, no further oxygen is required to complete the process of decomposition; depleted oxygen levels can depress fish growth and survival rates. To encourage communities to build expensive secondary treatment facilities, the federal government held out an alluring carrot: it would pay 75 percent of the construction costs and the rest was to come from state and local funds.

The nation's protective attitude toward the ocean was also mirrored in the EPA's efforts to regulate the dumping of industrial waste and sludge—the solid material left after sewage has been treated. For instance, EPA officials imposed a 1981 deadline for the termination of all ocean dumping of municipal sludge and industrial waste. The agency was successful in stopping the dumping activities of more than 100 small municipalities, but those dumpers accounted for only about 3 percent of the total municipal waste dumped in 1978. The EPA was more successful in its efforts to control the dumping of industrial waste. Between 1973 and 1980, the volume of industrial waste dumped in the ocean was cut by almost half—from 5 million tons to a little over 2.5 million tons. The EPA also took a strong stand against the dumping of low-level radioactive waste: no permits were issued for this type of disposal.

More Expensive By Land

Today, however, the public mood and the nation's regulatory climate are very different—as is the economic picture. Over the last 10 years, the costs of land-based disposal systems have soared for two primary reasons: the myriad environmental regulations and the diminishing availability of suitable sites. While many of these regulations are necessary to protect human health and the environment, they have made it difficult for some municipalities to convert to new disposal methods. New York State, for instance, has imposed a two-year moratorium on using sludge as an agricultural fertilizer out of concern that crops might absorb cadmium, a heavy metal, from the soil. A sewage district in Salem, Mass., recently spent $3 million to build an experimental incinerator facility to dispose of its sludge. But a test burn unexpectedly revealed that the resulting ash would be classified as hazardous waste under EPA regulations, and there are no hazardous-waste-disposal sites in Massachusetts. The city subsequently filed for and received a permit to discharge its waste into the ocean. The incinerator stands idle.

High energy costs have also made incineration a relatively expensive proposition. The recently required use of air-pollution-control technology has further increased the expense. Primarily because of high operating costs, nearly one-fifth of all sludge incinerators constructed since 1970 have ceased operation.

Furthermore, rising land costs as well as opposition from local residents are forcing many businesses and municipalities to transport their wastes to isolated sites farther and farther away. The resulting rise in transportation costs has motivated many disposers to look for cheaper alternatives.

As prices for disposal of waste on land rise, the cost differential between land and ocean disposal grows. Representatives from Orange County, which encompasses Los Angeles, recently told a congressional committee that the cost of discharging the county's

sewage (both effluent and sludge) into the ocean was one-fourth
the cost of disposing it on land. Ocean disposal, they testified, costs
between $13 and $21 dollars per ton, whereas landfilling would
run about $82 to $92 per ton. Boston, which seeks to continue discharging its sewage into the ocean under a special EPA waiver,
has estimated that ocean disposal costs between two and nine times
less than other alternatives. New York City has estimated that the
land-based alternatives for disposing of its sludge are about 10
times as expensive as its current practice of hauling the sludge 12
miles out to sea and dumping it.

The Path of Least Resistance

As mentioned, public opposition to land-based waste disposal
also presents major obstacles. In the mid-1970s, for instance, Nassau County, Long Island, which has dumped its sludge into the
ocean since 1963, was told by the EPA to stop dumping. The
county then constructed a $14 million composting facility, only to
be dissuaded from using it because of intense local opposition to
spreading the resulting compost on land. Ironically, there has been
no evidence suggesting that land spreading of composted sludge
would contaminate groundwater. But Nassau County continues
to dump its waste into the ocean, and county officials are considering using the multi-million-dollar composting facility as a parking
garage.

Some EPA regulations on ocean disposal have also been successfully challenged in court, preventing the agency from maintaining its strict policy of protecting the ocean. In 1980, for
instance, a number of municipalities in California and Alaska
sued the EPA, asserting that it was being overly restrictive in issuing waivers to the requirement that sewage be given secondary
treatment. These municipalities argued that building and operating costly secondary treatment plants was unnecessary, since they
could discharge their wastes into active ocean waters that rapidly
assimilate and disperse it. The Washington D.C. Circuit Court
agreed, in part, and directed the EPA to allow these and other municipalities to apply for permits to dispose by sea. Since the court
decision in 1982, more than 200 municipalities have applied for

such permits. The EPA is now in the process of reviewing the flood of applications.

The city of New York also mounted a successful court challenge of EPA regulations in 1981. City officials believed that the EPA had acted unreasonably because its 1981 deadline for terminating all ocean dumping had not taken into consideration the costs as well as the health and environmental risks of land-based alternatives. A federal district court agreed, ruling that EPA could not impose such a deadline without considering such factors.

In a highly unusual move, the EPA chose not to appeal the decision. Former EPA administrator Anne (Gorsuch) Burford said she wanted to let the ruling stand because it gave her agency needed flexibility. But U.S. Representative Norman D'Amours (D-N.H.) called her decision "a betrayal of congressional trust" and a "devastating blow to efforts to end harmful dumping practices." Having chosen not to appeal, the EPA is faced with the task of revising its now-obsolete regulations for ocean waste disposal. How they will be rewritten under the new administration of William Ruckelshaus, who was named to succeed Burford in May, remains to be seen.

Cuts in federal spending have also dampened the effort to protect the nation's waters. Under the Reagan administration, for instance, federal spending on the construction of sewage treatment facilities has declined by almost half—from $4.2 billion in 1979 to $2.4 billion in 1982.

Faced with mounting public opposition, increasing costs, and a haphazard regulatory environment, America's businesses and cities are taking the path of least resistance. Cities such as Philadelphia, which had been forced to end its ocean dumping, have indicated an interest in returning to the sea. And other cities that have never dumped before are now exploring the possibility of applying for an ocean dumping permit. In the meantime, the number of tons of municipal and industrial waste already being dumped in the ocean is on the rise. More than 7 million tons of sludge, for instance, were dumped in 1982, compared with approximately 4.8 million tons in 1973. Researchers at the National Oceanographic and Atmospheric Administration (NOAA) have estimated that the amount of sewage sludge dumped could increase by nearly 150 percent (to 17 million tons) by 1987.

The amount of material dredged from the bottom of harbors and channels and dumped in the ocean is also increasing. Between 1977 and 1979, for instance, the amount of dredged material dumped nearly doubled—from 41 million cubic yards to approximately 73 million cubic yards. Morever, as deep channels are constructed to increase access to U.S. ports over the next few years, the amount of dredged material to dispose of will increase. The planned expansion of existing coal ports alone may require dredging and disposing of more than six times the amount dumped in 1979.

There has also been a surge of interest in dumping low-level radioactive wastes into the ocean. In January of 1982, the U.S. Navy announced it was considering dumping decommissioned nuclear submarines in the ocean. The navy says more than 100 aging nuclear submarines will have to be disposed of at a rate of 3 to 4 annually over 30 years. Meanwhile, the Department of Energy is interested in the ocean disposal of soil contaminated by radionuclides as a result of the Manhattan Project during World War II. Under Burford, the EPA said it was planning to revise its regulations to permit ocean dumping of low-level radioactive wastes. Afraid the EPA might be moving ahead too quickly, Congress enacted a two-year moratorium on such dumping. That deadline is up next spring.

The Effects on Marine Life

A number of recent scientific studies have been used to buttress the argument that the ocean should be used as a dumpsite. But on closer inspection, these studies confirm the need to approach the disposal of wastes at sea with a cautious and soundly developed management policy.

The most comprehensive series of studies on the impact of ocean dumping on marine life has focused on the coastal areas around Los Angeles and San Diego. For more than a decade, five municipalities and countries in Southern California have discharged their sewage effluent and sludge into coastal waters. In the last two to three years alone, an average of a billion gallons of sewage effluent a day has been discharged there. The studies were conducted by the Southern California Coastal Water Research Project (SCCWRP) and funded primarily by the five local governments who use the dumpsite. The scientists surveyed algae, fish, and plankton as well as species of worms, clams, and crustaceans that live on the ocean bottom in these areas, comparing them to marine life in areas with no known pollution.

The researchers found both positive and negative changes. While some organisms grew bigger and more abundantly near the areas of discharge, other species disappeared or suffered from a greater incidence of disease. For instance, the scientists found significant fin erosion among the flatfish that lie on the bottom near the piped discharge. They also noticed thinning in the shells of eggs laid by pelicans living on a nearby island and a resulting decline in their population; the scientists attributed these these abnormalities to the discharge of DDT. More recently, the amount of DDT and other chlorinated hydrocarbons being discharged in municipal waste has declined owing to more stringent EPA regulations; the incidence of fin erosion and abnormalities in pelican eggs have declined as well.

In studying a major dump site on the East Coast, investigators also found evidence of significant degradation of marine life. The area they surveyed is located in the New York Bight apex in relatively shallow water (about 20 to 50 meters deep) 12 miles southeast of New York City. The investigators, who were affiliated with NOAA, the University of Rhode Island (URI), and the State University of New York at Stony Brook, found that animal communities living on the sea bottom were severely altered. As in Southern California, the flatfish suffered from fin erosion, and most fish species were contaminated with polychlorinated biphenyls (PCBs) and other highly toxic compounds. In response to these findings, the state of New Jersey recently issued a fish advisory suggesting that people not eat locally harvested fish more than once a week.

As early as 1970, the Food and Drug Administration had banned shellfishing with 11 kilometers of the same dumpsite after finding evidence that shellfish were contaminated with coliform bacteria. These bacteria come from human excrement and often indicate the presence of agents of infectious disease. In the late sev-

enties, other investigators found further evidence of coliform contamination. However, the New York Bight apex is polluted from
a number of sources, so it is not clear what portion of these effects
can be ascribed to the dumping of sludge.

Scientists at the Woods Hole Oceanographic Institution, URI,
and NOAA also studied the impact of dumping industrial waste
at a deep-water site much farther offshore. Here they found little
evidence of degradation of marine life. Since the late sixties, manufacturers have used the site, located 106 miles east of New York
City in waters about 2,000 meters deep, to dump wastes that contained sulphuric acid, ferrous sulphate, and small quantities of
other metals. Because of the EPA crackdown and the recent recession, the amount of industrial wastes dumped dropped from about
2 million tons in 1973 to 800,000 tons in 1982.

Studying the site in the late seventies, the researchers found
that increased concentrations of pollutants were temporary and
confined to the immediate area of dumping. These concentrations
were smaller than those found to be toxic in the laboratory, and
the investigators were unable to conclusively attribute the changes
they found in marine life to the material being dumped. The researchers think that the seeming absence of short-term effects is
due to the dynamic currents of the ocean in deep-water areas. As
Woods Hole biologist Judy Capuzzo notes, ocean waters at this
site have a much greater capacity to dilute wastes because of the
proximity to Gulf Stream currents and the depth of the water.
Wastes are often diluted to almost a millionth of their original
concentrations within a few days.

The problem is that most of today's ocean disposal is taking
place in areas much less equipped to handle wastes—such as the
Boston Harbor and New York Bight apex, which are shallow and
less active sites. Most municipal and industrial dumpers are reluctant to discharge waste at deeper sites further offshore for one simple reason: cost. It's much cheaper to dump waste a few miles
offshore than to haul it hundreds of miles out to sea.

Obstacles to Change

Overall, these results indicate that the ocean has some capacity to assimilate waste—particularly active, deep-water areas fairly far from shore. But the question of how much waste it can assimilate and at what specific sites has not yet been answered. And these answers may be difficult to come by, not only because of political and economic obstacles but also because of some scientific stumbling blocks. The fact is that our thermometer for measuring the effects of waste disposal is not very finely calibrated. We have not yet developed the tools with which to predict the ocean's capacity for waste. We haven't decided, for instance, which organisms to study: "pollution-sensitive" species such as amphipods, crustaceans that are among the first to die in a polluted area; "ecologically important" species such as zooplankton that are essential to the marine food chain; or commercially harvested species. We also haven't determined which effects should be used to assess environmental impact: changes in a particular organism's enzyme system; changes in its ability to grow and reproduce; the death of an individual organism; or the death of its entire population. We also haven't decided which area should be used to calculate damage—the dumpsite boundary itself, the zone of initial dilution from a specific dump, or some larger, as yet undefined boundary.

Furthermore, many of the methods now used to test toxicity in the lab tell us little about toxicity in the ocean. In the lab, researchers usually test different concentrations of chemicals on a particular marine species, calculating safe levels through repeated experiments. But we can't conclusively link the results of these laboratory tests to actual effects on organisms in the ocean.

It is also difficult to separate the effects of waste disposal from other environmental perturbations caused by humans. For instance, the region around the New York Bight apex receives pollutants from river flows, atmospheric fallout, landfill leaching, and the dumping of dredge spoils, dirt, and sludge. It is hard for scientists to determine whether a decrease in a particular fish population is due to sludge dumping or to air emissions from automobiles and industry.

Some scientists believe that a threshold for safe levels of waste can be determined for ocean dumping much like the threshold that is used for waste disposal in freshwater. According to that standard, fish can survive only in waters where the dissolved oxygen content is above 6 parts per million; disposers are prohibited from discharging wastes that will lower the oxygen content below that level. While this particular threshold has been effective in areas where simple organic wastes are discharged, much of today's sewage contains a variety of industrial contaminants. Consequently, a number of different thresholds will probably be required to accurately predict the level of danger to marine life.

Furthermore, developing thresholds for ocean dumping depends on how we define unacceptable consequences. For example, a coastal area will be able to assimilate more waste if we define our threshold as undesirable effects on commercially harvested species rather than undesirable effects on the marine ecology. And if we decide to concern ourselves only with edible fish, then we must determine what kind of change we consider unacceptable: the reduction, say, in a particular fish population of 1 percent, 10 percent, or 50 percent.

The Risks by Land versus Sea

In recent years, many scientists, politicians, and industry representatives have suggested we are being overly protective of our oceans at the expense of our groundwaters. In two separate reports, one released by the National Advisory Committee on Oceans and Atmosphere (NACOA), a presidential committee, and the other by the National Academy of Sciences (NAS), authorities have voiced the concern that our stringent policy of protecting the ocean is only increasing the danger to public health by forcing the disposal of all wastes on land. Some NACOA and NAS scientists expressed particular concern over the contamination of groundwater from the leakage of PCBs and other hazardous compounds dumped in lagoons and landfills.

There's no question that toxic wastes are seeping into groundwater and soil from dumpsites throughout the nation. But how do these potential hazards compare with the risks of dumping wastes into shallow water offshore?

Unfortunately, very few studies have attempted to answer that question. Perhaps the most extensive information comes from Nassau County, Long Island, an area where both fish and groundwater risks are high. Offshore lies the New York Bight, the nation's largest dumpsite for solid sludge; onshore, sandy soil and a particularly shallow aquifer combine to make groundwater contamination a problem as well. Based on data available from Nassau County officials, we have been able to compare the health risks posed by the daily consumption of locally harvested fish versus the daily consumption of groundwater.

First of all, the types of organic compounds that contaminate groundwater and fish are quite different. Small, soluble chemical compounds such as trichloroethylene and tetrachloroethylene are usually found in groundwater, having leaked from dumpsites; both are common industrial solvents. Conversely, large compounds such as PCBs dissolve poorly in groundwater and tend to cling to surface soils, but they are easily adsorbed and stored by fish. As a result, their concentration in fish is tens of thousands times their concentration in water. Both types of compounds are suspected carcinogens.

We have calculated the total risks of getting cancer from both types of contaminants by multiplying the degree of their potency by their estimated dose in humans. For an average individual weighing 155 pounds, the additional lifetime risk of getting cancer from drinking 2 liters of water a day is 34 in a million—a level of risk three times greater than the 10-in-a-million threshold considered acceptable by the EPA. For the same individual, the increased risk of getting cancer from eating 6.5 grams of fish per day (a mixture of flounder, lobster, and mussels averaged from a normal weekly portion) is 65 in a million. So even though most people drink much more water than they eat fish, the carcinogenic risks of doing either are about the same. For people who consume a large amount of striped bass, the risk of getting cancer is much higher: 2100 in a million. (Striped bass are more toxic because they migrate into the highly contaminated waters of the Hudson River.)

According to this limited assessment, we should be just as concerned about dumping chemical pollutants such as PCBs in shallow ocean waters as we are about dumping them on land. In fact, it might be safer to treat many of the insoluble organic compounds in active land-based systems. On the other hand, the ocean, with its large dilution capacity, is better equipped to handle wastes such as metals. And of course, some industrial pollutants such as dioxin and PCBs shouldn't be dumped at all. It would be much safer to destroy these compounds by incineration or develop substitute products or processes that would eliminate the need to dispose of these highly toxic substances.

An Economic Incentive for Safety

All these studies point to one conclusion: we need to make major changes in the way we regulate ocean disposal. The protectionist approach of the 1970s has backfired. Exceptions to restrictions on ocean dumping were granted and deadlines extended haphazardly, often as a reaction to political and economic forces. The United States must develop a regulatory program that recognizes that the ocean should be used for some waste disposal, yet provides an incentive for businesses and towns to control their ocean dumping activities.

One approach we advocate would be to charge a sliding fee for ocean disposal based on the amount dumped, the type of contaminants in the waste, and the location of disposal. Since it is far cheaper to dump wastes in the ocean than on land (no one, after all, can buy or lease the ocean for dumping), a fee system could bring ocean disposal into economic parity with other alternatives. Decisions on where to dispose of waste would then be more likely based on comparisons of environmental and health risks, not on the basis of economic or political expediency.

Under a fee system, disposers of innocuous materials such as seafood-cannery wastes, which contain easily degradable compounds, could be charged low, if any, fees, since uncontaminated organic material poses few threats to the marine environment. Disposers of contaminated wastes, on the other hand, would be taxed according to the type and concentration of pollutants in the waste. This kind of graduated fee would create an incentive for dumpers to either reduce the volume of waste dumped or pretreat it to decrease the amount of contaminants present. For instance, a municipality that was being charged a relatively high dumping fee because of the high concentrations of industrial contaminants in its waste would have an incentive to impose pretreatment requirements on local industries. Indeed, the Clean Water Act already gives municipalities the legal authority to do so.

A variable fee system would also give industry an incentive for developing innovative pretreatment and disposal techniques. The less contaminated the waste a company discharges, the lower the fee would be. Both industry and government could also save on fees (and make some additional income) by processing sludge into fertilizer and other useful products.

A variable fee system could also be used to encourage dumpers to use appropriate dumpsites. Under this system, dumping at deep-water sites shown to have a greater capacity to absorb waste would be charged much less than dumping at shallow coastal sites that are already heavily polluted. The fees could be structured in such a way as to counterbalance the increased cost of hauling wastes further offshore to deeper, more appropriate sites.

Furthermore, revenues generated from dumping fees could be put to valuable use. They could be earmarked for research of alternative waste-disposal techniques and used to finance studies aimed at finding safe deep-water dumping sites. Such revenues could also be used to fund a comprehensive program to monitor dumping and assess its effects on the marine environment. Since our knowledge of the marine environment is rudimentary, any effective system of ocean waste disposal must be accompanied by an ongoing monitoring program.

Finally, we believe a variable fee system would be more equitable than the current regulatory system. For example, the EPA phased out many small-volume municipal dumpers during the 1970s while allowing large-volume dumpers (such as New York City) to continue without penalty. The large municipalities had the legal and financial resources to find loopholes in the system, forcing the EPA to grant them special exceptions. A fee system based on tonnage and contamination levels would eliminate these inequities. In short, we believe such a system is a versatile regulatory tool that deserves serious consideration by America's policymakers.

THE RECYCLING OF CHEMICAL WASTE[6]

In place of landscaping, huge and unsightly ponds surround the Allied Corporation's chemical plant in Metropolis, Ill., a rural town on the Ohio River. The ponds are filled with a dull white liquid, thick as oatmeal, that would begin to burn the skin off a hapless wader within minutes.

The substance is calcium fluoride, an unwanted byproduct of chemical manufacturing that has accumulated at the Metropolis plant for seven years as hazardous waste. To keep it from human contact indefinitely—as Federal law requires—a network of five ponds, each as large as a football field and 10 feet deep, was built across the nearby fields and woodlands and surrounded by fence.

But a year ago, the pond-building stopped and Allied took a new tack. It invested $4.3 million in a "recovery plant" that recycles the waste into a safe raw material for the production of commercially valuable fluorine-based chemicals that are a specialty of Allied's Metropolis plant. The result: Allied saves $1 million annually on new storage ponds and also because it no longer needs to purchase as much raw material.

Allied's strategy at Metropolis is being matched throughout the chemical industry. Increasingly, the hazardous waste problem is being dealt with by recycling the waste into raw material—or by investment in new equipment that produces less waste. The technologies involved are not new, but until recently they were considered too costly to use.

That has changed as Federal regulations governing hazardous waste disposal have become more stringent—and more expensive. The proliferating rules have pushed up storage costs for hazardous chemical waste from about $24 a barrel in the late 1970s to more than $100 a barrel today, according to James Gutensohn,

[6]Reprint of an article by Steven J. Marcus, reporter. *New York Times.* p F 4. Ja. 8, '84. Copyright© 1984 by The New York Times Company. Reprinted by permission.

commissioner of the Massachusetts Department of Environmental Management.

The industry has also been pushed into recycling by the public outcry over inadequate or careless storage of chemical waste. Most recently, for example, the Federal Environmental Protection Agency charged that trichloroethylene—a suspected carcinogen—might be seeping into the Minneapolis water supply from a landfill site in Fridley, Minn., where containers of chemical waste once were buried.

That sort of publicity has reinforced the industry's growing belief that investment in recycling plants will turn out to be less costly than settling future lawsuits filed by people claiming they had developed cancer and other ailments from contact with stored chemical waste. "The bottom line is the basic unpredictability in the quality and endurance of chemical storage," said Robert D. Stephens, chief of the Hazardous Materials Laboratory of the California Health Department. "That's something nobody wants to bet on."

Others agree. A report released last year by Congress's Office of Technology Assessment, for example, estimated that "cleaning up a site and compensating victims might cost 10 to 100 times today's costs of preventing releases of hazardous waste."

The new activity has begun to show impressive results, the industry claims. The Chemical Manufacturers Association estimates that its member companies now "recycle, reuse or reclaim about a half-ton of hazardous waste for every ton discarded." A recent C.M.A. survey of 535 plants operated by 70 chemical companies found that from 1981 to 1982 the amount of hazardous waste buried or stored in barrels and tanks went down by 59 percent. The total volume of hazardous waste disposed of through burial, storage and other methods fell 42 percent in that year for these plants, according to the C.M.A. survey.

A recent Congressional survey appears to disagree with these industry findings. Congress's Office of Technology Assessment estimated that 80 percent of the nation's hazardous waste continues to be buried in barrels and sealed containers or otherwise stored long-term. "It's still the cheapest alternative and therefore not all people are rushing in the new direction," says William Wallace, director of solid and hazardous waste management at CH2M Hill Inc., a consulting firm.

Theoretically, recycling could eliminate all the millions of tons of hazardous waste that the nation's industries produce each year, solving a major environmental issue. But in fact, decades will be needed even to approach this goal. For one thing, most of the nation's factories were not designed to recycle their byproducts. Converting those factories is costly. In addition, there is no standard recycling procedure. Each type of carcinogenic or toxic chemical waste requires different techniques and different equipment, says Douglas Shooter, a senior consultant in the hazardous waste management group of Arthur D. Little Inc., a consulting firm. "We end up with many examples—successes in smaller and smaller packages—that are not transferable to other wastes." Adds Bob Bonczek, director of environmental affairs at E.I. du Pont de Nemours & Company: "Each technique requires great imagination and persistence, and none is a panacea."

At its Metropolis, Ill., plant, Allied has managed to recycle all of the calcium fluoride thrown off as a hazardous byproduct of the fluorine-based chemicals made there to produce gases for refrigerators and aid-conditioners. In fact, the company says that over the next decade, the network of pools in the nearby fields will be drained to feed the recycling plant and the land possibly restored. The Metropolis innovation earned Allied a National Environmental Industry Award last November, and the huge chemical company is also making changes at other plants. At Baton Rouge, La., for example, Allied dilutes acid waste, then mixes it with limestone to produce calcium chloride, a material used by the local oil and gas industries as a drilling fluid for rigs in the Gulf of Mexico. Before a recycling facility was built in 1981 to do this, 80,000 tons of chemical wastes were neutralized, the company said, and discharged into the Mississippi River.

At the Monsanto Company, which has its headquarters in St. Louis, the production of nylon spins off, as an unwanted byproduct, 30 million pounds a year of dibasic acid, a caustic material. It used to be stored in "deep-injection" wells, but now it is recycled and shipped to other plants as a raw material to make paints and solvents. It is also used in the scrubber systems of power plants to help reduce the emissions of sulfur dioxide into the air. The remaining dibasic acid is being concentrated and burned as a fuel, at a saving of $100,000 a year in Monsanto's fuel bill.

Earl Beaver, business development director for the Monsanto Fibers and Intermediates Company, estimates the company will sell five million pounds of recycled dibasic acid in 1984, for $1 million, enough to recover by 1985 the entire cost of the new recycling facility for the acid.

Mr. Beaver, who administers the company's Coproduct Utilization Program (Monsanto prefers to call the waste co-products rather than byproducts, he says, "because that implies additional value"), claims to have "found a home" in this manner for 70 million pounds of dibasic acid and other hazardous wastes thrown off last year by the manufacturing process.

Still, Monsanto's 1983 waste storage bill was high—$30 million to store 300,000 tons of hazardous waste, although that was down from nearly 400,000 tons in 1980. Even with this volume decline, the cost of hazardous waste disposal has tripled, from $10 million in the late 1970s, said Michael A. Pierle, Monsanto's director of regulatory management for hazardous waste. That is mostly a result of the cost of meeting Federal standards, he said.

The Minnesota Mining and Manufacturing Company estimates that 40 projects in its Pollution Prevention Pays program have eliminated 15,000 tons a year of hazardous wastes, yielding a total of $13.2 million in first-year savings. Sara Zoss, coordinator of the program, cites as an example the reuse of ammonium sulfate, a caustic material that is a byproduct of the manufacture of such products as videotape. The chemical is now sold as a raw material for fertilizer, saving 3M about $1 million in pollution-control equipment and producing revenues of $270,000 a year.

At 3M, a central incinerator in St. Paul burns 18,000 tons of hazardous waste a year, leaving a nonhazardous residue less than one-tenth the volume of the original material. The result has been savings in storage as well as a $1 million-a-year cutback in fuel costs.

Russell H. Susag, director of environmental operations at 3M, estimates that 90 percent of the company's hazardous wastes now are being eliminated, either through recycling or incineration. He said that the company's total cost of hazardous waste disposal has been reduced by as much as 75 percent, but he wouldn't cite dollar amounts.

Dow Chemical of Midland, Mich., also is recycling some hazardous wastes into useful products. Stacy Daniels, research leader in the company's Environmental Sciences Research Laboratory, talks of recycling "stillbottoms" from the production of caustic soda and chlorine into the useful raw material hydrochloric acid. But he says that Dow nevertheless relies on incineration to destroy most of its hazardous wastes.

Incineration is a major industry method of reducing the volume of hazardous wastes that must be stored indefinitely, with its attendant risk that seepage will contaminate the environment, creating future liability. But some experts say that incineration merely trades one type of pollution hazard for another. John Ehrenfeld, consultant in the hazardous-waste management group at Arthur D. Little, maintains that incineration "converts a small probability of high risk into low-level but continuous exposures" from air pollution emissions.

As for burial of waste in sealed containers, state legislation may eventually limit or end this alternative. California, for example, began last year to enforce a law that bans hazardous waste from landfills, and similar bans may soon appear at the national level. The Federal Resource Conservation and Recovery Act of 1976 is currently up for renewal in Congress, and experts predict a new law will most likely emerge that specifically prohibits the burial of some hazardous wastes.

Even in its present version, the Resource Conservation and Recovery Act has been a catalyst for change. The reduction of hazardous waste through recycling or incineration, said Mr. Stephens of the California Health Department, "is a very significant result of regulation."

Thus "some of the more forward-looking companies," Mr. Stephens said, "are sounding like environmentalists. People were calling us fuzzyheads a few years ago, but now companies like Getty, Dow and 3M, who know how chemicals behave and what to do with them, are speaking as we did."

In the last analysis, recycling or eliminating hazardous waste also depends heavily on a prosperous economy that will generate enough corporate revenue for the necessary capital investment, says Michael Overcash, professor of chemical engineering at North Carolina State University and a member of a National Academy of Sciences panel that is currently studying the hazardous waste issue. "The past few years haven't been too good for such investment," he says, "but the pace will quicken with recovery."

THE FUTURE

EDITOR'S INTRODUCTION

Where are current environmental policies leading us, and what will life be like in fifteen or twenty years? The final section reveals radical disagreement on this vital question.

William Ruckelshaus, leading the EPA for the second time in his career, describes, in a speech reprinted from the *EPA Journal,* the increasing difficulty of solving problems that science understands imperfectly. He advises that the competing claims of economic growth and conservation of nature may never be reconciled. In a speech reprinted from *High Country News,* Governor Richard Lamm of Colorado, assuming the role of Secretary of the Interior in a future administration, paints a wholly gloomy picture of the year 2005, by which time, he suggests, humanity will stand shoulder to shoulder and all natural resources will have been irrevocably destroyed by chemicals. However, Julian Simon, a spokesman for the diametrically opposed point of view, argues in an article reprinted from *The Futurist* that, on the contrary, the prospects for the preservation of natural resources have never looked better. Constance Holden, in an article from *Science* magazine, reviews the arguments of both optimists and pessimists, pointing out each side has ample evidence to support its conclusions.

The last two articles in this compilation assess the prospects for our two most vital resources—air and water. Kenneth Sheets, writing in *U.S. News & World Report,* describes the effects of the drought of 1983, which dramatized the need for a national water policy to allocate supplies and settle the disputes between western and southern states that need additional supplies to meet growing industrial and domestic needs. Finally Jerry Jasinowski, in an article from *USA Today,* describes the economic and social consequences of the Clean Air Act, and presents a case for amending some of its standards.

SCIENCE, RISK, AND PUBLIC POLICY[1]

We are now in a troubled and emotional period for pollution control; many communities are gripped by something approaching panic and the public discussion is dominated by personalities rather than substance. It is not important to assign blame for this. I appreciate that people are worried about public health and about economic survival, and legitimately so, but we must all reject the emotionalism that surrounds the current discourse and rescue ourselves from the paralysis of honest public policy that it breeds.

It is no accident that I am raising this subject here in the house of science. I believe that part of the solution to our distress lies with the idea enshrined in this building, the idea that disciplined minds can grapple with ignorance, and sometimes win: the idea of science. We will not recover our equilibrium without a concerted effort to more effectively engage the scientific community.

Somehow our democratic technological society must resolve the dissonance between science and the creation of public policy. Nowhere is this more troublesome than in the formal assessment of risk—the estimation of the association between the exposure to a substance and the incidence of some disease, based on scientific data.

Here is how the problem emerges at the Environmental Protection Agency. EPA is an instrument of public policy, whose mission is to protect the public health and environment in the manner laid down by its statutes. That manner is to set standards and enforce them; and our enforcement powers are strong and pervasive. But the standards we set, whether technology or health-related, must have a sound scientific base.

Science and the law are thus partners at EPA, but uneasy partners. It's a shotgun wedding. The main reason for the uneasiness lies, I think, in the conflict between the way science really works and the public's thirst for certitude that is written into EPA's laws. Science, as you all know, thrives on uncertainty. The

[1]Excerpted from a speech by William D. Ruckelshaus, EPA administrator, to the National Academy of Sciences, June 22, 1983. *EPA Journal.* 9:3–5. Jl. '83.

best young scientists flock into fields where great questions have been asked but nothing is known. The greatest triumph of a scientist is the crucial experiment that shatters the certainties of the past and opens up rich new pastures of ignorance.

But EPA's laws often assume, indeed demand, a certainty of protection greater than science can provide at the current state of knowledge. The laws do no more than reflect what the public believes and what it often hears from people with scientific credentials on the 6 o'clock news. The public thinks we know what *all* the bad pollutants are, *precisely* what adverse health or environmental effects they cause, how to measure them *exactly* and control them *absolutely*. Of course, the public and sometimes the law are wrong, but not all wrong. We do know a lot about some pollutants and we have controlled them effectively using the tools of the Clean Air Act and the Clean Water Act. These are the pollutants for which the scientific community can set safe levels and margins of safety for sensitive populations. If this were the case for all pollutants, we could breathe more easily (in both senses of the phrase); but it is not so.

When I left EPA over 10 years ago as its first Administrator, we had the Clean Air Act, the Clean Water Act, a solid waste law, a pesticide law and laws to control radiation and noise. Yet to come were the myriad of laws to control toxic substances from their manufacture to their disposal—but that they would pass was even then obvious.

When I departed a decade ago, the struggle over whether the Federal Government was to have a major role in protecting our health, safety and environment was ended. The American people had spoken. The laws had passed, the regulations were being written. The only remaining question was whether the statutory framework we had created for our journey made sense or whether, over time, we would adjust it.

Ten years ago I thought I knew the answer to that question as well. I believed it would become apparent to all that we could virtually eliminate the risks we call pollution if we wanted to spend enough money. When it also became apparent that enough money for all the pollutants was a lot of money, I further believed we would begin to examine the risks very carefully and structure a system which forced us to balance our desire to eliminate pollution against the costs of its control. This would entail some adjustment of the laws, but really not all that much, and it would happen by about 1976. I was wrong.

It may be that God is repaying me for my error by causing me to be reincarnated as Administrator of EPA. Whether God or President Reagan is the cause this time around, I am determined to improve our country's ability to cope with the risks of pollutants over where I left it 10 years ago.

It will not be easy, because we must now deal with a class of pollutants for which a safe level is difficult, if not impossible, to establish. These pollutants interfere with genetic processes and are associated with the diseases we fear most: cancer and reproductive disorders, including birth defects. The scientific consensus has it that any exposure, however small, to a genetically active substance embodies some risk of an effect. Since these substances are widespread in the environment, and since we can detect them down to very low levels, we must assume that life now takes place in a minefield of risks from hundreds, perhaps thousands, of substances. No more can we tell the public: you are home free with an adequate margin of safety.

This worries all of us, and it should. But when we examine the premises on which such estimates of risk are based, we find a confusing picture. In assessing a suspected carcinogen, for example, there are uncertainties at every point where an assumption must be made: in calculating exposure; in extrapolating from high doses where we have seen an effect to the low doses typical of environmental pollution; in what we may expect when humans are subjected to much lower doses of the same substance that causes tumors when given in high doses to laboratory animals; and finally, in the very mechanisms by which we suppose the disease to work.

One thing we clearly need to do is insure that our laws reflect these scientific realities. The Administrator of EPA should not be forced to represent that a margin of safety exists for a specific substance at a specific level of exposure where none can be scientifically established. This is particularly true where [that] forces the cessation of all use of a substance without any further evaluation.

It is my strong belief that where EPA or OSHA or any of the social regulatory agencies is charged with protecting public health, safety or the environment, we should be given, to the extent possible, a common statutory formula for accomplishing our tasks. This statutory formula may well weigh public health very heavily in the equation as the American people certainly do.

The formula should be as precise as possible and should include a responsibility to assess the risk and to weigh that, not only against the benefits of the continued use of the substance under examination, but against the risks associated with substitute substances and the risks associated with the transfer of the substance from one environmental medium to another via pollution control practices.

I recognize that legislative change in the current climate is difficult. It is up to those of us who seek change to make the case for its advisability.

I did not come here today to plead for statutory change. My purpose is to speak of risk assessment and risk management and science's role in both. It is important to distinguish these two essential functions. . . . Scientists assess a risk to find out what the problems are. The process of deciding what to do about the problems is risk management. [This] involves a much broader array of disciplines, and is aimed toward a decision about control.

Risk management assumes we have assessed the health risks of a suspect chemical. We must then factor in its benefits, the costs of the various methods available for its control, and the statutory framework for decision. These two functions [should] be separated as much as possible within a regulatory agency. This is what we now do at EPA and it makes sense.

I think we also need to strengthen our risk assessment capabilities. We need more research on the health effects of the substances we regulate. I intend to do everything in my power to make clear the importance of this scientific analysis at EPA. Given the necessity of acting in the face of enormous scientific uncertainties, it is more important than ever that our scientific analysis be rigorous and the quality of our data be high. We must take great pains not to mislead people regarding the risks to their health. We can help avoid confusion both by the quality of our science and the clarity of our language in explaining the hazards.

I intend to allocate some of EPA's increased resources, which everyone seems determined to give us, toward these ends. Our 1984 request contains significant increases for risk assessment and associated work. We have requested $31 million in supplemental appropriations for research and development and I would expect that risk assessment will be more strongly supported as a result of this increase as well.

I would also like to revitalize our long-term research program to develop a base for more adequately protecting the public health from toxic pollutants. I will be asking the advice of the outside scientific community how best to focus those research efforts.

Despite conflicting pressures, risk assessment at EPA must be based on scientific evidence and scientific consensus *only*. Nothing will erode public confidence faster than the suspicion that policy considerations have been allowed to influence the assessment of risk.

Although there is an objective way to assess risk, there is, of course, no purely objective way to manage it, nor can we ignore the subjective perception of risk in the ultimate management of a particular substance. To do so would be to place too much credence in our objective data and ignore the possibility that occasionally one's stomach is right. No amount of data is a substitute for judgment.

Further, we must search for ways of describing risk in ways the average citizen can comprehend. Telling a family living close to a manufacturing facility that no further controls are needed on the plant's emissions because according to our linear model their risk is *only* 10^6, is not very reassuring. We need to describe the suspect substances as clearly as possible, tell people what the known or suspected health problems are and help them compare that risk to those with which they are more familiar.

To effectively *manage* the risk, we must seek new ways to involve the public in the decision-making process. Whether we believe in participatory democracy or not, it is a part of our social regulatory fabric. Rather than praise or lament it, we should seek more imaginative ways to involve the various publics impacted by the substance at issue. They need to be involved early on and they need to be informed if their participation is to be meaningful. We will be searching for ways to make our participatory process work better.

For this to happen, scientists must be willing to take a larger role in explaining the risks to the public—including the uncertainties inherent in any risk assessment. What we need to hear more of from scientists is science. I am going to try to provide avenues at EPA for involvement in the public dialogue in which the scientific problems are described. Our country needs the clear unbiased voice of science.

Lest anyone misunderstand, I am not suggesting that all the elements of managing risk can be reduced to some neat mathematical formula. Going through a disciplined approach can help. It will assist in organizing our thoughts to include all the elements that should be weighed. We will build up a set of precedents that will assist later decision-making and provide more predictable outcomes for any social regulatory programs we adopt.

It is clear to me that in a society in which democratic principles so dominate, the perceptions of the public must be weighed. Instead of objective and subjective risks, the experts sometimes substitute "real" and "imaginary" risks. There is a certain arrogance in this—an elitism which has ill served us in the past. Rather than decry the ignorance of the public and seek to ignore their concerns, our governmental processes must accommodate the will of the people and recognize its occasional wisdom. As Thomas Jefferson observed: "If we think (the people) not enlightened enough to exercise their control with a wholesome discretion, the remedy is not to take it from them, but to inform their discretion."

Up to this point I have been suggesting how risks should be assessed and managed in EPA. Much needs to be done to coordinate the various EPA programs to assure a consistent approach. I have established a task force with that charter.

I further believe we should make uniform the way in which we manage risk across the Federal regulatory agencies. The public interest is not served by two Federal agencies taking diametrically opposed positions on the health risks of a given toxic substance and then arguing about it in the press. We should be able to coordinate our risk assessment procedures across all Federal agencies. The risk management strategy that flows from that assessment may indeed differ, depending on the agency's statutory mandate or the judgment of the ultimate decision maker.

But even at the management stage there is no reason why the approaches cannot be coordinated to achieve the goal of risk avoidance or minimization with the least societal disruption possible. In the last few weeks I have been exploring with the White House and the Office of Management and Budget the possibility of effecting a better intra-governmental coordination of the way in which we assess and manage risk.

To push this one step further, I believe it is in our nation's best interest to share our knowledge of risks and our approach to managing them with the other developed nations of the world. The environmental movement has taught us the interdependencies of the world's ecosystems. In coping with the legitimate concerns raised by environmentalism we must not forget that we cope in a world with interdependent economies. If our approach to the management of risk is not sufficiently in harmony with those of the other developed nations, we could save our health and risk our economy. I don't believe we need abandon either, but to insure it does not happen, we need to work hard to share scientific data and understand how to harmonize our management techniques with those of our sister nations.

I want to help achieve a better conceptual, statutory and societal framework to cope with risk in our country. To do that we need to get the emotion out of and the scientist into the process:

I need science's help.

I'll try to make it easier to access what we're doing at EPA. But if I can't do that, I need your help anyway.

What I'm after is a government-wide process for assessing and managing health, safety and environmental risks. This will take coordination, cooperation and good will within EPA, within the Executive Branch agencies and between the Congress and the Administration.

In other words, this will take a miracle.

Now I know science doesn't believe in miracles, but I need your help if this one's going to happen.

What's at stake is no less than whether this country works. It's worth the effort of all of us.

COLORADO'S GOVERNOR PEERS AHEAD[2]

As Secretary of the Interior, I am honored to be here on this momentous occasion to celebrate the 100th anniversary of the incorporation of the Audubon Society.

The President has sent me here to defend the record of this administration. We do not appreciate the strident, coercive and damaging criticism we are receiving from conservation groups in general or from this group specifically. The President is doing the best she can and has asked me to come and respond to your criticisms. I sincerely believe this President is a dedicated environmentalist. But unlike some of her predecessors in the Oval Office, she does not have the options that were available in the late 20th century.

You cannot believe and you cannot fully understand the problems we have in running a country of 430 million Americans as we enter the 21st century. We do not have the choices they had back in the 1970s, the 1980s, or even the 1990s. We live in a world that is crowded, hungry, poor and in conflict. These matters demand our total attention.

Let me start by saying that I really do sympathize with your viewpoints, but you must try to understand some of the problems we have running this country in a world that has over six billion people.

You and others have objected to the President's statement that "birds don't vote," comparing it to former President Reagan's statement that "if you've seen one redwood, you've seen them all." That is a tragically mistaken analogy. The President was acknowledging a political reality, not expressing a philosophical preference. Birds *don't* vote, and in an overcrowded, chaotic world, if you don't vote or have a sponsor who votes, then you don't count. Your political agendas are meaningless. Hungry and homeless people make birds and beasts expendable, make wilder-

[2]Reprint of a speech by Richard D. Lamm, governor of Colorado, to the National Audubon Society, August 30, 1983. *High Country News.* p 10–11. Ja. 23, '84. Copyright© by the High Country News Foundation. Reprinted by permission.

ness anachronistic, make scenery irrelevant and aesthetics super-fluous.

In order to provide even the most fundamental necessities to mankind in this crowded, polluted world, the realization of the Biblical prophecy that man will exercise "control over the earth and all living things" is essential. We do what we have to do. Although for a time during the 1970s and 1980s there existed a viable constituency for environmental issues, politics today is the science of accommodating people, not peregrines; humans, not hummingbirds. We are prisoners of decisions of policy-makers long dead.

You all know of the many problems just trying to feed America, the breadbasket of the world. The vast areas of prime farmland we once knew are mere history. Over 25 percent of the farmlands of 1980 are now devoid of the topsoil essential for high-yield production. We have lost 5 billion acres to desertification. The inexpert use of irrigation in the '80s and '90s created salinity problems we still are unable to solve. We as a planet wasted the one-time inheritance of a foot of the best topsoil that God ever gave anyone.

Of course, most farmland went to house our exploding population. Since 1980, we have added the equivalent of twenty Bangladeshes to an already hungry world. We add 2.5 people every second. When you sit down to dinner tonight there will be 50,000 more people to feed than when you got up from breakfast. We cannot worry about quality of life when we are worrying about the quantity of existence.

This Administration inherited a country and a world shaped by the tragic mistakes of previous generations. This Administration isn't responsible for making Canada an enemy by acid rain and predatory trade policy; we weren't in office when the nation's groundwater was poisoned by hazardous and toxic wastes. We cannot be blamed for the ruination of the world's fisheries by the failure to adopt the Law of the Sea Treaty.

Did we lose the People's Republic of Mexico or the Philippine Soviet? We did not. Mexico, Central America and the Philippines were lost long ago. Did we really think democracies that had corruption as a way of life, vast discrepancies between rich and poor, and populations that doubled every 15 years would survive? It wasn't *if* the revolution would take place, it was *when!*

And we didn't loan them all that money. We learned in the International Banking Crisis of 1986 that 300 million people in underdeveloped countries will *not* get up and go to work each morning for Chase Manhattan.

You must understand that we grieve the loss of environmental values with you. I was governor of this once beautiful state: governor before the high level toxic waste disposal site; before that ecological disaster known as synfuels; before acid rain ruined our alpine lakes. I grieve every time I return. I see these mountains I once climbed and rivers I once kayaked now despoiled. We didn't close Western Colorado's Recreational Areas because we wanted to, but because of the undeniable link between the cancer epidemic and spent shale. We have to live with and manage the results of another generation's myopia.

No one has forgotten the campaign of 1992—when the "Forests or Families" debate was carried on. But understand that my party neither had nor has anything against national forests— we merely believe that housing for people is more important. We've had to build as many housing units in the last 30 years as in the first 300 years of America's existence.

The President, however, is proposing an amendment to the recently passed *Forest Reduction Act*. This bill is patterned after the old Wilderness Act, which was repealed in 1990—and will exempt 5,000 acres in every state from harvesting. I'd also like to hear at least some praise for the fact that this administration has doubled the acres of urban parks in the nation by taking down the gravestones in cemeteries. We are trying.

Next, let me discuss the most controversial legislation now pending before Congress—the compulsory birth control amendment to the National Health Service Act. We can no longer tolerate the historic anachronism that the number of children a family has is strictly a private decision carrying no social consequences. The individual miracle of birth has become a collective tragedy.

The "right" you have to bear an unlimited number of children must be revoked. We are seeking to take away this freedom because people have abused it. No form of life has ever been able to breed indefinitely. All living things must inevitably come into balance with their environment; now man must come into balance with his. Your rights end at your neighbor's nose, and the human wave of population is already over our heads. The relentless geometry of population reminds me of Hegel's aphorism that "freedom is the recognition of necessity."

We think this law is clearly constitutional. If the law says you can have only one wife, why can't we say you can have only two children? This Administration wants to give you the maximum amount of human freedom—but our hands are tied. I can't understand why you extremists can't get that through your heads. We can't possibly allow you the freedom here in the year 2005 that your fathers and mothers had in 1970. We must have more restriction, more regimentation, and, of course, more rationing.

Speaking of rationing, another dark spot on the horizon is the Water Rationing Act. We were hoping to increase your allotment to two baths every week, but we have not had much success with our recycling programs.

Again, I resent being blamed for this conservation measure. Man has long known he clings precariously to the earth. As you history buffs know, until the late 20th century, 97.2% of the earth's water was in oceans, 2.15% locked up in ice caps, and only .65% was available to us as fresh water in our lakes, rivers, streams, underground water supplies, and atmospheric moisture. Since the Great World Drought of 1992, brought about by increasing global temperature, and since the substantial contamination of so much of the remaining water, our supply of fresh water has dropped dramatically below the 1990 level while demand has continued to increase. We do what we have to do.

I also want to mention the on-going foreign policy debate. As you know, I fully support the complete repeal of the Immigration Act and the Foreign Aid Act. I am as aware as you of the pitiful scenes we see daily on television of the current famine in Asia. But even as the deaths approach 200 million, the alleviation of this suffering is beyond our power. We made a mistake when we attempted to help earlier famines. We stretched our resources to the breaking point and merely delayed the day of reckoning a few years. Geometric curves are ravenous beasts that can never be sated.

I urge you to remember the Haitian refugee problems of the 1980s. We allowed a few boatloads of Haitian refugees into our country because they had destroyed their own environment. Their farms were no longer workable, they had no more forests, and they had nothing to eat. Soon we were accepting hundreds of thousands of refugees per year on top of the massive influx from South America, Central America, Asia and Europe. The people of Haiti were still producing children at the alarming rate of 2.2% per year, both in their country and in ours. Soon both the U.S. and Haiti had population problems, and still the people of Haiti had nothing to eat. The melting pot, like any pot, is finite. Clearly, the stork outflew the American eagle.

We do not have enough resources even for our own needs. We have picked the earth bare in order to support our bloated world population. The ship of state is being dismantled to feed the crew. Wilderness, birds and single family residences were fine in the 1960s when we had 200 million people and only three and a half billion people on earth; but today they are a luxury we cannot afford.

If mankind ever had a chance to save wildlife and preserve the environment, it passed with your fathers back in the '70s and '80s. Since then, we have lost over 200 species of animals—the California condor, the Spanish lynx, the New Zealand Kukapo, to name just a few—all lost because of poor environmental management. But the previous generation persisted in a naive belief that the forces of the marketplace would rescue us from resource shortages. Technology, they said, would provide ways of replacing the earth's natural resources and still improve quality of life without desecrating the environment. It was like giving blind men flashlights.

Whole geographic regions have had to be abandoned because of massive environmental destruction. Times Beach, once a thriving Missouri town, is vacant because dioxin and other chemicals have permeated the soil and groundwater in that area; the nuclear accident outside Paris only six years ago has made that area off-limits to humanity for at least another 50 years, possibly more; the coastline along northern England has become uninhabitable after the earthquake of 1996 threw many off-shore drilling rigs into the sea and released unquantified amounts of oil into the ocean and onto the beach.

How I wish we had seen the human predicament earlier. Forty years ago, a now-forgotten author named John McPhee sounded a very poignant warning: "What if the world's geologic time was compressed into the six days of creation of Genesis. On this scale, a day equals something like 660 million years—thus all day Monday and until Tuesday noon God was busy getting the earth going; life began Tuesday noon and developed over the next four days. At 4:00 p.m. Saturday, the big reptiles came. Five hours later, the redwoods appeared and there were no more big reptiles. At three minutes before midnight, man appeared. At one quarter of a second before midnight, Christ appeared. At one fortieth of a second before midnight the Industrial Revolution began. We are surrounded by people who think what we have been doing for 1/40 of a second can go on indefinitely. They are considered NORMAL, but they are STARK RAVING MAD."

John Locke said, "Hell is truth seen too late." And my hell—as Secretary of the Interior—is seeing the truth too late. Don't blame the President—blame our collective myopia.

There is a human imperative that makes man the most important species—not, perhaps, to geology; not perhaps, to theology, but clearly to the political process. We would have been much better off if birds did vote, but they don't—and they won't. And we never thought globally, nor did we act locally.

LIFE ON EARTH IS GETTING BETTER[3]

If we lift our gaze from the frightening daily headlines and look instead at wide-ranging scientific data as well as the evidence of our senses, we shall see that economic life in the United States and the rest of the world has been getting better rather than worse

[3]Excerpted from an article by Julian L. Simon, professor of economics and business administration at the University of Illinois at Urbana-Champaign. *The Futurist.* 17:7–12+. Ag. '83. Copyright© 1983 by the World Future Society, Bethesda, MD 20814-5089. Reprinted by permission.

during recent centuries and decades. There is, moreover, no persuasive reason to believe that these trends will not continue indefinitely.

But first: I am *not* saying that all is well everywhere, and I do not predict that all will be rosy in the future. Children are hungry and sick; people live out lives of physical or intellectual poverty, with little opportunity for improvement; war or some new pollution may finish us. What I *am* saying is that for most relevant economic matters I have checked, aggregate trends are improving rather than deteriorating. Also, I do not say that a better future will happen automatically or without effort. It will happen because men and women will use muscle and mind to struggle with problems that they will probably overcome, as they have in the past.

Longer and Healthier Lives

Life cannot be good unless you are alive. Plentiful resources and a clean environment have little value unless we and others are alive to enjoy them. The fact that your chances of living through any given age now are much better than in earlier times must therefore mean that life has gotten better. In France, for example, female life expectancy at birth rose from under 30 years in the 1740s to 75 years in the 1960s. And this trend has not yet run its course. The increases have been rapid in recent years in the United States: a 2.1-year gain between 1970 and 1976 versus a 0.8-year gain in the entire decade of the 1960s. This pattern is now being repeated in the poorer countries of the world as they improve their economic lot. Life expectancy at birth in low-income countries rose from an average of 35.2 years in 1950 to 49.9 years in 1978, a much bigger jump than the rise from 66.0 to 73.5 years in the industrialized countries.

The threat of our loved ones dying greatly affects our assessment of the quality of our lives. Infant mortality is a reasonable measure of child mortality generally. In Europe in the eighteenth and nineteenth centuries, 200 or more children of each thousand died during their first year. As late as 1900, infant mortality was 200 per 1000 or higher in Spain, Russia, Hungary, and even Germany. Now it is about 15 per 1000 or less in a great many countries.

Health has improved, too. The incidence of both chronic and acute conditions has declined. While a perceived "epidemic" of cancer indicates to some a drop in the quality of life, the data show no increase in cancer except for deaths due to smoking-caused lung cancer. As Philip Handler, president of the National Academy of Sciences, said:

The United States is not suffering an "epidemic of cancer," it is experiencing an "epidemic of life"—in that an ever greater fraction of the population survives to the advanced ages at which cancer has always been prevalent. The overall, age-corrected incidence of cancer has not been increasing; it has been declining slowly for some years.

Abating Pollution

About pollution now: The main air pollutants—particulates and sulfur dioxide—have declined since 1960 and 1970 respectively, the periods for which there is data in the U.S. The Environmental Protection Agency's Pollutant Standard Index, which takes into account all the most important air pollutants, shows that the number of days rated "unhealthful" has declined steadily since the index's inauguration in 1974. And the proportion of monitoring sites in the U.S. having good drinking water has greatly increased since record-keeping began in 1961.

Pollution in the less-developed countries is a different, though not necessarily discouraging, story. No worldwide pollution data are available. Nevertheless, it is reasonable to assume that pollution of various kinds has increased as poor countries have gotten somewhat less poor. Industrial pollution rises along with new factories. The same is true of consumer pollution—junked cars, plastic wrappers, and such oddments as the hundreds of discarded antibiotics vials I saw on the ground in an isolated Iranian village. Such industrial wastes do not exist in the poorest pre-industrial countries. And in the early stages of development, countries and people are not ready to pay for clean-up operations. But further increases in income almost surely will bring about pollution abatement, just as increases in income in the United States have provid-

ed the wherewithal for better garbage collection and cleaner air
and water.

The Myth of Finite Resources

Though natural resources are a smaller part of the economy
with every succeeding year, they are still important, and their
availability causes grave concern to many. Yet, measured by cost
or price, the scarcity of all raw materials except lumber and oil
has been *decreasing* rather than increasing over the long run.
There has been an enormous decline in the price of copper relative
to wages in the U.S.; this relative price is the most important measure of scarcity because it shows the cost of the material in the most
valuable of goods: human time. The price of copper has even been
declining relative to the consumer price index.

Perhaps surprisingly, oil also shows a downward cost trend in
the long run. The price rise in the 1970s was purely political; the
cost of producing a barrel of oil in the Persian Gulf is still only
perhaps 15 to 25 cents.

There is no reason to believe that the supply of energy is finite,
or that the price will not continue its long-run decrease. This
statement may sound less preposterous if you consider that for a
quantity to be finite it must be measurable. The future supply of
oil includes what we usually think of as oil, plus the oil that can
be produced from shale, tar sands, and coal. It also includes the
oil from plants that we grow, whose key input is sunlight. So the
measure of the future oil supply must therefore be at least as large
as the sun's 7 billion or so years of future life. And it may include
other suns whose energy might be exploited in the future. Even
if you believe that one can in principle measure the energy from
suns that will be available in the future—a belief that requires a
lot of confidence that the knowledge of the physical world we have
developed in the past century will not be superseded in the next
7 billion years, plus the belief that the universe is not expanding—
this measurement would hardly be relevant for any practical con-
temporary decision-making.

Energy provides a good example of the process by which resources become more abundant and hence cheaper. Seventeenth-

century England was full of alarm at an impending energy short-age due to the country's deforestation for firewood. People feared a scarcity of fuel for both heating and the vital iron industry. This impending scarcity led inventors and businessmen to develop coal.

Then, in the mid-1800s, the English came to worry about an impending coal crisis. . . . But spurred by the impending scarcity of coal (and of whale oil, whose story comes next), ingenious and profit-minded people developed oil into a more desirable fuel than coal ever was. And today England exports both coal and oil.

Another strand in the story: Because of increased demand due to population growth and increased income, the price of whale oil used in lamps jumped in the 1840s. Then the Civil War pushed it even higher, leading to a whale oil "crisis." The resulting high price provided an incentive for imaginative and enterprising peo-ple to discover and produce substitutes. First came oil from rape-seed, olives, linseed, and pine trees. Then inventors learned how to get coal oil from coal, which became a flourishing industry. Other ingenious persons produced kerosene from the rock oil that seeped to the surface. Kerosene was so desirable a product that its price rose from 75 cents to $2 a gallon, which stimulated enter-prisers to increase its supply. Finally, Edwin L. Drake sunk his famous oil well in Titusville, Pennsylvania. Learning how to re-fine the oil took a while, but in a few years there were hundreds of small refiners in the U.S. Soon the bottom dropped out of the whale oil market: the price fell from $2.50 or more a gallon at its peak around 1866 to well below a dollar.

Lumber has been cited as an exception to the general resource story of falling costs. For decades in the U.S., farmers clearing land disposed of trees as a nuisance. As lumber came to be more a commercial crop and a good for builders and railroad men, its price rose. For some time, resource economists expected the price to hit a plateau and then follow the course of other raw materials as the transition to a commercial crop would be completed. There was evidence consistent with this view in the increase, rather than the popularly supposed decrease, in the tree stock in the U.S., yet for some time the price did not fall. But now that expectation seems finally to have been realized as prices of lumber have fallen to a fourth of their peak in the late 1970s.

More Food for More People

Food is an especially important resource, and the evidence indicates that its supply is increasing despite rising population. The long-run prices of food relative to wages, and even relative to consumer goods, are down. Famine deaths have decreased in the past century even in absolute terms, let alone relative to the much larger population, a special boon for poor countries. Per person food production in the world is up over the last 30 years and more. And there are no data showing that the people at the bottom of the income distribution have fared worse, or have failed to share in the general improvement, as the average has improved. Africa's food production per capita is down, but that clearly stems from governmental blunders with price controls, subsidies, farm collectivization, and other institutional problems.

There is, of course, a food-production problem in the U.S. today: too much production. Prices are falling due to high productivity, falling consumer demand for meat in the U.S., and increased foreign competition in such crops as soybeans. In response to the farmers' complaints, the government will now foot an unprecedentedly heavy bill for keeping vast amounts of acreage out of production.

The Disappearing-Species Scare

Many are alarmed that the earth is losing large numbers of its species. For example, the *Global 2000 Report to the President* says: "Extinctions of plant and animal species will increase dramatically. Hundreds of thousands of species—perhaps as many as 20 percent of all species on earth—will be irretrievably lost as their habitats vanish, especially in tropical forests," by the year 2000.

The available facts, however, are not consistent with the level of concern expressed in *Global 2000*, nor do they warrant the various policies suggested to deal with the purported dangers.

The *Global 2000* projection is based upon a report by contributor Thomas Lovejoy, who estimates that between 437,000 and 1,875,000 extinctions will occur out of a present estimated total of 3 to 10 million species. Lovejoy's estimate is based on a linear relationship running from 0% species extinguished at 0% tropical forest cleared, to about 95% extinguished at 100% tropical forest cleared. (The main source of differences in the range of estimated losses is the range of 3 to 10 million species in the overall estimate.)

The basis of any useful projection must be a body of experience collected under a range of conditions that encompass the expected conditions, or that can reasonably be extrapolated to the expected conditions. But none of Lovejoy's references seems to contain any scientifically impressive body of experience.

A projected drop in the amount of tropical forests underlies Lovejoy's projection of species losses in the future. Yet to connect these two events as Lovejoy has done requires systematic evidence relating an amount of tropical forest removed to a rate of species reduction. Neither *Global 2000* nor any of the other sources I checked give such empirical evidence. If there is no better evidence for Lovejoy's projected rates, one could extrapolate almost any rate one chooses for the year 2000. Until more of the facts are in, we need not undertake alarmist protection policies. Rather, we need other sorts of data to estimate extinction rates and decide on policy. None of this is to say that we need not worry about endangered species. The planet's flora and fauna constitute a valuable natural endowment; we must guard them as we do our other physical and social assets. But we should also strive for a clear, unbiased view of this set of assets in order to make the best possible judgments about how much time and money to spend guarding them, in a world where this valuable activity must compete with other valuable activities, including the preservation of other assets and human life.

More Wealth from Less Work

One of the great trends of economic history is the shortening of the workweek coupled with increasing income. A shorter workweek represents an increase in one's freedom to dispose of that most treasured possession—time—as one wishes. In the U.S., the decline was from about 60 hours per week in 1870 to less than 40 hours at present. This benign trend is true for an array of countries in which the length of the workweek shows an inverse relationship with income.

With respect to progress in income generally, the most straightforward and meaningful index is the proportion of persons in the labor force working in agriculture. In 1800, the percentage in the U.S. was 73.6%, whereas in 1980 the proportion was 2.7%. That is, relative to population size, only 1/25 as many persons today are working in agriculture as in 1800. This suggests that the effort that produced one bushel of grain or one loaf of bread in 1800 will now produce the bushel of grain plus what 24 other bushels will buy in other goods, which is equivalent to an increase in income by a factor of 25.

Income in less-developed countries has not reached nearly so high a level as in the more-developed countries, by definition. But it would be utterly wrong to think that income in less-developed countries has stagnated rather than risen. In fact, income per person has increased at a proportional rate at least as fast, or faster, in less-developed than in more-developed countries since World War II.

The Ultimate Resource

What explains the enhancement of our material life in the face of supposed limits to growth? I offer an extended answer in my recent book, *The Ultimate Resource* (1981). In short, the source of our increased economic blessings is the human mind, and, all other things being equal, when there are more people, there are more productive minds. Productivity increases come directly from the additional minds that develop productive new ideas, as well as indirectly from the impact upon industrial productivity of the additional demand for goods. That is, population growth in the form of babies or immigrants helps in the long run to raise the standard of living because it brings increased productivity. Immigrants are the best deal of all because they usually migrate when they are young and strong; in the U.S., they contribute more in taxes to the public coffers than they take out in welfare services.

In the short run, of course, additional people mean lower income for other people because children must be fed and housed by their parents, and educated and equipped partly by the community. Even immigrants are a burden for a brief time until they find jobs. But after the children grow up and enter the work force, and contribute to the support of others as well as increasing productivity, their net effect upon others becomes positive. Over their lifetimes they are a boon to others.

I hope you will now agree that the long-run outlook is for a more abundant material life rather than for increased scarcity, in the U.S. and in the world as a whole. Of course, such progress does not come about automatically. And my message certainly is not one of complacency. In this I agree with the doomsayers—that our world needs the best efforts of all humanity to improve our lot. I part company with them in that they expect us to come to a bad end despite the efforts we make, whereas I expect a continuation of successful efforts. Their message is self-fulfilling because if you expect inexorable natural limits to stymie your efforts you are likely to feel resigned and give up. But if you recognize the possibility—indeed, the probability—of success, you can tap large reserves of energy and enthusiasm. Energy and enthusiasm, together with the human mind and spirit, constitute our solid hope for the economic future, just as they have been our salvation in ages past. With these forces at work, we will leave a richer, safer, and more beautiful world to our descendants, just as our ancestors improved the world that they bestowed upon us.

SIMON AND KAHN VERSUS GLOBAL 2000[4]

Futurist Herman Kahn, who died of a heart attack on 7 July, 1983, left behind a partially completed book that has attracted a good deal of attention even though it will not appear until some time next year. Coedited by Kahn and economist Julian Simon,

[4]Reprint of an article by Constance Holden, staff writer. *Science.* 221:341+. Jl. 22, '83. Copyright© 1983 by the American Association for the Advancement of Science. Reprinted by permission.

who shares Kahn's optimistic vision of the future of the globe, the book is an attempt to refute the conclusions of *Global 2000,* an influential report issued by the Carter Administration in 1980.

Global 2000 said that if present policies continue, the future in terms of population, resources, and the environment does not look good. Simon, who teaches at the University of Illinois, and Kahn, who headed the Hudson Institute, have argued, in contrast, that the trends by and large look fine and that the world will sort itself out if left to its own devices.

The two schools of thought have met in some preliminary skirmishes. . . . Presumably the debate will heat up when the book, christened *Global 2000 Revised* and financed by the Heritage Foundation, comes out. But whether it will instruct or further confuse the interested public is open to question.

Global 2000 is, in its way, confused enough. The three-volume study, which is the government's first attempt at a coordinated analysis of the global environment/resources picture, used the resources of 14 agencies and several outside sources to analyze 11 selected "elements," such as food, water, and energy. Although teeming with qualifications and alternate scenarios, it came out with a general picture which, while it steers clear of apocalyptic visions, is not too happy. It predicts that the world is likely to be confronted with ever higher prices for food, oil, minerals, and fertilizer. In less-developed countries (LDC's) it sees increasing soil erosion, little room for expansion of cropland, water shortages, deforestation, loss of species, more overcrowding, and more pollution.

Recommendations based on the report, *Global Future: A Time to Act,* came out in the last days of the Carter Administration and sank out of sight with Carter. As for the original report, it inspired the formation of a coalition called Global Tomorrow (chaired by Russell Peterson, chairman of the National Audubon Society), which recently held a conference in Washington on the report; and a Year 2000 Committee of prominent men (chaired by Russell Train, head of the World Wildlife Fund-U.S.), which is pushing global foresight legislation and doing studies of private sector global data use.

Global 2000 may have a "juggernaut" behind it (Simon's term), but Kahn and Simon have tried to balance it by gathering what Simon calls a group of "world class" authors for their book. The executive summary, which has been widely circulated, is far more provocative than the contributions. Written by Simon and Kahn, it explicitly contradicts the wording in *Global 2000,* saying, "If present trends continue, the world in 2000 will be less crowded, less polluted, more stable ecologically, and less vulnerable to resource-supply disruption than the world we live in now." Based on historical trends, it predicts declining scarcity, lowering prices and increased wealth. Trends in forests are "not worrisome," and "there is no evidence for the rapid loss of species." Simon frequently extrapolates from United States trends to predict developments in LDC's: For example, he says that as people get richer they will have more floor space in their homes. They will also have better roads and more vehicles. So they will have more room just as Americans have more than they did at the turn of the century.

As for the papers by the 23 authors, Simon and Kahn did not insist they toe the line and most of them eschew extreme positions. Nonetheless, despite the fact that *Global 2000* and *Global 2000 Revised* draw on many of the same original data sources, many findings are distinctly opposed.

Take, for comparison, the food and agriculture paper by D. Gale Johnson of the University of Chicago and the *Global 2000* food section. The two analyses differ markedly in their assessment of the role of fuel prices and environmental disruption in agriculture production. Johnson says that, according to the Food and Agriculture Organization (FAO), there will be an annual rise of 2.8 percent in food production in LDC's—more than enough for nutritional improvement. There is little need to bring new land into production because high yield practices (fertilizer, pesticides, and irrigation) are more efficient. Fertilizer prices, which have remained low, are not necessarily tied to petroleum prices, he says. Increases in per capita income make it implausible that an increasing share of resources will be into food production—as predicted by *Global 2000*—particularly since the percentage of the world's labor force engaged in agriculture has been declining. Prices of basic commodities such as grain and vegetable oils will stay low and may even decline. Increases in life expectancy indicate that malnutrition is declining. "Unavailability of food is no longer an important source of famine" (rather, it is war and strife). Johnson says that his projections are likely to prove valid if hindrances like trade restrictions and artificially low farm prices are removed.

Global 2000 used the government's grain-oilseed-livestock model to conclude that food production will increase at a 2.2 percent annual rate. Because of rising petroleum costs, however, it predicts a 95 percent increase in food prices. It sees rapid rises in costs of fertilizer, pesticides and fuel, and diminishing returns because of accelerated erosion, loss of soil fertility and irrigation damage. Cropland may increase by only 4 percent because the good land is already cultivated and quality land is being lost to urbanization. It says that the World Bank estimates the number of malnourished people in LDC's could rise to 1.3 billion in 2000 and a substantial increase in the share of the world's resources devoted to food production will be needed to meet demand.

There are similar conflicts between the two studies in their analysis of world fisheries. John Wise says that the world haul, now at 70 million tonnes a year, will probably continue to increase for the next two decades. It will reach the FAO-predicted total of 100 to 120 million tonnes by 2000. Primary gains could come from improved management and harvesting or lightly exploited stocks. Possible further gains could come from finding new ways to fish krill and other unconventional species; developing ways to use fish meal directly as human food, and reducing discards at sea, and spoilage. Although overfishing has been a problem, pollution has had little effect on large-scale marine fisheries.

Global 2000 asserts that traditional marine fish populations are now fully exploited, and the generally accepted annual potential of 100 million tonnes is unlikely on a sustained basis. Even if that figure is reached it would supply slightly less protein per capita—for a population of 6.35 billion—than it does now. (Wise, using the same figures, finds an increase in per capita protein.) Increasing ocean pollution is likely to effect significant reduction in yields, and improved technology has already masked real declines in fish populations. Increased harvest from lightly exploited areas and nontraditional species are inhibited by severe economic (that is, oil prices), technological, and management constraints.

An indication of the problems in forecasting fish catches is that the two analyses even differ on trends over the past decade, although they use the same set of figures. Wise, for example, maintains that the global haul rose by 10 percent in the 1970's, while *Global 2000* says the harvest leveled off in 1970.

Why the radical discrepancies, not only in future projections but in assessment of the current situation? There appear to be at least two explanations, one relating to the methodology, and the other to underlying assumptions.

In the Kahn-Simon book, the subjects are pretty much treated in isolation, with no reference to what may be pertinent trends outside the author's field. The creators of *Global 2000*, on the other hand, went through an agonizing process trying to integrate the data on each topic with data on everything else. This was extremely difficult because the computerized models used by each agency are generally devoted to narrow sectoral concerns or designed to justify particular policies. The energy model, for example, was intended to prove Project Independence would work by 1985.

Modelers often make assumptions about resources availability without referring to related efforts in other departments. Someone engaged in crop forecasting, for example, will assume the availability of a certain amount of water, which is also needed by an energy planner. So the two analysts may end up assuming 150 percent of the available water. . . .

Nonetheless, after coordinating all the diverse sources, the creators of *Global 2000* felt they had come up with the best data available.

Kahn and Simon are inclined to think *Global 2000*'s struggles were nothing but a huge waste of time. "Our philosophy is totally different," Kahn said last month. "We are hostile to big models . . . any attempt to have a global model to integrate everything becomes uncontrollable" and is "of dubious value." What about resolving inconsistencies? "If you find inconsistencies the model is better off without them." Simon agrees that the number of factors calibrated into an analysis has to be reasonably small or "you'll never get on with your work." For example, the Kahn-Simon summary says: "The future price of energy is not a key input for estimating the future price and quantity of food." They believe in trend analysis: extrapolating "simplistically with ruler and pencil" produces better results, said Kahn. All the global modelers get is *gigo*—"garbage in, gospel out."

Methodology, then, is one of the main areas where the two works differ. Another is in their concepts of the overall direction of human history. *Global 2000* depicts a time of historical discontinuity in which traditional ways of doing things and the old supply-demand equations will lead eventually to pillage and desecration of natural resources and increasing human misery. *Global 2000 Revised* reflects a belief in humanity's continuing ability to sort everything out for the best.

Global 2000 Revised also seems to put a lot more faith in man's ingenuity and the rate of technological advance than does *Global 2000*. For example, if the oil runs out, the former believes new substitutes will be found, whereas the latter is more likely to see higher prices and more pressures on the environment.

The free play of market forces—including natural ones—is fundamental to the Simon-Kahn vision, whereas the problems as *Global 2000* sees them would seem to call for government policy changes on every level.

The faith in the ability of market forces always to promote equilibrium is apparently why it was not deemed crucial to have a discussion of population growth in *Global 2000 Revised*. There is a paper by Mark Perlman of the University of Pittsburgh on the difficulties of making population projections, but according to Simon, the editors decided not to go into the implications of such growth because they did not want to divide the authors. Anyway, he said, populations level off by themselves when they reach a certain stage of economic well-being. Needless to say, *Global 2000* is not complacent about population growth.

Finally, as Kahn pointed out, there is a real difference in the way the two reports view nature. *Global 2000* is very much an environmentalist document; the subject is a core consideration in every topic discussed. Not so in the Simon-Kahn book: there is no mention of environmental considerations, for example, in the energy or agriculture articles. Kahn said the omission is appropriate:

he took the Old Testament view that "everything that creeps or crawls exists for man's benefit," which, he said, is basically the attitude of traditional western culture and one that is shared by the authors (with an exception for Roger Revelle of the University of California at La Jolla who gave permission for a paper on land to be reprinted but who is "not very enthusiastic" about their approach). Kahn argued that *Global 2000* reflects a trend toward eastern thinking in which every living thing is believed to have an intrinsic right to exist.

Simon and Kahn's views correspond in many respects to those of the Reagan Administration. Some of the ideas are explicitly stated in a paper drafted in January, reportedly by presidential adviser Danny J. Boggs, for the Global Issues Working Group, which advises the Cabinet Council on Natural Resources and Environment.

After quoting from the somber introduction of *Global 2000*, the paper says "Rather, from our experience . . . if the economies and societies of much of the world remain reasonably free, if technological advance is permitted to continue, and if prices are permitted to bring changes in supply and demand into equilibrium, the world in the year 2000 will, in general, be a better place for most people than it is today. Although there will be more people in the world, each of them should have more individual living space. . . . There will very likely be greter material output for each person. . . . In many cases, technological and economic advance will be the key . . . to . . . environmental progress."

The paper goes on to discuss the value of global modeling and the improvement of government "foresight" capability, which has become of particular concern to the *Global 2000* groups. People like Train and Peterson are pushing hard to get some kind of legislation passed that would improve the government's ability to make comprehensive analyses and recommendations related to global population, resource, and environmental trends. Proposals vary, but basically the idea is not to have a monolithic global model—which all agree would be undesirable—but to facilitate interaction among various models, get the assumptions documented, the data more compatible and the inconsistencies made explicit. There are currently two bills pending: one introduced by Representatives Albert Gore, Jr. (D-Tenn.), and Newt Gingrich (R-Ga.) would establish an "office of critical trends analysis" in the White House to evaluate trends and the impact of government policies on them. The other by Senator Mark Hatfield (D-Ore.) would establish a "council on global resources, the environment and population" to improve projections. It also calls for a national policy of population stabilization.

Innocuous as the legislation may seem, people have definitely political reasons for supporting or opposing it. Boggs, in the White House document, says the "tendency of such a centralization in an office would be to promote its capture and use by those who advocate a higher degree of governmental direction." He also notes that the "celebrated alarmist reports of the past . . . have underestimated the adjustive capacity and technological innovation of people" and have been "determinedly anti-market and anti-improvement by nongovernmental means."

Speaking at the conference held by the Global Tomorrow Coalition, Boggs pointed out that foresight can be wrong, as illustrated by such analyses as *Famine 75* by William and Paul Paddock and Paul Ehrlich's *Population Bomb*. "Would you want such an office run by Julian Simon or Herman Kahn?" he asked. Boggs later told *Science* he didn't think the problems of coordinating models was as great as *Global 2000* made out. He said "The notion that there is this commodity called foresight and if you will only buy a tube of it you'll come out with the right answers seems to me disingenuous." Supporters of the legislation, he felt, were saying "the world is going to hell in a handbasket and by passing this law we really want to confess it and say so."

Boggs is on target in the last remark. An environmentalist told *Science* the Administration disliked the idea because it knew improved foresight would present facts that did not fit its dogma.

The Global Issues Working Group is currently preparing a report on the appropriate governmental role in global issues—presumably an expanded version of the January document. In view of the political and methodological poles represented by *Global 2000* and *Global 2000 Revised,* it will be interesting to see what they come up with. Alan Hill, chairman of the Council on Environmental Quality (CEQ), who initiated the study, says it will be a general document on resource, environment, and population issues to come out around the first of the year. "We've avoided saying this will be our answer to *Global 2000*," he says, explaining that the data will be better, thanks to the spadework done in the course of preparing that report. CEQ has also commissioned the World Wildlife Fund to look at the global data needs of the private sector.

It appears then that *Global 2000*, while it has not had the intended impact on governmental policy, is serving as the basis for ever-widening circles of dialogue about global issues. Rather than scaring the public out of its wits, as critics have claimed, the growing coalition spawned by the report is provoking others to reexamine common assertions about the world situation. So market forces are at work on the commodity, knowledge.

WAR OVER WATER[5]

The drought and heat wave that scorched the nation this summer are intensifying already fierce competition over America's most precious and most wasted resource—water.

From bone-dry deserts of the West to lush fields of the Northeast, conflicts over water are erupting with increasing frequency. It is a war pitting region against region, state against state, city against city.

Farmers are competing with urban residents and industry for dwindling supplies. Indians have launched a campaign to recapture water rights taken from them more than a century ago. Some of the largest metropolitan centers, plagued by aging water mains and inadequate reservoirs, are walking a tightrope between barely adequate supplies and severe shortages. Publicly and privately owned power companies are scrapping over water to generate low-cost electricity.

[5]Reprint of an article by Kenneth Sheets, staff writer. *U.S. News* & *World Report*. 95:57–62. O. 31, '83. Copyright© 1983 by U.S. News & World Report, Inc. Reprinted by permission.

"The issue of water rights is like a bomb sitting there ready to explode," declares Ken Dickson, director of the Institute of Applied Sciences at North Texas State University in Denton.

Unlike showdowns of the frontier era, today's water wars are waged not by cattlemen and sodbusters armed with guns but by lawyers, lobbyists and politicians fighting in courtrooms, legislatures and the halls of Congress. The disputes are complex, the political and economic stakes enormous.

Without more water, booming urban hubs such as Los Angeles and Phoenix will stop growing and could even shrivel. The massive shift of industry from the Northeast and Midwest to the sun belt could grind to a halt. Huge agricultural empires might revert to desert. One thing is certain: In the end, everyone will be paying more for water as competition for clean, plentiful supplies increases.

Mother Nature's Pranks

Statistically, at least, the U.S. should not have a water problem at all. About 4.2 trillion gallons of rain and snow fall on the contiguous 48 states on a typical day, while Americans use only 450 billion gallons daily. But the supply is unevenly distributed, most of it concentrated in the eastern half of the country and in the Pacific Northwest. Even there, reserves are being stretched thin as more rivers, lakes and aquifers become polluted and undrinkable.

Since the beginning of this century, the U.S. population has increased about 200 percent while per capita water use has shot up 500 to 800 percent. By 1980, water use reached some 2,000 gallons a day for each man, woman and child in the U.S.—a 22 percent increase from 1970. Americans use three times as much water per capita as the Japanese.

Notes Larry Silverman, executive director of the American Clean Water Association: "The nation's water consumption is increasing faster than our population growth."

Many experts compare today's water problems to the energy crunch of the 1970s. Water, they predict, will be "the resource crisis of the '80s."

California: North vs. South

A crisis over water already exists in California, scene of a battle between the arid, fast-growing southern end of the state and the water-rich north. The fight has raged for decades, and peace is nowhere in sight.

Northern California receives more than two thirds of the state's rainfall, but more than 60 percent of the population lives in the desertlike south. Southern Californians claim their northern neighbors are allowing "surplus" water to flow out to sea unused. Those living in the north contend that any water shipped south would be wasted on filling swimming pools and watering lawns.

The latest round was fought in 1982, when voters soundly rejected a plan to build a 43-mile earthen ditch—called the Peripheral Canal—that would have diverted water from the Sacramento-San Joaquin River Delta and pumped it south through aqueducts and waterways.

Southern California claims it desperately needs to divert water from the north, since it soon will lose by court decree some of the water it now is drawing from the Colorado River. Environmentalists also have filed lawsuits to cut Los Angeles's take from the Owens Valley and Mono Lake Basin, which supplies 80 percent of the city's water.

Already, Southern California is eying new ways to divert water from the north. Says an official of the Los Angeles Metropolitan Water District: "The question is not whether surplus water that originates in the north will be sent to the south. The question is how." Responds Stanford University's Prof. Joseph Franzini, an expert on water problems: "Does it make any sense to have millions of people living in Southern California, where the water has to be brought immense distances at incredible cost? If you keep providing them with water, the millions will continue to grow, and the problem will become larger. Maybe the time has come to put a moratorium on any further extension of water supply to new areas in the desert."

Shrinking Farms

Another water conflict is forcing major changes in California's San Joaquin Valley and eventually could affect 148,000 farmers in 17 Western states who now receive cheap water from federal projects.

The struggle began more than a decade ago when a coalition of environmentalists, small farmers and agrarian reformers persuaded the courts to strictly enforce the Reclamation Act of 1902, which aimed to bring irrigation water to the arid West and settle small family farmers on 160-acre tracts. Over the years, the government looked the other way as farmers ignored the 160-acre limit and built huge spreads covering thousands of acres. Many of the farms receiving federally subsidized water are owned by absentee landlords and big corporations.

In an effort to avoid strict enforcement of the 160-acre limit, big landowners mounted a counterattack in Congress, where lobbyists reportedly spent up to $250,000 a month to get favorable legislation. What emerged was a compromise: A limit of 960 acres on individual landholdings and higher water rates for those who continue farming more than that. Many large farms will be unaffected, because a family will be entitled to 960 acres per adult member. But corporate farmers such as the Southern Pacific Transportation Company, which owns 106,000 acres in the big Westlands Water District, will be forced to sell some of their holdings.

Farmers in the San Joaquin Valley still are trying to decide how to deal with the changes, but Representative George Miller (D-Calif.) predicts they will lead to "a revolution in Western water use, conservation and agriculture."

The Precious Colorado

Southern California faces its current predicament because it lost a long, bitter campaign when the Supreme Court affirmed Arizona's right to some of the Colorado River water now flowing to the Los Angeles area.

By the mid-1980s, when the Central Arizona Project is complete, Arizona will be able to transport Colorado River water to Phoenix, Tucson and other metropolitan areas by a series of canals and aqueducts. The water Arizona will get now provides about half the water used by 13 million people in Southern California. In times of drought, it has been the only source of supply.

"If we have dry years after we lose the Colorado River water, the people in the south will be in a pinch," says Don Owen, an official of the California Department of Water Resources. "There will be water rationing."

Arizona says it needs Colorado River water for its growing population and industry. The state now gets most of its water from aquifers that are being rapidly depleted, mostly by agricultural demands. Every year, Arizonans pump twice as much water out of the ground as nature returns to it.

Since there is not enough water to meet all the needs of competing interests—even with water from the Colorado—Arizona farmers are losing the fight for survival.

Under a plan enacted in 1980, farmers are being required to pay sharply higher prices for water to irrigate their cotton, alfalfa, pecan groves and citrus trees. The goal is to force them to sell their land for other uses by the year 2006. If not enough farmers sell out by then, the state will begin buying up farmlands to retire them from production.

Arizonans are betting that an influx of high-technology industries will make up for the loss of agriculture, which now contributes 2 billion dollars a year to the economy.

New Mexico: Surrounded

Although one of the driest states in the U.S., New Mexico is being attacked from all sides by water-hungry neighbors.

The most controversial encounter involves New Mexico and El Paso, a Texas city of 425,000 with a faltering water supply. El Paso has obtained water rights in southern New Mexico and plans to drill wells and pipe water across the border.

In response to what it called this act of "piracy," New Mexico invoked a law that banned the export of water. However, a federal court ruled last January that the law was an unconstitutional interference with interstate commerce. New Mexico lawmakers promptly passed new legislation to circumvent the court's decision. El Paso is suing to get the new law declared unconstitutional, too.

Says John Sapolek, an official of the Elephant Butte, N.M., irrigation district: "As far as we're concerned, this is nothing less than a well-planned invasion by a foreign country, and we'd rather spend our last dollar fighting El Paso than lie down."

New Mexico and Texas also are battling over how to divide water from the Pecos River and the Rio Grande. On another front, New Mexico is locked in combat with Colorado over use of the Vermejo River, which originates in the mountains of southern Colorado and flows through New Mexico.

Eyes of Texas

Faced with chronic water problems, especially in the arid western half of the state, Texas is casting covetous glances at its more fortunate neighbors.

The state needs water to replace supplies now being drawn from the Ogallala aquifer, a huge underground lake sprawling from northern Texas through parts of Oklahoma, New Mexico, Kansas, Colorado, Nebraska, Wyoming and South Dakota.

The Ogallala provides irrigation water pumped through 170,000 wells for 14.3 million acres of land that produce 15 percent of the nation's total value of wheat, corn, sorghum and cotton and 38 percent of the livestock.

The huge demand for water is rapidly draining the Ogallala. About 24 million acre-feet a year are being withdrawn, while nature is replacing only 3 million. An acre-foot is the liquid it takes to cover 1 acre of land to a depth of 1 foot—325,851 gallons. Experts warn that many parts of the aquifer will be drained early in the next century.

To avoid that, Texas has talked for years about importing water, preferably from the Mississippi River, only to run into opposition from Arkansas and Louisiana. Even Texas voters have rejected proposals that would have financed a water-importation scheme, contending that it was not worth the estimated 20.6-billion-dollar price tag.

Colorado's Search for Peace

Like California's, Colorado's water problems stem from lopsided population and moisture patterns. While 80 percent of the population lives east of the Rockies, mainly in Denver, almost 70 percent of the water supply is west of the Continental Divide. Result: Constant bickering among water-starved Denver, the state's west slope and environmentalists.

Colorado is trying a unique approach to mediating disputes before they get out of hand. The vehicle is the Metropolitan Water Roundtable, a 30-member group created in 1981 to formulate plans for meeting Denver's future water needs without acrimony. The roundtable includes representatives from all interested parties, including environmentalists and west-slope governments.

So far, the mediation effort has resulted in an agreement that would permit Denver to divert water from the west slope. In exchange, Denver has agreed to implement a major water-conservation program and build a reservoir on the west slope to offset the impact of diversion.

"The history of state water development was an eye-for-an-eye, tooth-for-a-tooth situation that had left us all toothless and blind," says Colorado Governor Richard Lamm, chairman of the roundtable.

Adds Bob Golten, an attorney for the National Wildlife Federation: "This far surpasses litigation as a means for grappling with this thing."

High Plains Shoot-Out

In a major confrontation on the upper Great Plains, South Dakota is pitted against Iowa, Missouri and Nebraska over diversion of water from the Missouri River.

The fight started in 1981, when South Dakota sold water rights from the Missouri to a coal-slurry-pipeline company, Energy Transportation Systems, Inc., for 9 million dollars a year. The pipeline, intended to stretch from Wyoming's coal-rich Powder River basin to electric-power plants in Arkansas and Louisiana, would require 20,000 acre-feet of water from the Missouri each year—about one tenth of 1 percent of the river's annual flow of 20 million acre-feet.

The three downriver states filed suit against the Interior Department, which approved the sale. Also suing to halt the pipeline are the Kansas City Southern Railway, the Sierra Club and three chapters of the National Farmers Union.

Declares Missouri Atty. Gen. John Ashcroft: "The Missouri River provides water for drinking, agricultural production, generation of electricity and commerce. It is too important a commodity for Missourians to stand idly by while the federal government allows the river to be siphoned off."

Warren Neufeld of the South Dakota Department of Water and Natural Resources denies that the coal-slurry pipeline is a threat to the river's flow. "People downstream are exaggerating the problem beyond belief," he declares.

Another High Plains water dispute is raging over the Garrison Diversion project, a 1.1-billion-dollar network of work to irrigate 250,000 acres of farmland in central and eastern North Dakota.

First authorized by Congress in 1965, the project is only 15 percent complete and is facing mounting opposition in Congress. Because the Garrison Diversion would connect with the Hudson Bay Drainage Basin, the Canadian government fears that it would allow pollutants and trash fish to infiltrate north of the border.

"Garrison would do as much environmental damage as any water project in the U.S. today," asserts Brent Blackwelder of the Environmental Policy Center.

Retorts Senator Quentin Burdick (D-N.D.): "The main question is, do we get our fair share of the water? Missouri water is our right. They can't take that away from us."

The Indian Factor

Indian tribes recently have opened a new front in the nation's water wars that could upset the entire pattern of water use in the West.

Indians have filed about 55 lawsuits claiming rights to vast amounts of water they contend is due them under terms of peace treaties signed more than a century ago. Jim Bush, an attorney for the Western Regional Council, a coalition of Rocky Mountain business interests, says the lawsuits involve "every major water-user system and source in the West."

The problem goes back to 1908, when the Supreme Court ruled that Indians were entitled to enough water to irrigate the reservations created by treaty or executive action in the late 1800s. The concept, known as the Winters Doctrine, established Indian water rights as "senior" to virtually every other use.

If this concept is carried to the limit in Arizona, for instance, critics say, the Indians could lay claim to five times the amount of water available to the entire state.

"If Indians are given water rights on the basis of the irrigable-acres test, it would just create chaos in the Southwest," warns Wesley Steiner, director of the Arizona Department of Water Resources.

Says George Christopulos, state engineer for Wyoming: "It's as if you bought a house and later someone else claims they own it."

Joe Sparks, attorney for the San Carlos Apache and Tonto Apache tribes in Arizona argues: "At stake is the ability of Indians to participate in the economy of the U.S. in a way equivalent to non-Indians. Without water rights, Indians will be unable to do that and thus be doomed to desolation, unemployment and everything else that comes with poverty. So we're talking about the Indians' very existence and survival."

Litigation is expected to drag on for years. Meanwhile, water rights throughout the West will remain in doubt.

"Any claim not settled is a black cloud overhanging future development," asserts Arizona Governor Bruce Babbitt.

The Water Belt Fights Back

Nervously aware that the booming sun belt is eying their vast water supplies, states in the upper Midwest are moving to head off raids on the Great Lakes, which constitute the largest body of fresh water on earth.

Already, states along the Great Lakes have been approached about providing water for coal-slurry pipelines. Other planners have dreamed for decades of gigantic canal projects that would transport Great Lakes water to the Southwest. Although high costs make these projects unfeasible for now, the mere fact that they are on the drawing boards makes Great Lakes states uneasy.

One newly formed group, the Council of Great Lakes Governors, has vowed to be "unyielding in our opposition to any effort to divert our water resources to other states." Ontario's Natural Resources Minister Alan Pope has warned that Canada also will fight any plan to remove water from the Great Lakes.

Some Midwestern governors believe the region's ample water supply eventually will help regain some of the economic edge it has lost to the sunbelt over the past two decades because of a cold climate and high labor costs.

Says Ohio Governor Richard Celeste: "I hope this region becomes known as the water belt of our nation, for we are just that. And in the competition—national and global during the coming decade—we who live in the water belt . . . should have a substantial advantage if we are determined to seize it."

The East: Where Tensions Grow

Although blessed with plenty of rain and snow, even the eastern half of the U.S. is beginning to feel some of the pressures that are triggering water wars elsewhere.

In many areas, pollution of rivers, lakes and aquifers is putting a premium on supplies of clean water for drinking and recreation.

Authorities in New York City have nightmares that one of the two tunnels—built in 1917 and 1937—that bring water from reservoirs will fail before a badly needed third tunnel can be completed around the turn of the century. Failure of even one tunnel would bring what one official calls "a scenario for disaster"—people going thirsty, Wall Street and other business centers shut down, fires raging unabated.

Many older Eastern cities that have been hit hard by the recession and flight of industry to the sun belt are strapped for money to repair or replace old water mains, some of them more than a century old and made of wood. Leaking pipes cause some communities in New Jersey to lose up to 40 percent of their water before it reaches the tap.

In Massachusetts, at least 40 communities ordered curbs on water usage for a time this year because of shortages. The major problem: Not enough storage capacity. "You can have all the precipitation in the world, but it doesn't do any good if you can't store it," observes Dick Sullivan of the state's Department of Environmental Quality Engineering.

In water-rich Pennsylvania, the State Legislature is considering a law that would allow the government to allocate water among competing users. Police in Bucks County, Pa., recently arrested 46 protesters trying to halt work on a pumping station that will divert 95 million gallons of water a day from the Delaware River for use by Bucks and Montgomery counties and a nuclear power plant being built near Philadelphia.

Florida is pumping water from aquifers at such a furious rate to meet the needs of its mushrooming population that the Everglades are drying up and the ground is collapsing in some areas to create huge sinkholes. In the quest for more water, booming Tampa is trying to tap the Suwannee River, only to run into heavy opposition from county governments in northern Florida.

In addition, a new front has opened that will have widespread repercussions everywhere.

The controversy—pitting private power companies against public utilities—revolves around federally licensed hydroelectric projects that provide cheap electricity for millions of consumers. The Federal Water Power Act of 1920 and subsequent regulatory rulings give preference to utilities owned by municipalities and rural cooperatives. Even so, hundreds of hydroelectric licenses were granted to private as well as public utilities. The permits usually run for 50 years, and many are coming up for renewal over the next decade. Public utilities see this as an opening to take over private hydroelectric facilities.

At least 11 public power companies, claiming preference status, have applied for licenses now held by private utilities. The Edison Electric Institute, representing private utilities, warns that this is only the opening shot in a much bigger war. The institute says licenses for an additional 157 hydro projects will expire in the next 10 years, and more will be up for relicensing after 1993.

Higher Prices Ahead

No matter who wins in the growing struggle over water resources, this much is clear: American consumers will be paying sharply higher prices for water in coming decades.

Says Stanford's Professor Franzini: "Some cities don't even meter their water use. We should charge people the actual cost of providing them with water."

Even people living in damper climates will be forced to pay higher rates to finance construction of new reservoirs and pipelines and to repair decaying facilities.

Agriculture will be hit hardest. Many farmers could be forced out of business as they pay more of the real cost of water. John Harris, owner of a large farm in California's San Joaquin Valley, estimates that changes in the 1902 Reclamation Act will double his water bill, to 1.6 million dollars a year "without assurances of better yields or better prices."

In Texas, many farmers are switching to dry-land farming because of the high cost of pumping water. "Irrigation costs have tripled in the last five or six years," observes rancher James Mitchell of Wolfforth.

Many experts advocate higher prices to force consumers to conserve water. They note there is little logic to current rates 53 cents per 1,000 gallons in water-short El Paso and $1.78 in Philadelphia where water is abundant.

"Our water is either underpriced or not charged for at all," says Irwin Remon, a California water expert. "The most important conservation technique is to charge for water what it costs to produce."

The twin challenges of allocating ever scarcer supplies and bringing order to the pricing system guarantee that the escalating war over water will drag on for decades. Deciding who wins and who loses will go far toward shaping the U.S. of the 21st century.

IMPROVING THE BALANCE BETWEEN JOBS AND CLEAN AIR[6]

Throughout history, men and women have struggled to produce the basic essentials of food, clothing, and shelter by controlling their environment. Waste product have inevitably resulted from this struggle, and environmental quality has suffered. People slowly became aware that pollution could pose a threat to public health.

This heightened public awareness set in motion courses of action that have resulted in a cleaner environment. Legislation has been passed that prohibits the fouling of our water and air and the destruction of our natural treasures. One such piece of legislation is the Clean Air Act, originally passed in 1963. The Clean Air Act has been eminently successful—our air is considerably cleaner than it was 20 years ago. Unfortunately, the cost of implementing the act has been high, and it will continue to be costly unless the act is amended.

The 1963 act was the first significant clean air legislation. It defined the role of the Federal government as primarily a researcher on the nature of air quality. The development and implementation of emission controls on stationary sources (plants and factories) were placed with state and local officials, with local governments given the major authority. In 1965, the act was amended to address the question of auto emissions, and the Federal government stepped in as overseer.

Congress shifted to a regional approach in air quality control in 1967, but then abandoned the concept in favor of national controls with the 1970 Clean Air Act Amendments. The role of the Federal government was expanded to include the establishment of national standards for air quality—in addition to research and technical assistance to the states. Amendments passed in 1971 further increased the Federal government's role.

[6]Reprint of an article by Jerry J. Jasinowski, senior vice president and chief economist of the National Association of Manufacturers. *USA Today* [magazine]. 111:47–9. My. '83. Copyright© 1983 by the Society for the Advancement of Education. Reprinted by permission.

Since 1971, there has been increasing concern that the costs of implementing the act far outweigh the benefits. The Clean Air Act has a particularly profound impact on manufacturing operations and the economic considerations which motivate manufacturers and consumers. Unfortunately, the law is lengthy and complex, inspiring litigation and creating difficult administrative problems for both the states and the Federal government. Manufacturers who have attempted to deal with the act's complexities report frustration, inefficiency, and waste. The paperwork and cost of compliance are prohibitive. The act also places substantial hurdles before manufacturers. Rather than building new, more pollution-efficient plants, they are forced to continue operating less efficient ones. Rather than being able to provide more jobs and a better working environment, they are forced to retain the *status quo*.

A pristine environment is a worthy goal, but it is time to temper our goals with common sense. We are undergoing tough economic times, and there must be a balance between the environment and the economic health of the country. The business community has long been aware of this fact. Even Congress is beginning to take a more balanced view of the Clean Air Act—a balance that is necessary and long overdue.

Implementing Clean Air Goals

The clean air regulations take their present form largely from the 1970 Clean Air Act Amendments. That legislation defined clean air goals from three perspectives: air quality management, limits on emissions from stationary sources, and limits on emissions from mobile sources—primarily cars and trucks.

The 1977 amendments introduced two additional concepts: restrictions on industrial growth and expansion in areas where national air quality standards have not been met—called nonattainment areas; and limitations on industrial growth in areas where the air quality is better than the national standards—termed Prevention of Significant Deterioration (PSD).

The organizational framework by which these clean air goals are implemented is the State Implementation Plan (SIP). Each state is required to survey every major source of emissions within its borders and develop strategies to insure compliance with the guidelines set down by the legislation. The Environmental Protection Agency (EPA) is required to approve each state plan.

The SIP process is greatly complicated by special regulations dealing with regions that do not meet the national air quality standards and with areas where the air is cleaner than average. State plans must also be constantly revised to reflect changing rules and regulations and altered conditions in a state, and these revisions must also be approved by the EPA.

Air quality management. The major goal of the legislation passed in 1970 was to control the seven most common "criteria" air pollutants. EPA was given the task of determining the maximum allowable concentrations of each. The agency set limits for all seven: particulates, sulfur dioxide, nitrogen dioxide, hydrocarbons, ozone, carbon monoxide, and lead. Specific legislative guidelines were provided for development of the standards by which limits were set. These standards are called National Ambient Air Quality Standards (NAAQS), and they are the core of air quality management.

EPA has set two types of NAAQS—primary and secondary. Primary standards focus on public health and are intended to provide the country with an adequate margin of safety. This margin of safety has been defined to include a representative sample of certain sensitive populations, such as the elderly and asthmatics. The target date for compliance with primary standards is Dec. 31, 1982, with a five-year extension available in areas with a major automobile pollution problem. Primary standards are set without regard for cost of the availability of control technology—based on the concept that the cost and technology should not be considered when health is the issue.

Secondary air quality standards are concerned with crops, visibility, and buildings, rather than health. No deadlines have been set for their compliance.

In addition to regulating the seven major pollutants and setting NAAQS, EPA was charged with developing emission standards for hazardous pollutants such as asbestos, beryllium, mercury, and vinyl chloride. These differ from ambient air pollu-

tants in that they are usually localized and can be technically difficult and costly to control.

Limiting stationary emissions. Along with managing and
policing air quality, EPA is also responsible for developing regulations setting maximum emission limits for plants and factories.
So far, the agency has established five major control categories:
• New Source Performance Standards apply to "newly constructed or modified buildings, facilities, and installations" that could
potentially emit 100 or more tons of pollutants per year.
• Control   Technique   Guidelines   focus   on
retrofitting technology for existing plants in areas that meet
NAAQS.
• Reasonably Available Control Technology is concerned with retrofitting existing facilities in areas that do not meet NAAQS.
• Lowest Achievable Emission Rates (LAER) is mandated in areas where the ambient air does not meet national standards (non-
attainment areas).
• Best Available Control Technology is designed for use in PSD
areas.

Non-Attainment, attainment, and PSD. For enforcement
purposes, the nation is divided into 247 air quality control regions.
Each region is classified as an attainment or non-attainment area
for each of the common pollutants. A region, for example, might
be an attainment area for carbon monoxide, but fail to meet the
standards for sulfur dioxide.

Companies building or expanding plants in non-attainment
areas are required to meet the LAER's mentioned above. In addition, new industrial construction is not allowed unless a company
first obtains "offsets." A company is required to *more than offset*
any emission that will be produced by the new construction by up-
grading or closing existing, polluting facilities. In some instances,
companies have had to purchase and close operating plants to obtain the necessary offsets.

For those areas designated attainment areas, a complex system
of regulations has been developed to achieve PSD. The regulations
break PSD areas into three classes, each allowing a different level
of pollution increases termed "increments." Class I allows virtually no increases in emission, Class II allows modest incremental in-

creases, and Class III provides for considerable growth and permits quality levels to increase up to the NAAQS limits.

Companies wishing to construct facilities that could affect air quality in a PSD area must first obtain permission to use part of that region's increments—assigned on a first-come, first-served basis. The company must also demonstrate, through computer modeling studies and air quality monitoring surveys, that emissions from the new facility will not exceed the assigned increments.

Limiting mobile emissions. Clean air efforts have singled out emissions from moving sources—primarily automobiles—for special attention. The 1970 legislation mandated a 90% reduction in auto emissions of pollutants by the mid-1970's. This deadline was postponed twice, primarily for fuel efficiency reasons.

By 1980, the 90% reduction standard was met for hydrocarbons, and for carbon monoxide in 1981. The 75% standard for nitrogen oxides was also reached in 1981. These reductions are significant, since autos account for a large share of air pollutants.

Emerging Issues

A number of emerging concerns are not directly addressed by the air quality regulations. One is the developing problem of indoor pollution, where energy goals and clean air goals seem to be working at cross-purposes. Another concern is the long-range transport of air pollution, resulting in what is called acid rain.

Acid rain and snow are created when sulfur and nitrogen oxides combine with water vapor in the atmosphere. There is some evidence that the sulfur and nitrogen emissions originate from coal-burning facilities, but the evidence is inconclusive. It is a complex problem, and Congress has authorized a major study to determine its dimensions. In the meantime, many advise caution until the investigation can be completed and the causes of acid precipitation adequately defined.

The effects of the effort to improve America's air quality can be measured from two perspectives. One considers changes in air quality; the other the impact of this undertaking on economic growth, jobs, and productivity.

In a December, 1980, report, the Council on Environmental Quality observed that "the nation's air quality is continuing to improve." The report summarized information on air quality. Among its findings:

• Combined data from 23 major urban areas indicates that the number of so-called "unhealthful" days declined 18% between 1974 and 1978.

• The aggregate number of "very unhealthful" and "hazardous" days in the 23 areas dropped from 547 to 358 during this same period—a reduction of 35% . . .

• The total number of "hazardous" days fell from 33 to 15—a 55% decrease.

The council concludes that "The overall improvement has been quite steady, with the total number of days in which the air was unhealthful or worse decreasing each year." EPA agrees. The agency estimates that, in the nine years from 1970 through 1978, with the exception of nitrogen oxides, total emissions of the seven major pollutants either decreased or remained constant.

Ninety-three per cent of industry is now in compliance with air quality regulations. For particulates, produced mainly by fuel combustion at factories and power plants, estimated annual emissions dropped 46.1%, but the cost has been high.

Economic Impact

The Council on Environmental Quality predicts that expenditures for meeting the nation's clean air goals will total $278,900,000,000,000 between 1978 and 1987 (in 1978 dollars); $138,600,000,000 in capital costs and $140,300,000,000 for operation and maintenance. A Business Roundtable report concludes that, between 1970 and 1987, industry will spend $400,000,000,000 on air pollution abatement—money that must ultimately be included in the price of goods and services.

In addition to direct expenditures for the purchase, operation, and maintenance of emission control equipment, meeting the nation's clean air goals has significant indirect costs on the following areas:

Economic growth. A study conducted by the Roundtable revealed that it can take some industries, particularly heavy industries such as steel and automotive manufacturers, three or more years and $250,000 to $300,000 to obtain the permits necessary to construct a single new plant. This has caused some manufacturers to purchase existing plants that may be outmoded, or to build outside the U.S.

Energy self-sufficiency. It is well-known that the U.S. has an abundance of coal. Three presidents have urged approximately 100 electric utilities capable of generating electricity from coal—but now using oil or natural gas—to convert back to coal. To date, because of the cost and difficulty of meeting clean air standards for coal-fired plants, very few have switched.

U.S. competitiveness in world trade. In 1950, Ameican industry ranked first among the world's machine tool builders, producing 47% of the world's raw steel and 76% of its autos. Today, the U.S. ranks third as a builder of machine tools, produces only 18.7% of the world's steel, and the condition of the auto industry is well-known. A significant factor in the decreasing competitiveness of U.S. goods in international markets is the failure to devote sufficient capital to modernize and expand American industry.

Small businesses. Small companies often face special problems relating to environmental goals. This is because they are generally required to meet the same standards—and fill out the same forms—as large companies. The Federal Paperwork Commission reports that over 5,000,000 small businesses spend more than $3,000 each per year to complete Federal forms—many relating to clean air regulations.

Clearly, the nation's air is cleaner. However, as Douglas M. Costle, former administrator of EPA, pointed out in *Congressional Quarterly,* "To achieve that seemingly simple goal costs American industry billions of dollars each year and affects nearly all industrial energy production, transportation, and real estate activities in the country."

Public opinion strongly supports protection of the environment, but only 27% of the respondents in a recent poll commissioned by the Council on Environmental Quality agreed that economic growth should be sacrificed for clean air and water. This response is down sharply from 1978, when 58% would have accepted slower economic progress to protect the environment.

America's clean air programs originated in the desire to protect the public health and enhance the quality of life. These goals are worth while and are widely supported by the public.

There is little question that the programs have been successful. America's air is cleaner. There is also little question that this effort has carried a high price tag—in terms of direct costs and reduced economic growth.

The public is beginning to suspect that perhaps the nation's clean air goals can be achieved within a framework of a more positive approach that will lower the costs of air quality programs. Better scientific data, more careful economic analysis, increased attention to local and regional needs, added flexibility, and a sensible attitude that concentrates on reducing the complexities of the clean air regulations could help reduce their impact on the economy. The Council on Environmental Quality estimated that, unless the present system of regulations is revised, Federal environmental regulations alone could cost the U.S. $518,000,000,000 between 1977 and 1988.

Perhaps it is time for America to consider other national priorities. The single-minded pursuit of environmental programs may have caused this nation to lose sight of the need to provide jobs for an expanding work force, to achieve greater energy self-sufficiency, and to increase productivity—the source of funds for essential social services and real increases in earnings.

Perhaps it is time to seek a better balance among our national goals. By amending the Clean Air Act, we can tip the scales toward that balance.

BIBLIOGRAPHY

An asterisk (*) preceding a reference indicates that the article or part of it has been reprinted in this book.

BOOKS AND PAMPHLETS

Baxter, William F. People or penguins: the case for optimal pollution. Columbia University Press. '74.

Beckerman, Wilfred. Two cheers for the Affluent Society: a spirited defense of economic growth. Saint Martin's Press. '75.

Brown, Lester R. The Twenty-ninth day: accommodating human needs and numbers to the earth's resources. Norton. '78.

Brown, Michael M. Laying waste: the poisoning of America by toxic chemicals. Pantheon Books. '80.

Carson, Rachel. Silent spring. Houghton Mifflin. '62.

Carter, Vernon G. and Dale, Tom. Topsoil and civilization. Oklahoma University Press. '74.

Congressional Office of Technology Assessment. Technologies and management strategies for hazardous waste control. U.S. Government Printing Office. Mr. 16, '83.

Council on Environmental Quality and the Department of State. The Global 2000 Report to the President—entering the 21st century. U.S. Government Printing Office. '80.

Cousteau, Jacques Y. and the staff of the Cousteau Society. The Cousteau Almanac: an inventory of life on our water planet. Doubleday. '81.

Eckholm, Erik P. Down to earth: environment and human needs. Norton. '82.

Ehrlich, Paul. The population bomb. Ballantine Books. '68.

Eisenbud, Merril. Environment, technology, and health: human ecology in historical perspective. New York University Press. '78.

Epstein, Samuel S., Brown, Lester O., and Pope, Carl. Hazardous waste in America. Sierra Club Books. '82.

*Foreign Policy Association Editors. Protecting world resources: Is time running out? Great decisions '82. Foreign Policy Association. '82.

Glassner, Martin I., ed. Global resources: challenges of interdependence. Published for the Foreign Policy Association by Praeger. '83.

Hardin, Garrett and Baden, John, eds. Managing the commons. W.H. Freeman. '77.

Highland, Joseph E. and others of the Environment Defense Fund and Boyle, Robert H. Malignant neglect. Knopf. '79.

Holdgate, Martin W. and White, Gilbert F., eds. Environmental issues. John Wiley and Sons. '77.

Lake, Laura. Environmental regulation: the political effects of implementation. Praeger. '82.

Lamm, Richard D. and McCarthy, Michael. The angry West: a vulnerable land and its future. Houghton Mifflin. '82.

Lebedoff, David. The new elite. Franklin Watts. '81.

Mackarness, Richard. Living safely in a polluted world: how to protect yourself and your children from chemicals in your food and environment. Stein and Day. '81.

Magat, Wesley A. ed. Reform of environmental regulation. Ballinger. '82.

Meadows, Donella and others. The limits to growth: a report for the Club of Rome Project on the predicament of mankind. New American Library. '72.

Mills, Edwin S. The economics of environmental quality. Norton. '78.

Mitchell, John G. Losing ground. Sierra Club Books. '75.

Moran, Joseph M. and Morgan, Michael D. Introduction to environmental science. W.H. Freeman. '80.

Nebel, Bernard J. Environmental science, the way the world works. Prentice-Hall. '81.

Odell, Rice. Environmental awakening: the new revolution to protect the earth. Ballinger. '80.

Office of Technology Assessment. Cancer risk: assessing and reducing the dangers in our society. Westview Press. '82.

Orr, David W. and Soroos, Martin S., eds. The global predicament: ecological perspectives on world order. The University of North Carolina Press. '79.

Panel on Energy, Natural Resources, and the Environment. Energy, natural resources, and the environment in the eighties. President's Commission for a National Agenda for the 1980s. U.S. Government Printing Office. '80.

Passmore, John. Man's responsibility for nature: ecological problems and Western traditions. Scribner. '74.

Peskin, Henry M. and others, eds. Environmental regulation and the U.S. economy. Johns Hopkins University Press. '81.

Pringle, Laurence. Lives at stake: the science and politics of environmental health. Macmillan. '80.

*Regenstein, Lewis. American the poisoned. Acropolis Books. '82.

Schelling, Thomas C., ed. Incentives for environmental protection. Massachusetts Institute of Technology Press. '83.

Schumacher, E. F. Small is beautiful. Harper & Row. '73.

Simon, Julian. The ultimate resource. Princeton University Press. '81.

Skjei, Eric and Whorton, M. Donald. Of mice and molecules: technology and human survival. Dial Press. '83.

Stoddard, Charles H. Looking forward: planning America's future. Macmillan. '82.

Stone, Christopher D. Should trees have standing? Toward legal rights for natural objects. Avon Books. '75.

Thurow, Lester. The zero-sum society. Basic Books. '80.

*Tucker, William. Progress and privilege: America in the age of environmentalism. Anchor Press/Doubleday. '82.

Wenner, Lettie M. The environmental decade in court. Indiana University Press. '82.

PERIODICALS

Atlantic. 249:22+. Jl. '82. Environmental deregulation. D. Osborne.

Atlantic. 252:80-8+. Jl. '83. The future of water. P. Rogers.

Audubon. 85:122+. Jl. '83. Thinking globally. B. Evans.

Audubon. 85:8+. Jl. '83. Underdogs. P. Steinhart.

Audubon. 85:38+. S. '83. Dead forests and acid bananas. J. R. Luoma.

Audubon. 85:4. S. '83. You can make a difference. R. W. Peterson.

Barrons. 63:11. F. 21, '83. Despite the witch doctors, environmental regulatory reform remains a must. R. M. Bleiberg.

Barrons. 63:11. My. 2, '83. America the beautiful; private ownership of natural resources is the way to go. J. Baden.
EXCERPT FROM Natural resources: bureaucratic myths and environmental management.

BioScience. 32:728-9. O. '82. Environmental degradation and the tyranny of small decisions. W. E. Odum.

BioScience. 33:418-22. Jl./Ag. '83. Acid rain clouds U.S. and Canadian relations. L. Roberts.

BioScience. 33:536-7. O. '83. Acid rain controls: the case grows stronger. L. Roberts.

*Blair & Ketchum's Country Journal. 10:38-44. Ap. '83. Environmental protection: assessing the record. John G. Mitchell.

Bulletin of the Atomic Scientists. 39:59-60. N. '83. Paradigm comflict R. E. Dunlap.

Business Week. p 86. Ja. 24, '83. Secretary Watt fires back at his critics. EXCERPT FROM Environmentalists: more of a political force.

Business Week. p 80-2. N. 28, '83. Deregulating America.

Chemical Week. 132:15. Ap. 13, '83. Panel: let the states do it.

Chemical Week. 132:15. Je. 1. '83. Myth of greener pastures.

*Common Cause Magazine. My./Je. '83. Playing politics with pollution. Deborah Baldwin.

Environment. 24:14-20+. My. '82. Trends in public opinion on the environment. R. Anthony.

Environment. 25:6-12+. Je. '83. Examining the role of science in the regulatory process: a roundtable discussions of science at EPA.

Environment. 25:6-11+. Jl./Ag. '83. Responding to the double standard of worker/public protection. P. Derr and others.

Environment. 25:25-32. O. '83. Acid deposition and the materials damage questions. S. R. Scholla.

*Environment. D. '83. The toxics boomerang. Lewis Regenstein.

*EPA Journal. 9:3-5. Jl. '83. Science, risk, and public policy. W. D. Ruckelshaus.

Esquire: 100:118-20. Ag. '83. Poison waters. G. Norman.

Field and Stream. 88:21-2. S. '83. Of wheels and deals. G. Reiger.

Fortune. 108:58-60+. Ag. 8, '83. How acid rain might dampen the utilities. M. Magnet.

Fortune. 108:85+. Ag. 22, '83. Acid rain dissolves the lobbies.

*Fortune. 108:158-60+. O. 31, '83. The hazards of helping toxic waste victims. J. Main.

Futurist. 17:61-2. Je. '83. Reindustrialization and the environment.

Futurist. 17:16-22. Ag. '83. The cornucopian fallacies: the myth of perpetual growth. L. Grant.

*Futurist. 17:7-12+. Ag. '83. Life on earth is getting better, not worse. Julian L. Simon.

Futurist. 17:85. O. '83. America's number one environmental problem.

Harper's. 264:27-36. Mr. '82. Is nature too good for us? W. Tucker. EXCERPT FROM Progress and privilege.

Harper's. 267:34-40+. N. '83. Second thoughts about the third world. EXCERPT FROM The economics and politics of race.

*High Country News. p 10-11. Ja. 23, '84. Colorado's governor peers ahead and finds life dismal. It is the year 2005. . . . Speech by Richard D. Lamm.

Industry Week. 218:45-46+. My. 2, '83. Air pollution: the "inside" story. G. Johnson.

Industry Week. 218:46-53. Jl. 11, '83. Are environmentalists talking truce? W. H. Miller.

International Wildlife. 13:24B. Jl./Ag. '82. Let's resolve the quality-versus-quantity debate. J. D. Hair.

Macleans. 96:38-9. Mr. 7, '83. Distrust across the border.

National Review. 35:924-6+. Ag. 5, '83. The greening of James Watt. N. Shute.

*Nation's Business. 71:56-8. Mr. '83. Behind the campaign against Watt.

Nation's Business. 71:26-9. Ap. '83. Environmentalists take the offensive. H. Eason.

Nation's Business. 71:28-29. Ag. '83. How to survive an EPA inspection. S. N. Klein.

Nation's Business. 71:60-1. S. '83. Don't pull the plug on economic growth.

*Nation's Business. 71:70+. N. '83. Environmental gridlock. M. M. Wantuck.

Natural History. 91:33-48. Je. '82. Human wants and misused lands. E. P. Eckholm.
EXCERPT FROM Down to earth.

Natural History. 92:4. Ag. '83. Catastrophe on Camels Hump, cont. E. Eckholm.

Natural History. 92:82+. S. '83. Gone with the trees. D. S. Wilcove and R. F. Whitcomb.

National Parks. 57:42. Jl./Ag. '83. Acid rain costs U.S. $5 billion annually. D. Kaufman.

National Parks. 57:20-1. Jl./Ag. '83. Endangered species: the illusion of stewardship. M. J. Bean.

National Parks. 57:8-11+. S./O. '83. Wheeling and dealing our public land assets. B. Shanks.

National Wildlife. 21:4-11. Je./Jl. '83. How dangerous is acid rain? M. Hornblower.

New York. 16:88+. Ag. 29, '83. Quiet . . . please! S. A. Newman.

New York Times. p D 9. Ja. 2, '83. Risk assessment techniques used by various federal agencies to determine safety of chemicals.

New York Times. p A 15. Ja. 14, '83. Brookings Institute study finds federal failure to use relevant scientific data in regulatory decisions on the environment.

New York Times. p A 10. F. 12, '83. Concern growing about dioxin; Reagan administration sees no emergency.

New York Times. p K 2. F. 13, '83. N.J. researchers find indoor home levels of pollutants high.

New York Times. p A 31. F. 16, '83. Watt's economic folly. T. A. Barron.

New York Times. p A 1. F. 17, '83. Steven R. Weisman analysis of anti-EPA charges, context of entire dispute.

New York Times. p D 16. F. 20, '83. Editorial: Watts and Gorsuch. New York Times. p A 9. F. 26, '83. Analysis of Reagan's defensive attempts to control EPA controversy.

New York Times. p A 22. F. 26, '83. The EPA wasteland.

New York Times. p D 1. F. 27, '83. Review of political crisis at EPA: Concern in Washington—is enough done to safeguard U.S. against environmental hazards?

New York Times. p A 22. Mr. 1, '83. Misconceptions in a "diatribe" against Secretary Watt. J. V. Hansen.

New York Times. p A 12. Mr. 5, '83. Outline of EPA/Burford dispute.

New York Times. p A 1. Mr. 6, '83. Environmental agency: deep and persisting woes.

New York Times. p A 1. Mr. 10, '83. Head of EPA, Burford, resigns.

New York Times. p A 1. Mr. 10, '83. Reagan's EPA retreat: capitulation on the agency's chief and data gives Democrats a sharp political edge. H. Smith.

New York Times. p A 8. Mr. 12, '83. Transcript of Reagan news conference.

New York Times. p C 2. Mr. 13, '83. The price of cleaning up toxic wastes: billions of dollars and new ideas. S. S. Epstein.

New York Times. p A 36. Mr. 13, '83. Congressional inquiry into EPA centers on four subjects.

New York Times. p D 1. Mr. 13, '83. Saving face and cleaning up. W. Williams.

New York Times. p A 1. Mr. 15, '83. Concern over toxic chemicals in food supply.

New York Times. p A 20. Mr. 16, '83. Consensus emerging among experts that land burial of hazardous waste is least safe in long run, though low immediate cost. Alternatives.

New York Times. p A 19. Mr. 17, '83. Did the ancient Romans suffer from lead poisoning?

New York Times. p B 14. Mr. 17. '83. Congress's Office of Technology Assessment study says Federal regulations on toxic waste disposal do not assure protection of human health.

New York Times. p D 1. Mr. 17. '83. Hazardous waste.

New York Times. p D 1. Mr. 20. '83. Review of Reagan administration EPA controversies and appointments.

New York Times. p A 21. Mr. 22, '83. Movement to center. H. Smith.

New York Times. p A 1. Mr. 22, '83. Ruckelshaus named to EPA, Reagan adopts conciliatory tone.

New York Times. p A 8. Mr. 26, '83. EPA employees hold champagne parties after resignation of 5 senior officials.

New York Times. p E 5. Mr. 27, '83. EPA's recent past may overshadow its future. P. Shabecoff.

New York Times. p A 14. Mr. 28, '83. Poisons that are boomeranged out of the U.S. (letter). L. Regenstein.

New York Times. p C 3. Mr. 29, '83. U.S. scientist who toured dioxin-sprayed forests in Vietnam says they have recovered faster than thought.

New York Times. p A 14. Mr. 30, '83. Reagan in interview denies unresponse to the environment.

New York Times. p A 1. My 5, '83. Ruckelshaus talks of EPA; what he will do, past problems.

New York Times. p B 3. Je. 2, '83. Ruckelshaus and EPA morale.

New York Times. p A 1. Jl. 27, '83. EPA administrator says Reagan administration "confused" public's desires on environment.

New York Times. p A 3. O. 10, '83. Secretary of Interior James Watt resigns; analysis.

New York Times. p B 12. O. 13, '83. Environmentalists come of age. P. Shabecoff.

*New York Times. p F 4. Ja. 8, '84. The recycling of chemical waste. Steven J. Marcus.

New York Times. p B 8. F. 21, '84. Calmer seas with Clark at helm.

New York Times. p A 10. Mr. 3, '84. Few chemicals tasted for hazards, report finds. P. Boffey.

New York Times. p A 1. Mr. 3, '84. U.S. imposes curbs on EDB in fruit.

New York Times. p A 17. Mr. 5, '84. Federal callousness on dangers of EDB. G. Miller.

New York Times. p A 16. Mr. 5, '84. Gasoline storage tanks that leak EDB into groundwater. (letter) Phil Jalbert.

New York Times Magazine. p 26-7+. O. 31, '83. Laissez-faire landscape. R. W. Peterson.

Newsweek. 101:35. Ap. 11, '83. Watt's truth crusade. M. A. Lerner.

*Newsweek. 102:22-4+. Jl. 25, '83. Battle over the wilderness. M. Beck. REPRINTED IN THIS VOLUME: interview with former secretary of Interior James Watt.

Newsweek. 102:45-6. N. 21, '83. A life-and-death choice.

*Public Relations Journal. Winter '83. Industry and the environment; a communication gap. Gerald Prout.

Science. 220:1003. Je. 3, '83. Waste management. P. H. Abelson.

Science. 221:9-17. Jl. 1, '83. Indoor air pollution: a public health perspective. J. D. Spengler and K. Sexton.

*Science. 221:341-3. Jl. 22, '83. Simon and Kahn versus Global 2000. C. Holden.

Science. 221:713-18. Ag. 19, '83. Ground water contamination in the U.S. V. I. Pye and R. Patrick.

Science. 222:125. O. 14, '83. Workers at risk. D. Nelkin.

Science News. 123:390. Jl. 18, '83. Acid rain report blames man-made pollution. I. Peterson.

Sierra. 68:35-45+. Ja./F. '83. The 1982 elections: an environmental impact statement.

Society. 20:11-17. N./D. '82. Irreducible uncertainties. K. E. Boulding.

Sports Illustrated. 59:66-70+. S. 26, '83. Inside Interior: an abrupt turn. B. Gilbert.

Sports Illustrated. 59:98-111. O. 3, '83. Special report: inside Interior. B. Gilbert.

Sports Illustrated. 59:15. O. 10, '83. In this sad fish story, the numbers simply don't lie. J. Underwood.

Technology Review. 85:32-7. Ja. '83. Exploring environmental impacts: beyond quantity to quality. L. S. Bacow.

*Technology Review. 86:14-16. Jl. '83. Controlling health hazards without Uncle Sam. J. R. Miyares.

*Technology Review. 86:60-8. Ag./S. '83. The case for ocean waste disposal. William Lahey and Michael Connor.

Time. 120:84-86. D. 6, '82. Storm over a deadly downpour. F. Golden.

Time. 122:19. Jl. 11, '83. Confronting the acid test.

USA Today [magazine]. 111:41-3. Jl. '82. The Reagan administration and the environment. R. Pomerance and T. Turner.

*USA Today [magazine]. 111:47-9. My. '83. Improving the balance between jobs and clean air. Jerry J. Jasinowski.

U.S. News & World Report. 93:57-9. Ag. 30, '82. Why Reagan is on griddle over the environment. R. A. Taylor.

U.S. News & World Report. 95:57-9. Jl. 4, '82. When the U.S. plows under a poisoned community: more and more families are being uprooted to flee contamination—at taxpayer expense. Joseph L. Gallsway.

U.S. News & World Report. 95:23-4. Ag. 15, '83. Nuclear-waste war cry: not here, you don't! S. N. Wellbron.

U.S. News & World Report. 96:51-52. Ap. 2, '84. Do environmentalists care about poor people? R. A. Taylor.

*U.S. News & World Report. 95:57-62. O. 31, '83. War over water: crisis of the '80s. K. R. Sheets.

U.S. News & World Report. 95:71. N. 14, '83. City on the spot: give up jobs or risk health. K. M. Chrysler.

*Vital Speeches of the Day. 48:235-41. F. 1, '82. The Environmental community; address, November 19, 1981. Brock Evans.

Wall Street Journal. p 1. Ap. 1, '83. Watt increasingly isolated, challenged both by Reaganites and environmentalists.

Wall Street Journal. p 2. Je. 2, '83. Ruckelshaus, head of EPA, bluntly warns industry leaders to forget about significant easing of antipollution laws in near future; concedes White House erred.

Wall Street Journal. p 1. Je. 6, '83. Waiving the rules. Reaganites find plans for deregulation stall after EPA revelations but effort continues; how an official relieves pain of aspirin makers.

Wall Street Journal. p 5. Je. 23, '83. Ruckelshaus, head of EPA, calls for partnership between scientists and the federal government to protect public from toxic chemicals.

Wall Street Journal. p 15. Ag. 9, '83. Presicent Reagan's policies spur big revival of environmental community, says president of Shell Oil.

Wall Street Journal. p 19. Ag. 15, '83. High costs, contradictory regulations, and lack of will on part of producers and disposers hamper spread of better waste disposal methods.

Wall Street Journal. p 10. S. 1, '83. EPA says American industry generates about 1500 lbs. of hazardous waste per person in the U.S. each year.

Wall Street Journal. p 30. O. 19, '83. Can the EPA be made rational?

Wall Street Journal. p 4. N. 10, '83. Nationwide survey of 263 top business executives indicates that two-thirds want to protect environment even if economic growth slows.

*Weekly Compilation of Presidential Documents. 19:428-432. Mr. 21, '83. (Ronald Reagan) Remarks and a question-and-answer session on the nomination of William D. Ruckelshaus to be administrator of the Environmental Protection Agency.

*Weekly Compilation of Presidential Documents. 19:863-4. Je. 20, '83.
    (Ronald Reagan) Environmental and natural resources manage-
    ment. In defense of James Watt: radio address to the nation.
*Weekly Compilation of Presidential Documents. 19:1617-1618. D. 5,
    '83. (Ronald Reagan) Clark is appointed. President's radio address
    to nation.
Wilderness. 47:2-38. Summer '83. The national forests.
Wilderness. 47:2-38. Fall '83. The wildlife refuges.